The Right Word in Chinese

漢語指南

Hànyǔ zhǐnán

Irene Saunders

The Right Word in Chinese

漢語指南

Hànyǔ zhǐnán

Irene Saunders

THE COMMERCIAL PRESS
Ⓦ *Westinghouse Electric (China) S.A.*

漢語指南
THE RIGHT WORD IN CHINESE
Compiled by Irene Saunders

Published by
THE COMMERCIAL PRESS, LTD.
4/F, Kiu Ying Bldg., 2D Finnie St., Quarry Bay, H.K.

Printed by
C & C JOINT PRINTING CO., (H.K.) LTD.
75, Pau Chung Street, Kowloon, Hong Kong.

First Edition January 1986
Second printing July 1987
ISBN 962 07 1062 2

DEDICATION TO
CHINA WILDLIFE CONSERVATION ASSOCIATION

This dictionary, which is intended to be useful to people associated with China's modernisation programme, will help fulfil another important need, by raising funds for wildlife conservation in China.

Modernisation and conservation should, in fact, be closely linked. China is in the unique position of having the opportunity to co-ordinate the development of industry while ensuring that this does not upset the ecological balance. Thus many of the conservation problems encountered by previously industrialised nations may be avoided. Strong and successful industrial development can also give effective support to conservation of wildlife and the environment.

Westinghouse is in China to do business, not only today, but in the future when China emerges as a major industrial power. China's widely announced conservation goals match Westinghouse's philosophy and practice – a healthy long term development, sustained by a love of nature and concern for the environment.

It has been my personal pleasure to be involved with World Wildlife Fund (W.W.F.) and the newly formed China Wildlife Conservation Association (C.W.C.A.), both of which organisations are engaged in the conservation effort in the People's Republic of China. Let us wish them every success.

June 1985   L.C. Saunders

INTRODUCTION

THE RIGHT WORD IN CHINESE is a dictionary compiled to help make the language accessible to foreigners visiting China for either business or pleasure.

The vocabulary covers both everyday language and business and technical terms. The English entries are followed by Pinyin romanisations and the complicated traditional Chinese characters as well as the simplified ones commonly used today. These are included to help people avoid the frustrations I experienced when I first came to China. My knowledge of Putonghua was very limited, and I was not always able to pronounce it so that people could understand what I was trying to say. The dictionary is designed so that those who know nothing of the language can look up a word, pronounce it according to the Pinyin romanisation, or if this fails simply show the entry to the Chinese friend or colleague they are trying to communicate with. People who already know some Chinese may find it useful in expanding their vocabulary, particularly when they run into difficulties over technical terms.

As the dictionary is the first of its kind, it is bound to have shortcomings. Any criticisms and suggestions will be appreciated so that improvements can be made to future editions.

The compilation of this book was funded by Westinghouse Electric (China) S.A., which is donating all proceeds from sales to the China Wildlife Conservation Association (C.W.C.A.).

June 1985   Irene Saunders

Table of Contents

Part One

Everyday Vocabulary

A

abbreviation	suōxiě 縮寫(缩写)
abdomen	dùzi 肚子
abide by	zūnshǒu 遵守
abilities, talent	cáinéng 才能
ability	nénglì 能力
able	néng 能
about	zhōuwéi 周圍(周围)
about, approximately	dàyuē 大約(大约); chà bu duō 差不多
about, on, concerning, with regard to	guānyú 關於(关于)
about to, on the point of	gāng…de shíhòu 剛…的時候 (刚…的时候)
above	zài…zhīshàng 在…之上
above, on top	shàng 上; shàngbian 上邊(上边)
above (used with temperature and age)	…duō …多
abroad	guówài 國外(国外)
absolute	juéduì 絕對(绝对)
absorbed, concentrated	zhuānxīn 專心(专心)
abundant	fēngfùde 豐富的(丰富的)
academic education	zhìyù 智育
academic knowledge	xuéshù 學術(学术); xuéwèn 學問(学问)
accent	kǒuyīn 口音
accept, receive	shōu 收; jiēshōu 接收; jiēshòu 接受
acceptable	xíng 行; kěyǐjiēshòu 可以接受
accessories	fùjiàn 附件

1

accident	yìwài 意外; shìgù 事故
accompany	péi 陪; péitóng 陪同
accomplish	wánchéng 完成
according to	ànzhào 按照
account (bank)	zhàngmù 賬目(帐目); zhànghù 賬戶(帐户)
accurate, precise, exact	zhǔnquède 準確的(准确的)
ache	téng 疼
achieve	huòdé 獲得(获得)
achievement	chéngjì 成績(成绩); chéngjiù 成就
acid	suān 酸
acquaintance	shúrén 熟人
acquaint (with), recognize	rènshi 認識(认识)
acrobat	zájìyǎnyuán 雜技演員(杂技演员)
across	guò過(过); héngguò 橫過(横过)
act (in a play)	mù 幕
action, activity, to act	xíngdòng 行動(行动)
activities	huódòng 活動(活动)
actor, actress	yǎnyuán 演員(演员)
actual, in actuality	shíjì 實際(实际); shíjìshàng 實際上(实际上)
actually, after all	dàodǐ 到底
acupuncture	zhēnjiǔ 針灸(针灸)
add, append	tiān 添; jiā 加
additional, supplementary	fùjiāde 附加的
address	dìzhǐ 地址; zài…shang xiě dìzhǐ 在…上寫地址(在…上写地址)
adhere to, attach to	tiē 貼(贴)
adjacent, neighboring	fùjìnde 附近的
adjust, correct	duìzhǔn 對準(对准); tiáozhěng 調整

2

	調整(调整)
administer, manage	guǎnlǐ 管理
admiral	hǎijūn shàngjiàng 海軍上將(海軍上将)
adorn, dress	dǎbàn 打扮
adult	dàrén 大人; chéngrén 成人
advance	qiánjìn 前進(前进)
in advance	yùxiān 預先(预先)
advanced	xiānjìnde 先進的(先进的)
advertise	zuòguǎnggào 做廣告(做广告)
advertisement	guǎnggào 廣告(广告)
advertising company	guǎnggào gōngsī 廣告公司(广告公司)
adviser	gùwèn 顧問(顾问)
aerated water	qìshuǐ 汽水
aeroplane	fēijī 飛機(飞机)
affair	shìqing 事情
affix	fùshàng 附上; qiānshàng 簽上(签上)
afraid	pà 怕; hàipà 害怕
Africa	Fēizhōu 非洲
after, later	yǐhòu 以後(以后); zhīhòu 之後(之后)
after, following, next to	jiēzhe…zhīhòu 接着…之後(接着……之后)
after all	bìjìng 畢竟(毕竟); fǎnzhèng 反正; bùguǎn zěnyàng 不管怎樣(不管怎样)
after all, at last	dàodǐ 到底; zhōngyú 終於(终于)
afternoon	xiàwǔ 下午
after school	fàngxué yǐhòu 放學以後(放学以

后)

afterwards	yǐhòu 以後(以后); ránhòu 然後 (然后); hòulái 後來(后来)
again, once more	yòu 又; zàiyícì 再一次
age	suì 歲(岁);niánjì 年紀(年纪)
age, period, era	shídài 時代(时代)
agency	dàilǐchù代理處(代理处); jīgòu 機構(机构)
agent	dàilǐrén 代理人
agitated, anxious	zháojí 着急
ago	yǐqián 以前
agreement, written contract	xiéyì 協議(协议); qìyuē 契約 (契约)
agree to, consent to	tóngyì 同意
agriculture	nóngyè 農業(农业)
agricultural products	nóngchǎnpǐn 農產品(农产品)
agricultural tools	nóngjù 農具(农具)
ahead, first	xiān 先; zàiqián 在前
ahead of	zài…zhīqián 在…之前
aim, objective	mùdì 目的; mùbiāo 目標(目标)
air	kōngqì 空氣(空气)
air conditioner	kōngtiáojī 空調機(空调机)
air force	kōngjūn 空軍(空军)
air hostess	kōngzhōng xiǎojiě 空中小姐
air mail	hángjì 航寄; hángyóu 航郵(航邮)
airplane	fēijī 飛機(飞机)
airport, airfield	fēijīchǎng 飛機場(飞机场)
alike, same	xiāngtóng 相同; yíyàng 一樣 (一样)
alike, similar	xiāngsì 相似
all	dōu 都; suǒyǒude 所有的; yíqiè

4

	一切; quán 全
all at once, all of a sudden, in one go, in one stroke	yíxiàzi 一下子
allergy	guòmǐn 過敏(过敏)
alley	hútòng 胡同
allocate	fēnpèi 分配
allocation	bōkuǎn 撥欸(拨款); fēnpèié 分配額(分配额)
all of you	zhūwèi 諸位(诸位)
all one's life	yìshēng 一生; bìshēng 畢生(毕生)
all over, finished	quánbù jiéshù 全部結束(全部结束)
allow	ràng 讓(让); yǔnxǔ 允許(允许)
all the rest	shèngxiàde 剩下的
all the time	yìzhí 一直; yíguàn 一貫(一贯)
almost, mostly	dàbùfen 大部分
almost, nearly	chàyìdiǎnr差一點兒(差一点儿); chàbùduō 差不多
alone	dāndú 單獨(单独)
along, along the way	yánzhe 沿着; yán 沿
along with, as well as	háiyǒu 還有(还有)
aloud	dàshēng 大聲(大声)
alphabet	zìmǔbiǎo 字母表
capital letter	dàxiě 大寫(大写)
lower case letter	xiǎoxiě 小寫(小写)
already	yǐjīng 已經(已经)
also	yě 也
also, more over	érqiě 而且
alter	biàngēng 變更(变更); gǎibiàn 改變(改变)

although, though	jīnguǎn 儘管(尽管); suírán 雖然(虽然)
although…yet	suírán…dànshì 雖然…但是(虽然…但是)
altogether	yígòng 一共
always, forever	zǒngshì 總是(总是); yǒngyuǎn 永遠(永远)
am	shì 是
amaze	lìngrén jīngqí 令人驚奇(令人惊奇)
ambassador	dàshǐ 大使
ambulance	jiùhùchē 救護車(救护车)
American	Měiguórén (the people) 美國人(美国人); Měiguóde (of America) 美國的(美国的)
among	zài qízhōng 在其中
amount	shùliàng 數量(数量); héjì 合計(合计)
ample	fēngfùde 豐富的(丰富的)
amuse oneself	wán(r) 玩兒(玩儿); yúlè 娛樂(娱乐)
analyze	fēnxī 分析
ancient	gǔdàide 古代的; gǔ 古
ancient relic	gǔwù 古物
ancient sites	gǔjī 古迹
ancient times	gǔdài 古代
and	hé 和; gēn 跟
and so on, etc.	děng 等; děngděng 等等
anew	chóngxīn 重新
angel	shénxiān 神仙; tiānshǐ 天使
angry	shēngqì 生氣(生气)
animal	dòngwù 動物(动物)

6

anniversary	zhōunián jìniàn 週年紀念(周年紀念)
another	lìngyígè 另一個(另一个)
answer, respond	huídá 回答; xiǎngyìng 響應(響應)
antibiotic	kàngshēngsù 抗生素
antique	gǔwán 古玩; gǔdǒng 古董
any	rènhé 任何
anyone	rènhérén 任何人
anytime	rènhé shíjiān 任何時間(任何時間)
anxious	zháojí 着急
anxious (worried) about …	wèi…zháojí 爲…着急(爲…着急)
apart from	chúle 除了
apartment, flat	yítào zhùfáng 一套住房
apologetic	guòyìbúqù 過意不去(過意不去)
apologize	dàoqiàn 道歉
apparently	xiǎnrán 顯然(顯然)
appeal, call for	hàozhāo 號召(号召)
appear, come out	chūxiàn 出現(出现)
appear (to be), look	xiǎnde 顯得(显得)
appearance, by the look of it	wàibiǎo 外表; yàngzi 樣子(樣子); shìyàngr 式樣兒(式樣兒)
appetite	shíyù 食欲; wèikǒu 胃口
applaud	pāishǒu 拍手; hècǎi 喝彩
apple	píngguǒ 蘋果(苹果)
appliance, electrical equipment	diànqì 電器(电器)
application	shēnqǐng 申請(申请)
application form	shēnqǐngbiǎo 申請表(申请表)

appoint, arrange	ānpái 安排
appointment	yuēhuì 約會(约会)
appreciate, enjoy	xīnshǎng 欣賞(欣赏)
approach	jiējìn 接近
approval, to approve	pīzhǔn 批准; zànchéng 贊成(赞成)
approximately, about	dàyuē 大約(大约)
April	sìyuè 四月
architect	jiànzhùshī 建築師(建筑师)
architecture	jiànzhùwù 建築物(建筑物)
area	miànjī 面積(面积)
area, (location)	dìqū 地區(地区)
armed forces	jūnduì 軍隊(军队)
army	lùjūn 陸軍(陆军)
aroma, scent	xiāng 香
around, about	zuǒyòu, dàyuē 左右;大約(大约)
around, surrounding	zhōuwéi 周圍(周围)
arouse, stimulate	jīqǐ 激起; yǐnqǐ 引起
arrange, dispose	ānpái 安排;bùzhì 布置
arrange, put in order	zhěnglǐ 整理
arrive	dàodá 到達(到达); láidào 來到(来到)
art	yìshù 藝術(艺术)
articles, necessities	yòngpǐn 用品
artist	yìshùjiā 藝術家(艺术家)
ascend	dēngshàng 登上
ash tray	yānhuīgāng 烟灰缸
Asia	Yàzhōu 亞洲(亚洲)
ask	wèn 問
ask, demand	yāoqiú 要求
ask for a favor from	qǐng…bāngmáng 請…幫忙(请…帮忙)

aspect, respect	fāngmiàn 方面
aspiration, desire	yuànwàng 願望(愿望)
aspirin	āsīpǐlín 阿司匹林
assembly, mass rally	jíhuì 集會(集会)
assiduous, hard-working	kèkǔde 刻苦的
assign（someone）	pài 派
assignment	gōngzuò 工作
assistant	zhùshǒu 助手
as soon as	yī…jiù… 一…就…
at all times, always	cónglái 從來(从来);zǒngshì 總是(总是)
at, by	páng 旁; zài…páng 在…旁
at, in	zài 在
athlete, sportsman, player	yùndòngyuán 運動員(运动员)
athletics, sports	yùndòng 運動(运动)
atlas	dìtújí 地圖集(地图集)
at once, immediately	lìkè 立刻
at one go, at a stretch	yìkǒuqìde 一口氣地(一口气地); yíxiàzi 一下子
attach	fù 縛(缚); fùshàng 附上
attached, enclosed	fùyǒu 附有
attend	chūxí 出席; cānjiā 參加
attend a class	shàngkè 上課(上课)
attendant	fúwùyuán 服務員(服务员)
attention	zhùyì 注意
at that time, then	nàshí 那時(那时);yúshì 於是(于是)
at the same time, simultaneously	tóngshí 同時(同时)
attract	xīyǐn 吸引
attractive	xīyǐnrénde 吸引人的;yǒuměilide

有魅力的

audience	tīngzhòng 聽眾(听众)
audience, spectators	guānzhòng 觀眾(观众)
auditorium	lǐtáng 禮堂(礼堂)
August	bāyuè 八月
authentic, genuine	kěkàode 可靠的; zhēnde 眞的
author	zuòzhě 作者; zuòjiā 作家
automatic	zìdòngde 自動的(自动的)
automobile	qìchē 汽車(汽车)
autumn	qiūtiān 秋天
average	píngjūn 平均
aviation	hángkōng 航空
awake, wake up	huànxǐng 喚醒(唤醒)
away	líkāi 離開(离开)
awful	kěpàde 可怕的
awhile	yīhuìr 一會兒(一会儿)
ax	fǔzi 斧子

B

baby	yīngér 嬰兒(婴儿)
back	huí 回
bring back	dàilái 帶來(带来)
come back	huídào 回到; huílaī 回來(回来)
go back	huíqù 回去
take back	dàihuí 帶回(带回)
back, behind	hòumiàn 後面(后面); hòutóu 後頭(后头)
background	bèijǐng 背景
backwards and forwards	láihuí 來回(来回)
bad	huài 壞(坏)
worse	bǐjiàohuài 比較壞(比较坏)

worst	zuìhuài 最壞(最坏)
bad (quality), inferior	chà 差; cì 次
bad, spoiled, damaged	huàide 壞的(坏的)
badminton	yǔmáoqiú 羽毛球
badminton rackets	yǔmáoqiúpāi 羽毛球拍
badminton shuttlecock	yǔmáoqiú 羽毛球
bad person, evil-doer	huàirén 壞人(坏人)
bag, sack	kǒudai 口袋
baggage	xíngli 行李
baggage check	xínglǐtuōyùndān 行李托運單(行李托运单)
balance	chèng 稱(称)
balance, equilibrium	pínghéng 平衡
balance (to balance on scale)	chēng 稱(称)
balcony	yángtái 陽臺(阳台)
ball	qiú 球
ballet	bāléiwǔ 芭蕾舞
ball games	qiúlèi 球類(球类)
ball-point pen	yuánzhūbǐ 圓珠筆(圆珠笔)
bamboo	zhúzi 竹子
bandage(n.)	bēngdài 繃帶(绷带)
bandage(v.)	bāozā 包扎
bank	yínháng 銀行(银行)
banquet	yànhuì 宴會(宴会)
barbecue, grill	kǎo 烤
barber shop	lǐfàdiàn 理髮店(理发店)
bar drinks	yǐnliào 飲料(饮料)
barely	jǐnjǐn 僅僅(仅仅)
barrel, tub, pail	tǒng 桶
bas-relief	fúdiāo 浮雕
baseball	bàngqiú 棒球

play baseball	dǎ bàngqiú 打棒球
basic	jīchǔde 基礎的(基础的)
basically, mainly	zhǔyào 主要
basis	gēnjù 根據(根据)
basketball	lánqiú 籃球(篮球)
play basketball	dǎ lánqiú 打籃球(打篮球)
basket, container	lánzi 籃子(篮子)
basket (waste paper)	zhǐlǒu 紙簍(纸篓)
bat (for ball)	qiúpāi 球拍
bath, take a bath	xǐzǎo 洗澡
bathroom	xǐzǎojiān 洗澡間(洗澡间);yùshì 浴室
bath tub	zǎopén 澡盆
battering (from wind and rain)	fēng chuī yǔ dǎ 風吹雨打(风吹雨打)
battery	diànchí 電池(电池)
battleground	zhànchǎng 戰場(战场)
bay	hǎiwān 海灣(海湾)
beach, seashore	hǎitān 海灘(海滩)
beacon	dēngtǎ 燈塔(灯塔)
bear, tolerate	rěnnài 忍耐
beat, hit	dǎ 打
beat, win	yíng 贏
beautiful	měilìde 美麗的(美丽的); piàoliàngde 漂亮的
beauty (man-made)	réngōngměi 人工美
beauty (natural)	zìránměi 自然美
beauty spots, famous sites	míngshèng 名勝(名胜)
because, as	yīnwéi 因為(因为)
because of, owing to, due to	yóuyú 由於(由于)

become, turn into	chéngwéi 成爲(成为)；biàn-chéng 變成(变成)
bed	chuáng 床
bedroom	wòshì 臥室
bed sheet	chuángdān 床單(床单)
beer	píjiǔ 啤酒
before, formerly, once upon a time	cóngqián 從前(从前)
begin	kāishǐ 開始(开始)
be going to, will take time	yào 要
behave	biǎoxiàn 表現(表现)
behind	hòubiān 後邊(后边)
behind	zài…zhīhòu 在…之後(在…之後)
Beijing	Běijīng 北京
believe	xiāngxìn 相信
bell	líng 鈴(铃)
press a bell	àn líng 按鈴(按铃)
belong	shǔyú 屬於(属于)
below	xiàmian 下面
bend	wān 彎(弯)
bend over	wānxiàqù 彎下去(弯下去)
benevolence, mercy	rénci 仁慈
beside, next to	pángbiān 旁邊(旁边)
besides	chú…zhīwài 除…之外
best	zuìhǎo 最好
better	bǐjiàohǎo 比較好(比较好)；gènghǎo 更好
between	zài…zhījiān 在…之間(在…之間)
bicycle	zìxíngchē 自行車(自行车)

13

big, large, great	dà 大
bill	zhàngdān 賬單(帐单)
bill, make out a bill	suànzhàng 算賬(算帐)
bind, tie	kǔn 捆
biology	shēngwùxué 生物學(生物学)
bird	niǎo 鳥(鸟)
birth（to give birth to）	shēng 生
birth control	jiéyù 節育(节育)
birthday	shēngri 生日
biscuit	bǐnggān 餅乾(饼干)
bite, snap at	yǎo 咬
bitter	kǔ 苦
black, dark	hēi 黑
black-and-white	hēibái 黑白
blackboard	hēibǎn 黑板
bland	wēnhéde 溫和的
blanket	máotǎn 毛毯; tǎnzi 毯子
blast	chuī 吹
block	dǎngzhù 擋住(挡住)
blood	xiě, xuè 血
blood pressure	xuèyā 血壓(血压)
blouse	nǔchènyī 女襯衣(女衬衣)
blow	chuī 吹
blue	lán 藍(蓝)
blunt	dùn 鈍(钝); màn 慢
boat	chuán 船
body	shēn 身
boil	zhǔ 煮
boiled water	kāishuǐ 開水(开水)
boisterous	rènào 熱鬧(热闹); chǎonào 吵鬧(吵闹)
bone	gútou 骨頭(骨头)

14

bonsai	pénjǐng 盆景
book	shū 書(书)
book (Chinese brocade signature)	qiānmíngbù 簽名簿(签名簿)
book of paintings	huàcè 畫册(画册)
bookshelf	shūjià 書架(书架)
bookslip (from library)	jièshūdān 借書單(借书单)
bookstore	shūdiàn 書店(书店)
boots	xuēzi 靴子
border	biānjiè 邊界(边界)
bordering	yánzhe 沿着
bored	yànfán 厭煩(厌烦)
born	shēng 生
borrow	jiè 借
boss	lǎobǎn 老闆(老板)
both	dōu 都
both…and…	jì…yě… 既…也…
bothersome	máfan 麻煩(麻烦)
both sides	liǎngbiān 兩邊(兩边); liǎngcè 兩側(兩侧)
bottle stopper, lid, cover	gài 蓋(盖)
bottom	xiàbiān 下邊(下边); dǐ 底
boundary	biānjiè 邊界(边界)
bound for	kāiwǎng 開往(开往)
bouquet	huāshù 花束
bowl	wǎn 碗
box (large)	xiāngzi 箱子
box (small)	hézi 盒子
boy	nánháir 男孩兒(男孩儿)
brain	nǎozi 腦子(脑子)
brake (n.)	zhá 閘(闸)
brake (v.)	shāchē 刹車(刹车)

branch manager	fēnbù jīnglǐ 分部經理(分部经理)
brand, trade mark	pái 牌; páihào 牌號(牌号)
brandy	báilándì 白蘭地(白兰地)
brave, courageous	yǒnggǎnde 勇敢的
bread	miànbāo 麵包(面包)
break	lònghuài 弄壞(弄坏); pòhuài 破壞(破坏)
break down	huàile 壞了(坏了)
breakfast	zǎofàn 早飯(早饭)
break off, sever	duàn 斷(断)
breathe	hūxī 呼吸
breeze	wēifēng 微風(微风)
brick	zhuān 磚(砖)
bride	xīnniáng 新娘
bridegroom	xīnláng 新郎
bridge	qiáo 橋(桥)
bridge game	qiáopái 橋牌(桥牌)
briefcase, portfolio	gōngshìbāo 公事包
bright	míngliàngde 明亮的
bright, brilliant (of intellect)	cōngmingde 聰明的(聪明的)
bright, cheerful (of mood)	gāoxìngde 高興的(高兴的)
bright, clear (of sky)	qínglǎngde 晴朗的
bright (of color)	xiānyànde 鮮艷的(鲜艳的)
bring	dàilái 帶來(带来)
bring, carry by hand	ná 拿
brisk, spry	qīngkuài 輕快(轻快)
broad, spacious	kuānde 寬的(宽的)
brocade	zhījǐn 織錦(织锦)
broken, out of order	huàile 壞了(坏了)

16

brow	méitóu 眉頭(眉头)
brown (from cooking)	jiāohuáng 焦黄
brush (n.)	shuāzi 刷子
brush (v.)	shuā 刷
bucket	tǒng 桶
Buddha	Fó 佛
Buddhism	Fójiào 佛教
buffet	zìzhùcān 自助餐
buffet dinner	zìzhù wǎncān 自助晚餐
buffet lunch	zìzhù wǔcān 自助午餐
bug	chòuchóng 臭蟲(臭虫)
build, construct	jiànshè 建設(建设)
build, establish	jiànlì 建立
building, (more than one storey)	lóu 樓(楼)
building, structure, edifice	jiànzhùwù 建築物(建筑物)
bumper yield field	fēngchǎntián 豐產田(丰产田)
burn	ránshāo 燃燒(燃烧); shāoshāng 燒傷(烧伤)
bus	gōnggòng qìchē 公共汽車(公共汽车)
bus (long-distance)	chángtú qìchē 長途汽車(长途汽车)
business	mǎimài 買賣(买卖); shēngyì 生意
bustling, boisterous	rènào 熱鬧(热闹)
busy	máng 忙
busy, have no time	méiyǒu shíjiān 沒有時間(没有時間); méi shíjiān 沒時間(没時間)
but	kěshì 可是; dànshì 但是

but, on the contrary	fǎn'ér 反而
butter	huángyóu 黃油
butterfly	húdié 蝴蝶
buy	mǎi 買(买)
by, according to	ànzhào 按照
by, at (the door, etc.)	zài…páng 在…旁
by all means	yídìng 一定; wùbì 務必
by means of, with the help of	jiè 借; píngjiè 憑借(凭借); yīkào 依靠
by (the time of)	zài…zhīqián 在…之前

C

cabinet	guìzi 櫃子(柜子)
cadre	gànbù 幹部(干部)
cake	bǐng 餅(饼); dàngāo 蛋糕
calculate	jìsuàn 計算(计算)
calculator, computer	jìsuànjī 計算機(计算机)
calendar	rìlì 日曆(日历)
lunar calendar	yīnlì 陰曆(阴历)
call (v.)	jiàohǎn 叫喊
call, appeal	hàozhào 號召(号召)
call (of birds, insects)	jiào 叫
call, to be called	jiào 叫; jiàozuò 叫做
calm, steady, sure	wěn 穩(稳)
calm, still	píngjìng 平靜
calorie	kǎlùlǐ 卡路里
camera	zhàoxiàngjī 照相機(照相机)
camera lens	jìngtóu 鏡頭(镜头)
can	huì (through learning) 會(会); néng (by natural talent) 能; kěyǐ (by permission) 可以

18

Canada	Jiānádà 加拿大
canal	yùnhé 運河(运河)
cancer	ái 癌
candle	làzhú 蠟燭(蜡烛)
candy	táng 糖
cannot but, can only	zhǐhǎo 祇好(只好)
capability	nénglì 能力
capacity	róngliàng 容量; nénglì 能力
capacity, seating	zuòwèishù 座位數(座位数)
capital (city)	shǒudū 首都; jīngchéng 京城
capital, fund	zījīn 資金(资金)
captain	duìzhǎng 隊長(队长);shàngwèi 上尉
captain (of plane)	jīzhǎng 機長(机长)
captain (of ship)	chuánzhǎng 船長(船长)
caption	biāotí 標題(标题)
car	xiǎoqìchē 小汽車(小汽车)
card	kǎpiàn 卡片
careful, attentive	zǐxìde 仔細的(仔细的)
be careful about	liúshén 留神
careful, cautious	xiǎoxīn 小心
carpet	dìtǎn 地毯
carry	dài 帶(带)
carry, deliver, take to	sòng 送
carry, take	ná 拿
carry in one's arms	bào 抱
carry on, go on with	jìnxíng 進行(进行)
carry on one's shoulder, shoulder	káng 扛
cart (n.)	dàzhē 大車(大车)
cart (v.)	tuīchē 推車(推车)
carve, engrave	diāokè 雕刻

cassette player	lùyīnjī 錄音機(录音机)
cassette tape	lùyīndài 錄音帶(录音带)
cast, throw	pāo 拋
cat	māo 貓(猫)
catalogue, list	mùlù 目錄(目录)
catch!	jiēzhù! 接住!
catch, grip	zhuāzhù 抓住
catch a chill	dòngzhe 凍着(冻着)
catch up, keep pace with	gēnshàng 跟上
catty (＝0.5 kg.)	jīn 斤
cause	shǐ 使; lìng 令
cause, reason	yuányīn 原因
cause, undertaking	shìyè 事業(事业)
caution, cautious	shènzhòng 慎重; xiǎoxīn 小心
cave	yándòng 岩洞; yáodòng 窰洞
caviar	yúzǐjiàng 魚子醬(鱼子酱)
cease, stop	tíngzhǐ 停止
celebrate	qìngzhù 慶祝(庆祝)
celebrate (spend) the New Year	guònián 過年(过年)
cent	fēn 分
center	zhōngxīn 中心; zhèngzhōng 正中
center on	wéirǎo 圍繞(围绕)
centigrade	shèshì 攝氏(摄氏)
central	zhōngxīnde 中心的; zhǔyàode 主要的
central heating	nuǎnqì 暖氣(暖气)
century	shìjì 世紀(世纪)
ceramics	táocíxué 陶瓷學(陶瓷学); zhì- táoshù 製陶術(制陶术)
ceremony	yíshì 儀式(仪式)

ceremony, opening	kāimùshì 開幕式(开幕式)
certain, definite	yídìng 一定
(a) certain (thing or person)	mǒu 某
certificate	zhèngmíng 證明(证明); zhèng-shū 證書(证书)
chair	yǐzi 椅子
armchair	fúshǒuyǐ 扶手椅
chairman, chairwoman, chairperson	zhǔxí 主席
chalk	fěnbǐ 粉筆(粉笔)
champion	guànjūn 冠軍(冠军)
championship	jǐnbiāosài 錦標賽(锦标赛)
chance, opportunity	jīhuì 機會(机会)
by chance, opportunely	pèngqiǎo 碰巧(碰巧)
change	gǎi 改
change, exchange	huàn 換(换); jiāohuàn 交換(交换)
change, odd coins	língqián 零錢(零钱)
change, vary	biànhuà 變化(变化)
chaos, disorder	hùnluàn 混亂(混乱)
character	rénwù 人物
characteristic	tèdiǎn 特點(特点)
charge, responsibility	zérèn 責任(责任)
be in charge of, take charge of	guǎn 管
charge d'affaires	dàibàn 代辦(代办)
charges, fees	fèi 費(费)
chase, pursue	gǎn 趕(赶)
chat, talk	tányìtan 談一談(谈一谈); liáotiānr 聊天兒(聊天儿)

cheap, inexpensive	piányi 便宜
check(n.)	zhīpiào 支票; zhàngdān 賬單(帐单)
check(v.)	jiǎnchá 檢查(检查)
cheerful, happy	kuàilè 快樂(快乐)
cheering on	jiāyóu 加油
cheers	gānbēi 乾杯(干杯)
cheese	nǎilào 奶酪; gānlào 乾酪(干酪)
chemistry	huàxué 化學(化学)
chess	qí 棋; xiàngqí 象棋
chess board	qípán 棋盤(棋盘)
chess piece	qízǐr 棋子兒(棋子儿)
chest, trunk	xiāngzi 箱子
chest pain	xiōngkǒu téng 胸口疼
child, children	háizi 孩子
children	háizimen 孩子們(孩子们)
China	Zhōngguó 中國(中国)
China Daily	Zhōngguórìbào 中國日報(中国日报)
Chinese-American	měijí huárén 美籍華人(美籍华人)
Chinese-British	yīngjí huárén 英籍華人(英籍华人)
Chinese brush pen	máobǐ 毛筆(毛笔)
Chinese character	Hànzì 漢字(汉字)
Chinese food	Zhōngcān 中餐
Chinese ink stick	mò 墨
Chinese language	Hànyǔ 漢語(汉语)
Chinese people	Zhōngguórén 中國人(中国人)
chocolate	qiǎokèlì 巧克力
choose, select	xuǎnzé 選擇(选择)
chop, cut	kǎn 砍

chopsticks	kuàizi 筷子
Christ, Son of God	Jīdū 基督
Christmas	shèngdànjié 聖誕節(圣诞节)
church	jiàotáng 教堂
cicada	chán 蟬(蝉)
cigarette	xiāngyān 香烟
cinema, film	diànyǐng 電影(电影)
circle, ring	yuánquān 圓圈(圆圈)
circular, round, spherical	yuánde 圓的(圆的)
circumstance, condition	qíngkuàng 情况
circumstances, environ- ment, surroundings	huánjìng 環境(环境)
citizen	gōngmín 公民
city, town	chéngshì 城市
city-gate tower	chénglóu 城樓(城楼)
city hall	dàhuìtáng 大會堂(大会堂)
civilian	píngmín 平民; lǎobǎixìng 老百姓
claim, demand	yāoqiú 要求
class	kè 課(课); bān 班
after class	kèhòu 課後(课后)
go to class	shàngkè 上課(上课)
class (social)	jiējí 階級(阶级); jiēcéng 階層(阶层)
class, species	zhonglei 種類(种类)
classical	gǔdiǎn 古典
class is over	xiàkè 下課(下课)
classmate	tóngxué 同學(同学)
class papers	jiǎngyì 講義(讲义)
class-room	jiàoshì 教室
class year	niánjí 年級(年级)
clay figurine	níréner 泥人兒(泥人儿)

23

clean (adj.)	gānjìng 乾淨(干净)
clean (v.)	dǎsǎo 打掃(打扫)
clear	míngbai 明白
clear, distinct	qīngchǔ 清楚
clear and definite, clear-cut, explicit	míngquè 明確(明确)
clear away, take away	chèxiàqù 撤下去
clear day	qíngtiān 晴天
clerk	yíngyèyuán 營業員(营业员)
clever, intelligent	cōngming 聰明(聪明)
climate	qìhòu 氣候(气候)
climb	pá 爬
clinic	zhěnsuǒ 診所(诊所)
clip	jiǎn 剪
clippers	jiǎnzi 剪子
clock	zhōng 鐘(钟)
cloisonné	jǐngtàilán 景泰藍(景泰蓝)
close, intimate	jǐnmì 緊密(紧密); qīnmì 親密 (亲密)
close, shut	guān 關(关)
close down	guān 關(关); guāndiào 關掉(关掉)
closet	bìchú 壁櫥
close to, near by	kuàiyào 快要; jìn 近
cloth	bù 布
clothes	yīfu 衣服
clothing	yīfu 衣服
cloud	yún 雲(云)
cloudy	tiānyīn 天陰(天阴)
clove	dīngxiāng 丁香
club	jùlèbù 俱樂部(俱乐部)
clumsy	bènzhuō 笨拙

coach, teach	fǔdǎo 輔導(辅导)
coal	méi 煤
coast line	hǎiànxiàn 海岸綫(海岸线)
coat	dàyī 大衣
Coca Cola	Kěkǒukělè 可口可樂(可口可乐)
cock, hen, chicken	jī 鷄(鸡)
cocktail	jīwěijiǔ 鷄尾酒(鸡尾酒)
cocktail party	jīwěijiǔhuì 鷄尾酒會(鸡尾酒会)
coffee	kāfēi 咖啡
coincidental, opportune, as it happens	qiǎohé 巧合; gāngqiǎo 剛巧(刚巧)
coincidentally, by chance	pèngqiǎo 碰巧(碰巧)
cold, catch cold	zháoliáng 着涼; gǎnmào 感冒
cold, frosty	lěng 冷
collapse	dǎotā 倒塌; bēngkuì 崩潰(崩溃)
colleague	tóngshì 同事
college, institute	xuéyuàn 學院(学院)
college, university	dàxué 大學(大学)
collect	shōují 收集
colorful	duōcǎisède 多彩色的; huāde 花的
combine	jiānyǒu 兼有
combustion	ránshāo 燃燒(燃烧)
come	lái 來(来)
come along	gēnlái 跟來(跟来)
come back	huílái 回來(回来)
come in	jìn 進(进);jìnlái 進來(进来)
come out, appear	chūlái 出來(出来)
come to the end, finish	wánshì 完事
come to visit (someone)	láikàn 來看(来看)

25

comfort, console	ānwèi 安慰
comfortable	shūfu 舒服
comma	dòuhào 逗號(逗号)
commemorate, mark, commemoration	jìniàn 紀念(纪念)
commerce, trade	màoyì 貿易(贸易)
commit (a mistake, a crime)	fàn 犯
common, ordinary	pǔtōng 普通; píngcháng 平常
common people, ordinary civilian	lǎobǎixìng 老百姓
commonplace	píngfánde 平凡的
commune	gōngshè 公社
commune member	shèyuán 社員(社员)
communication	jiāotōng 交通
Communist Party	Gòngchǎndǎng 共產黨(共产党)
companion	tóngbàn 同伴
company, corporation	gōngsī 公司
compare	bǐjiào 比較(比较)
compared with, against	bǐ 比
compass	luópán 羅盤(罗盘); zhǐnánzhēn 指南針(指南针)
compel, force	bī 逼; qiángpò 強迫
competition, match	bǐsài 比賽(比赛); jìngzhēng 競爭(竞争)
compile	biānxiě 編寫(编写)
complete, accomplish, fulfil	wánchéng 完成
completely	wánquán 完全
complicated	fùzáde 複雜的(复杂的)
compose, be composed of	zǔchéng 組成(组成)

26

composition, essay, writing	zuòwén 作文
computer	jìsuànjī 計算機(计算机);diànnǎo 電腦(电脑)
comrade	tóngzhì 同志
concern	guānxīn 關心(关心)
concerning, regarding	guānyú 關於(关于)
condition	tiáojiàn 條件(条件)
conditions, circumstances	qíngkuàng 情況
conductor (of an orchestra)	zhǐhuī 指揮(指挥)
conductor, ticket sellor	shòupiàoyuán 售票員(售票员)
confess	jiāodài 交代; tǎnbái 坦白
confidence	xìnxīn 信心
conflict, struggle	dòuzhēng 鬥爭(斗争)
conform, be in keeping with	fúhé 符合
confused, disorderly	luàn 亂(乱); hùnluàn 混亂(混乱)
confused, distressed	kǔnǎo 苦惱(苦恼)
congratulation	gōngxǐ 恭喜
connect, join, link	liánjiē 連結(连结)
connect (for telephone)	jiētōng 接通
connection, relevance	guānxì 關係(关系)
conscience	liángxīn 良心
conscientious	rènzhēn 認眞(认真)
conscript	zhēngmù 徵募(征募)
consent, agree	tóngyì 同意
consequence	hòuguǒ 後果(后果)
conservation	shēngwù bǎohù 生物保護(生物保护)
conserve	bǎocún 保存
consider, think, regard as	rènwéi 認爲(认为)

consider, think of a way, suppose	xiǎng 想
consistently	yíxiàng 一向
console, comfort	ānwèi 安慰
constant	búbiànde 不變的（不变的）
constant, non-stop	jīngchángde 經常的（经常的）; búduànde 不斷的
constitute, make up, form	gòuchéng 構成（构成）
construct, build	jiànzào 建造
construction	jiànshè 建設（建设）; jiànzào 建造; jiànzhù 建築（建筑）
consul	lǐngshì 領事（领事）
consulate	lǐngshìguǎn 領事館（领事馆）
consult, ask for advice	qǐngjiào 請教（请教）
consumer	xiāofèizhě 消費者（消费者）
contact, get in touch with, connect ties, connection	liánxì 聯繫（联系）
contain, accomodate	róngnà 容納（容纳）
contain, hold, pack	zhuāng 裝（装）
container	róngqì 容器
contend over, fight for	dòuzhēng 鬥爭（斗争）
content, substance	nèiróng 內容
content with oneself	zìdé 自得
contents, list, catalogue	mùlù 目錄（目录）
contest, match	bǐsài 比賽（比赛）
continent (land mass)	zhōu 洲
contingent, troops	duìwǔ 隊伍
continue (in close succession)	jiēzhe 接着
continue, resume	jìxù 繼續（继续）
contract, a written agree-	qìyuē 契約（契约）; hétong 合同

28

ment

contribute, render service to, contribution	gòngxiàn 貢獻（贡献）
control, direct	guǎn 管; kòngzhì 控制
convenient	fāngbiàn 方便
convention, mass meeting	dàhuì 大會（大会）
cook (n.)	chúshī 廚師（厨师）
cook (v.)	zuòfàn 做飯（做饭）
cooked	shúde 熟的
cooking-pot	guō 鍋（锅）
cool	liáng 凉
cope with	duìfu 對付（对付）
copy	yìfèn 一份
copy, (make a copy of)	fùyìn 復印（复印）
cord, string	shéng 繩（绳）
corn	yùmǐ 玉米
corner (of a room)	jiǎoluò 角落
corner (of a street)	guǎijiǎo 拐角
corner (of a table, etc.)	jíjiǎo 犄角；…jiǎo …角
correct (an error)	gǎizhèng 改正
correct, redress (a wrong)	jiūzhèng 糾正（纠正）
correct, right, correctly	zhèngquè 正確（正确）
correct, that's right	duì 對（对）
corridor	zǒuláng 走廊
cost, price	jiàqian 價錢（价钱）
cotton	miánhuā 棉花
cotton cloth	miánbù 棉布
cough	késòu 咳嗽
could not help doing something	bùyóude 不由得

counsellor	cānzàn 參贊(参赞)
count	shǔ 數(数)
counter (sales)	guìtái 櫃臺(柜台)
counter (service)	fúwùtái 朋務臺(服务台)
country	guó 國(国); guójiā 國家(国家)
countryside	nóngcūn 農村(农村)
county	xiàn 縣(县)
couple (married)	fūfù 夫婦(夫妇)
couple, two	liǎng 兩(两)
courage	dǎnzi 膽子(胆子); yǒngqì 勇氣 (勇气)
course, curriculum	kèchéng 課程(课程)
courtesy	lǐmào 禮貌(礼貌)
courtyard	tíngyuàn 庭院
cover, lid, stopper	gài 蓋(盖)
cover, put on	tào 套; gài 蓋(盖)
cover, shade	zhē 遮
cover all over	pūmǎn 鋪滿(铺满)
cow	niú 牛
crab (sea)	hǎixiè 海蟹; pángxiè 螃蟹
crab (fresh water)	héxiè 河蟹; pángxiè 螃蟹
crackers	bǐnggān 餅乾(饼干)
craft products	gōngyìpǐn 工藝品(工艺品)
craftsmanship, technology	gōngyì 工藝(工艺)
crash into	zhuàng 撞; chuǎng 闖(闯)
cream	nǎiyóu 奶油
cream (face)	miànshuāng 面霜; miànyóu 面 油
credit, trust worthiness	xìnyòng 信用
crisp	cuì 脆
crops	nóngzuòwù 農作物(农作物)
crowd	qún 羣; rénqún 人羣

crowd, jostle, throng	jī 擠(挤)
crowded	yōngjǐ 擁擠(拥挤)
crude, natural (oil, wood, etc.)	tiānránde 天然的
crude (poorly made)	cūzhìde 粗製的(粗制的)
crush, press	yā 壓(压)
cry, crying	kū 哭
cry out, shout	jiàohǎn 叫喊
crystallization	jiéjīng 結晶(结晶)
cultural	wénhuàde 文化的
cultural relics	wénwù 文物
cultural exchange	wénhuàjiāoliú 文化交流
culture	wénhuà 文化
cup	bēizi 杯子
cure (n.)	liáofǎ 療法(疗法)
cure (v.)	zhìhǎo 治好
curry (favor)	tǎohǎo 討好(讨好); qiúchǒng 求寵(求宠)
cursorily	zǒumǎ kàn huā 走馬看花(走马看花)
curtain (of theater, etc.)	mù 幕
curtain (of window, etc.)	chuāngliánr 窗簾兒(窗帘儿)
customer	gùkè 顧客(顾客)
custom, habit	xíguàn 習慣(习惯)
customs, customs house	hǎiguān 海關(海关)
cut, cut apart	qiē 切

D

daily	měitiān 每天
daily paper	rìbào 日報(日报)
damp	cháoshī 潮濕(潮湿)
dance (n.)	wǔdǎo 舞蹈
dance (v.)	tiàowǔ 跳舞

31

dance troupe	wǔjùyuàn 舞劇院 (舞剧院)
dangerous	wēixiǎnde 危險的 (危险的)
dare	gǎn 敢
daring, bold vision	qìpò 氣魄 (气魄)
dark, black	àn 暗; hēi 黑
dark (color)	shēn 深
date	rìzi 日子; rìqī 日期;hào 號 (号)
daughter	nǚer 女兒 (女儿)
daughter-in-law	érxifù 兒媳婦 (儿媳妇)
day	tiān 天
another day	gǎitiān 改天
once a day	yītiān yīcì 一天一次
one day, once	yǒuyītiān 有一天
that day	nèitiān 那天
the following day	dìertiān 第二天
day after tomorrow	hòutiān 後天 (后天)
day before yesterday	qiántiān 前天
day of the month	jǐhào 幾號 (几号)
day of the week	xīngqījǐ 星期幾 (星期几)
Monday	Xīngqīyī 星期一
Tuesday	Xīngqīèr 星期二
Wednesday	Xīngqīsān 星期三
Thursday	Xīngqīsì 星期四
Friday	Xīngqīwǔ 星期五
Saturday	Xīngqīliù 星期六
Sunday	Xīngqītiān 星期天
daytime	báitiān 白天
deaf	lóng 聾 (聋)
deal with, cope with	yìngfù 應付 (应付)
deal with, manage	bàn 辦 (办)
dear, loved	qīnàide 親愛的 (亲爱的)
death	sǐ 死; sǐwáng 死亡

decay	fǔxiǔ 腐朽
December	shíèryuè 十二月
decide	juédìng 決定
decidedly, certainly	díquè 的確(的确); yídìng 一定
decimal point	xiǎoshùdiǎn 小數點(小数点)
deduct	jiǎn 減(减); kòuchú 扣除
deep, profound	shēn 深; shēnkè 深刻
deer	lù 鹿
defeat	dǎbài 打敗(打败)
defect, change sides	pànbiàn 叛變(叛变); bèipàn 背叛
defect, flaw	quēdiǎn 缺點(缺点)
defence	fángwèi 防衞(防卫)
defend	shǒu 守; bǎowèi 保衞(保卫)
definitely, precisely	quèqiède 確切地(确切地)
definitely, sure	yídìng 一定
degree	jí 級(级)
degree (college)	xuéwèi 學位(学位)
B.A. or B.S.	xuéshì 學士(学士)
M.A. or M.S.	shuòshì 碩士(硕士)
Ph.D.	bóshì 博士
degree, level	chéngdù 程度
degree (of temperature)	wēndù 溫度
delay, postpone	yánhuǎn 延緩(延缓); yánqī 延期; dānge 耽擱(耽搁)
delegate, representative	dàibiǎo 代表
delegation	dàibiǎotuán 代表團(代表团)
delegation leader	tuánzhǎng 團長(团长)
deliberately	yǒuyì 有意
delicate, dainty	xiǎoqiǎode 小巧的
delicious	hǎochīde 好吃的
delighted	gāoxìng 高興(高兴)

deliver	jiāo 交; sòng 送
demand, require	yāoqiú 要求
demonstrate, prove	zhèngshí 證實(证实)
demonstration	shìwēi 示威
democracy	mínzhǔ 民主
depart, walk, travel	zǒu 走; qǐchéng 起程
department (of government, store, etc.)	bù 部; bùmén 部門(部门)
department (of university, etc.)	xì 系
department store	bǎihuòshāngchǎng 百貨商場 (百货商场)
dependable	kěkàode 可靠的
deposit (n.)	bǎozhèngjīn 保證金(保证金)
deposit (v.)	cúnfàng 存放
deposit money in a bank	cúnqián 存錢(存钱)
deposits, savings	cúnkuǎn 存欵
deputy	fùshǒu 副手
descend	xiàjiàng 下降
describe, portray	miáoxiě 描寫(描写);xíngróng 形容
describe, tell	jiǎng yì jiǎng 講一講(讲一讲)
design, pattern	huāyàng 花樣(花样)
design, plan	shèjì 設計(设计)
desire, want (n.)	yuànwàng 願望(愿望); yāoqiú 要求
desire, want (v.)	xiǎngyào 想要
desk	shūzhuō 書桌(书桌)
desk lamp	táidēng 檯燈(台灯)
despatch, send	pàiqiǎn 派遣
despatch, transport	sòng 送
dessert	gāodiǎn 糕點(糕点); tiánshí 甜

食

destination	mùdìdì 目的地; zhōngdiǎn 終點 (终点)
destroy	huǐ 毀; pòhuài 破壞(破坏)
details, particulars	xìjié 細節(细节)
detect	kànchūlái 看出來(看出来); chájué 察覺(察觉)
determine, decide	juédìng 決定
develop (a film)	chōngxǐ 沖洗
develop, extend	fāzhǎn 發展(发展)
development	kāifā 開發(开发)
deviate from, leave	líkāi 離開(离开)
diary	rìjì 日記(日记)
dictate, dictation	kǒushù 口述
dictionary	zìdiǎn 字典
die	sǐ 死
die away, extinguish	xī熄; xīmiè 熄滅(熄灭)
diesel engine	cháiyóujī 柴油機(柴油机)
diesel oil	cháiyóu 柴油
differ from	bùtóng 不同
different	bùtóng 不同
difficult	nán 難(难)
difficulty	kùnnan 困難(困难)
dig	wā 挖; wājué 挖掘
diluted	xībó 稀薄
dim, dull, dark	àn 暗
dime	máo 毛; jiǎo 角
dining car	cānchē 餐車(餐车)
dining hall	cāntīng 餐廳(餐厅)
dining room	cānshì 餐室
dinner	wǎnfàn 晚飯(晚饭)
dinner party	wǎnyàn 晚宴

35

diplomatic, diplomacy	wàijiāo 外交
direct	zhíjiē 直接
directly	zhíjiē 直接地
direction, orientation	fāngxiàng 方向
directory inquiry, information	cháhàotái 查號臺 (查号台)
dirt	zāngdōngxi 髒東西 (脏东西)
dirty	zāng 髒 (脏)
disabled	cánfèi 殘廢 (残废)
disaster, calamity	zāinàn 災難 (灾难)
discover	fāxiàn 發現 (发现)
discuss, discussion	tǎolùn 討論 (讨论); zuòtán 座談 (座谈); shāngyì 商議 (商议)
dish, plate	pánzi 盤子 (盘子)
dish(es) of food	cài 菜
dislike	bùxǐhuān 不喜歡 (不喜欢)
disorder, chaos	hùnluàn 混亂 (混乱)
disorderly, confused	luàn 亂 (乱)
disperse, scatter	fēnsàn 分散; sànkāi 散開 (散开)
display, be on show	zhǎnchū 展出
distance	jùlí 距離 (距离)
distinct	dútède 獨特的 (独特的); xiǎnzhùde 顯著的 (显著的)
distress, suffering	kǔnàn 苦難 (苦难)
disturb, trouble	dǎrǎo 打擾 (打扰); dǎjiǎo 打攪 (打搅)
diverting, amusing	hǎowánr 好玩兒 (好玩儿)
divide	fēn 分; fēnwéi 分爲 (分为)
do	zuò 做
do, handle, tackle	bàn 辦 (办)
do, work, make	gàn 幹 (干)
do not	bié 別; búyào 不要

doctor	yīshēng 醫生(医生); dàifu 大夫
doctor (Chinese traditional)	zhōngyī 中醫(中医)
doctor (Western trained)	xīyī 西醫(西医)
document	wénjiàn 文件
dog	gǒu 狗
dollar	yuán 圓(圆)
donkey	lǘ 驢(驴)
door, gate	mén 門(门)
doorway	ménkǒu 門口(门口)
dormitory	sùshè 宿舍
double room	shuāngrénfáng 雙人房(双人房)
doubt, suspect	huáiyí 懷疑(怀疑)
down	wǎngxià 往下; xià 下
downstairs	lóuxià 樓下(楼下)
drag, pull	qiān 牽(牵)
dragon	lóng 龍(龙)
drain, empty	fànggān 放乾(放干)
drama, play	huàjù 話劇(话剧)
draw, attract	xīyǐn 吸引
draw, paint	huà 畫(画)
draw, smoke	xī 吸
drawer	chōuti 抽屜
drawing, painting	huà 畫(画)
drawnwork	chōushā 抽紗(抽纱)
dream	mèng 夢(梦)
dress (n.)	yīfu 衣服; fúzhuāng 服裝(服装)
dress (v.)	chuān 穿
dress, adorn	dǎbàn 打扮
drink (n.)	yǐnliào 飲料(饮料)
drink (v.)	hē 喝
drinking straw	xīguǎnr 吸管兒(吸管儿)

drill ground	cāochǎng 操場(操场)
drive (a car)	kāichē 開車(开车)
drive, smash (tennis, etc.)	chōu 抽
driver	sījī 司機(司机)
drizzle	máomaoyǔ 毛毛雨
drop, lose	diūdiào 丟掉
drunk, tipsy	zuì 醉
dry	gānzào 乾燥(干燥); gān 乾(干)
dry (for wine)	dàn 淡; bùtián 不甜
dry clean	gānxǐ 乾洗(干洗)
duck	yāzi 鴨子(鸭子)
due to	yóuyú 由於(由于)
dull, dim, dark	àn 暗
dumpling	jiǎozi 餃子(饺子)
duplicate	fùyìnběn 復印本(复印本); fùběn 副本
during	zài…qījiān 在…期間(在…期间)
dusk	huánghūn 黃昏
dust (n.)	chéntǔ 塵土(尘土); tǔ 土
dust (v.)	dǎn 撣(掸)
dwell, stay overnight	sù 宿
dynasty	cháodài 朝代

E

each, everyone	měi 每; měiyígè 每一個(每一个)
each other	hùxiāng 互相
ear	ěrduo 耳朵
earliest	zuìzǎo 最早
early	zǎo 早

early, first, ahead	xiān 先; qián 前
early, near the beginning	chū 初
earn, gain	yíngdé 贏得
earn（money）	zhuàn（qián）賺（錢）（赚（钱））
earnest	rènzhēn 認眞(认真)
earphone	ěrjī 耳機(耳机)
earth	tǔ 土
earth, globe	dìqiú 地球
earthen mound, hill	qiūlíng 丘陵
east	dōng 東(东)
east side	dōngbian 東邊(东边)
easy	róngyì 容易
eat	chī 吃
eat one's fill	chībǎo 吃飽(吃饱)
eat up	chīguāng 吃光
economy, economic	jīngjì 經濟(经济); jīngjìde 經濟的(经济的)
edge	biān 邊(边)
educate, education	jiàoyù 教育
effect, influence	yǐngxiǎng 影響(影响)
effect, result	xiàoguǒ 效果
effective	yǒuxiàode 有效的
efficiency	xiàolù 效率
effort	nǔlì 努力
eight	bā 八
eighteen	shíbā 十八
eighth	dìbā 第八
eighty	bāshí 八十
either…or…	búshì…jiùshì… 不是…就是…; huò…huò… 或…或…
elated, exulted, pleased with oneself	déyì 得意

electric	diànde 電的(电的)
electrical equipment, appliances	diàn qì 電器(电器)
electric generator	fādiànjī 發電機(发电机)
electric heater	diànrèqì 電熱器(电热器)
electrician	diàngōng 電工(电工)
electricity	diàn 電(电)
electric light	diàndēng 電燈(电灯)
electric machinery plant	diànjīchǎng 電機廠(电机厂)
electric plug	diànchātóu 電插頭(电插头)
electronic games	diànzǐ yóuxì 電子遊戲(电子游戏)
elegant, refined	wényǎde 文雅的
elephant	dàxiàng 大象
elevator	diàntī 電梯(电梯)
eleven	shíyī 十一
elm tree	yúshù 榆樹(榆树)
embarrass	wéinán 爲難(为难)
embassy	dàshǐguǎn 大使館(大使馆)
embroider	xiùhuā 繡花(绣花)
embroidery	xiùhuā 繡花(绣花); xiùzhìpǐn 繡製品(绣制品)
emergency	jǐnjíshìjiàn 緊急事件(紧急事件)
emperor	huángdì 皇帝
employ	gù 雇
employee	gōngzuò rényuán 工作人員(工作人员); gùyuán 雇員(雇员)
Empress	nǚhuáng 女皇; huánghòu 皇后
empty	kōngde 空的
enable	shǐ…nénggòu 使…能夠
enclosed, attached	fùyǒu 附有

40

encounter, meet	yùjiàn 遇見(遇见)
end, bring to an end, settle	liǎojié 了結(了结)
end, conclude	jiéshù 結束(结束)
(to the) end, to the finish	dàodǐ 到底
enemy	dírén 敵人(敌人)
energetic	yǒulìde 有力的
energy	néngliàng 能量
engage in	cóngshì 從事(从事)
engine, machine	jīqì 機器(机器)
engineer	gōngchéngshī 工程師(工程师)
engineering course	gōngkē 工科
England	Yīngguó 英國(英国)
English	Yīngwén 英文; Yīngyǔ 英語(英语)
engrave, carve	diāokè 雕刻
enjoy	xiǎngshòu 享受
enjoy, appreciate	xīnshǎng 欣賞(欣赏)
enjoyable, happy	yúkuàide 愉快的
enjoy oneself	guòdéyúkuài 過得愉快(过得愉快)
enough, sufficient	gòu 夠; gòule 夠了
enter	jìn 進(进)
enter (a place)	zǒujìn 走進(走进)
entertain guests	dàikè 待客
enthusiastic	rèliè 熱烈(热烈); rèxīn 熱心(热心)
entire, complete	wánquán 完全
entire, whole	zhěnggè 整個(整个)
entrance (the act of entering)	jìnrù 進入(进入)

41

entrance (in a building)	rùkǒu 入口
envelope (for letter, papers, etc.)	xìnfēng 信封
equal, be equal to	děngyú 等於(等于); xiāngtóng 相同
equipment, facilities	shèbèi 設備(设备)
equivalent to	zhéhé 折合; xiāngdāng 相當(相当)
era, period, age	shídài 時代(时代)
erect	shùzhíde 豎直的(竖直的)
erect, build	shùlì 樹立(树立)
error, fault, mistake	cuòwù 錯誤(错误)
escalator	zìdòng fútī 自動扶梯(自动扶梯)
especially, exceptionally	géwài 格外
especially, specially	tèbié 特別
essay, thesis	lùnwén 論文(论文)
establish, set up	chénglì 成立; jiànlì 建立
etc.	děng 等
Europe	Ōuzhōu 歐洲(欧洲)
European	Ōuzhōurén 歐洲人(欧洲人)
even	lián…dōu 連…都(连…都); shènzhì 甚至
even, level	píngde 平的
even go so far as to	shèněr 甚而
even if	jíshǐ 即使
even more, still more	géng 更; hái 還(还)
even so much so that	shènzhì 甚至
evening	wǎnshàng 晚上
evening dinner party	wǎncānhuì 晚餐會(晚餐会)
evenly matched	shìjūnlìdí 勢均力敵(势均力敌)
event	shìjiàn 事件

event (in a sports competition)	xiàngmù 項目(项目)
every	měi 每; gè 各
every, all	suǒyǒude 所有的; měiyīgè 每一個(每一个)
everybody, everyone	suǒyǒuderén 所有的人; yígèrén 每一個人(每一个人)
everyday	měitiān 每天
everything	yíqiè 一切; fánshì 凡事
every time when, whenever	měidāng 每當(每当)
everywhere	měiyígè dìfang 每一個地方(每一个地方); chùchù 處處(处处)
exact, precise, accurate	zhǔnquè 準確(准确)
exactly, exactly right	zhèngshì 正是
exactly the same	yìmóyíyàng 一模一樣(一模一样)
exam, test, quiz	kǎoshì 考試(考试)
examine, insepect	jiǎnchá 檢查(检查)
example	lìzi 例子
for example	lìrú 例如
example, model	bǎngyàng 榜樣
excavate	wājué 挖掘; wāchūtǔ 挖出土
excellent	hǎojíle 好極子(好极了)
except, with the exception of, in addition to, besides	chúle…yǐwài 除了…以外
exceptional	tèbié 特別
exceptionally	fēicháng 非常; géwài 格外
excessive	tài 太; guòfèn 過份(过分)

excess, surplus	guòliàng 過量(过量)
exchange	jiāoliú 交流
exchange (cultural)	wénhuà jiāoliú 文化交流
exchange (money)	huànqián 換錢(换钱)
exchange, swop	jiāohuàn 交換
excited	xīngfèn 興奮(兴奋); jīdòng 激動(激动)
exclamatory mark	gǎntànhào 感嘆號(感叹号)
excuse me	duìbuqǐ 對不起(对不起)
exercise	liànxí 練習(练习)
exercise, athletics, sport	yùndòng 運動(运动)
exercise-book	běnzi 本子; liànxíběn 練習本(练习本)
exercise (physical)	duànliàn shēntǐ 鍛煉(锻炼)
exert one's strength	yònglì 用力
exhibition	zhǎnlǎn 展覽(展览)
exhibition hall	zhǎnlǎnguǎn 展覽館(展览馆)
exist	cúnzài 存在
exit (n.)	chūkǒu 出口
exit (v.)	tuìchū 退出
expand	kuòzhǎn 擴展(扩展)
expect, hope	xīwàng 希望
as expected	guǒrán 果然
expense, fee	fèiyòng 費用(费用)
expensive	guì 貴(贵)
experience	jīngyàn 經驗(经验); jīnglì 經歷(经历)
experienced, skilled	shúliànde 熟練的(熟练的)
expert, practiced	shúliànde 熟練的(熟练的)
explain	jiěshì 解釋(解释)
explain, show, illustrate	shuōmíng 說明(说明)
explanation, explanatory	zhùshì 注釋(注释)

44

notes

exploit, deed, merit	gōngjì 功績(功绩)
exploit (resources)	kāifā 開發(开发)
export	chūkǒu 出口; shūchū 輸出(输出)
export goods	chūkǒuhuò 出口貨(出口货)
express, indicate	biǎoshì 表示
express, show	biǎoxiànchū 表現出(表现出)
express, urgent	jiājíde 加急的
express, voice, convey	biǎodá 表達(表达)
expression (of emotion)	biǎoqíng 表情
exquisite	jīngměi 精美
extend	shēnzhǎn 伸展; kuòdà 擴大(扩大)
extend, develop	fāzhǎn 發展(发展)
extension (telephone)	fēnjī 分機(分机)
extinguish	xī 熄; xīmiè 熄滅(熄灭)
extra	éwàide 額外的(额外的)
extracurricular	kèwài 課外的(课外的)
extraordinarily	fēicháng 非常
extraordinary, tremendous	liǎobuqǐde 了不起的
extravagent	shēchǐde 奢侈的
extreme	jíduānde 極端的(极端的); fēichángde 非常的
extremely	jíduānde 極端地(极端地); fēichángde 非常地
eye	yǎn 眼; yǎnjīng 眼睛
eye glasses	yǎnjìng 眼鏡(眼镜)

F

fable	yùyán 寓言
face	liǎn 臉(脸)
face, confront	miànduì 面對(面对); miànlín 面臨(面临)
face, looks on	miànxiàng 面向
facial expression	biǎoqíng 表情
facing, opposite	duìmiàn 對面(对面)
fact	shìshí 事實(事实)
factory	gōngchǎng 工廠(工厂)
factory building	chǎngfáng 廠房(厂房)
faculty, department	xì 系
faculty (teaching staff)	jiàozhíyuán 教職員(教职员)
fade, lose color	diàoshǎi 掉色
fail	shībài 失敗(失败)
fairly, quite	xiāngdāng 相當(相当)
fall, autumn	qiūtiān 秋天
fall, stumble	diējiāo 跌跤
fall down	dǎo 倒
fall to, drop to	jiàng 降; jiàngdào 降到
false, fake	jiǎ 假
false, not correct	búduì 不對(不对)
familiar with, knowing well	shúxī 熟悉
family	jiā 家
famine	jīhuāng 饑荒(饥荒)
famous, well-known	yǒumíng 有名
fan	shànzi 扇子
fan (v.)	shān 搧(扇)
far	yuǎn 遠(远)
far away, remote	yáoyuǎn 遙遠(遥远)
Far East	yuǎndōng 遠東(远东)
farm	nóngchǎng 農場(农场)

farmer	nóngmín 農民(农民); nóngfū 農夫(农夫); nóngchǎngzhǔ 農場主(农场主)
farming	gēngzhòng 耕種(耕种)
fashion	shímáo 時髦(时髦); fēngshàng 風尚(风尚)
fashion, way, manner	fāngshì 方式
fast, quick	kuài 快
fat (n.)	féiròu 肥肉
fat, obese	pàng 胖
father	bàba 爸爸; fùqīn 父親(父亲); diē 爹
fear, be afraid of	pà 怕
fearful, frightful, terrible	kěpà 可怕
feather	yǔmáo 羽毛
features	yàngzi 樣子(样子)
February	èryuè 二月
feed, raise, keep	wèi 餵(喂)
fee, expense	fèiyong 費用(费用)
feel, sense, perceive	juéde 覺得(觉得); gǎndào 感到
feel, touch	mō 摸
feel faint	tóuyūn 頭暈(头晕)
feelings, mood	xīnqíng 心情
feet	jiǎo 腳
feet (British measure)	yīngchǐ 英尺; chǐ 呎
female	nǚ 女
fertilizer	féiliào 肥料
festival	jiérì 節日(节日)
fetch, collect	qǔ 取
feudalism	fēngjiàn 封建
fever	fāshāo 發燒(发烧)
few, little	shǎo 少

47

a few, some	jǐgè 幾個(几个); yìxiē 一些
fiancé	wèihūnfū 未婚夫
fiancée	wèihūnqī 未婚妻
fiction, novel	xiǎoshuō 小說(小说)
field, farmland	tián 田
field (of studies)	xuékē 學科(学科)
fierce, powerful	lìhaide 厲害的(厉害的)
fierce, violent	měngde 猛的
fifteen	shíwǔ 十五
fifth	dìwǔ 第五
fifty	wǔshí 五十
fight, combat	zhàndòu 戰鬥(战斗)
fight for, contend over	zhēng 爭(争)
figure, calculate	suàn 算(祘); shǔ 數(数)
figure, form, image	xíngxiàng 形像(形象)
figures, numbers	shùzì 數字(数字)
fill, load, pack	zhuāngmǎn 裝滿(装满)
fill an office, serve as	dānrèn 擔任; dāng 當(当)
fill in, stuff	tián 填; sāi 塞
fill in, write	tiánxiě 填寫(填写)
fill in a blank	tiánkòng 填空
film	diànyǐng 電影(电影)
shoot a film	pāishè diànyǐng 拍攝電影(拍摄电影)
film (a roll of)	jiāojuǎn 膠捲(胶卷)
final, last, ultimate	zuìhòu 最後(最后)
finally, in the end	zhōngyú 終於(终于)
finally, lastly	zuìhòu 最後(最后)
finals (in sports, tests, etc.)	juésài 決賽(决赛)
find	zhǎodào 找到
find, discover	fāxiàn 發現(发现)

48

fine, clear (weather)	qíng 晴
fine, good	hǎode 好的
fine, tiny, minute	xìwēide 細微的
fine art	měishù 美術（美术）
finger	shǒuzhǐ 手指
finish, complete, accomplish	wánchéng 完成; zuòwán 做完
finish (a job)	wánchéng 完成
finish classes	shàngwánkè 上完課（上完课）
finished, having come to the end	wánle 完了; wánshì 完事
finished, ready	hǎole 好了
fire	huǒ 火
light a fire	shēnghuǒ 生火
firecrackers	biānpào 鞭炮
firewood	chái 柴
first	dìyī 第一
at first	zuìchū 最初
first, ahead, early	xiān 先
first of all, above all, in the first place	shǒuxiān 首先
first time	chūcì 初次
fish	yú 魚
fisherman	yúmín 漁民
fishery	yúyè 漁業（渔业）
fishing boat	yúchuán 漁船
fit, suitable, just right	zhènghǎo 正好
fitting (for clothes)	shǐ 試（试）; shìyíshì 試一試（试一试）
fittings, furnishings	jiajù 傢具（家具）; bǎishè 擺設（摆设）
five	wǔ 伍, 五

49

fix, fixed, stable	gùdìng 固定
flag	qízi 旗子
flash	shǎn 閃(闪)
flash cards	shēngcí kǎpiàn 生詞卡片(生词卡片)
flash light	diàntǒng 電筒(电筒)
flash of lightning	shǎndiàn 閃電(闪电)
flashlight	shǒudiàntǒng 手電筒(手电筒)
flat, apartment	gōngyù 公寓
flat, even, level	píng 平
flatter, compliment	gōngwéi 恭維(恭维)
flavor	wèidao 味道
flavor, flavoring, flavored	tiáowèi 調味(调味)
flaw, defect	quēdiǎn 缺點(缺点)
flee, escape, run away	táo 逃
fling, cast away	rēng 扔; shuāi 摔
flood, submerge	yān 淹; yānmò 淹沒
floor (in a room)	dìxia 地下; dìbǎn 地板
floors (in a building)	céng 層(层)
flour	miànfěn 麵粉(面粉)
flower	huā 花
flu	gǎnmào 感冒
fluent	shúliàn 熟練(熟练); liúlì 流利
flurried, flustered	huāngzhāng 慌張(慌张)
fly (n.)	cāngying 蒼蠅(苍蝇)
fly (v.)	fēi 飛(飞)
fog, mist	wù 霧(雾)
follow	gēnsuí 跟隨(跟随)
following, listed after	xiàliè 下列
following after, thereupon	gēnzhe 跟着
fond of	ài 愛(爱); xǐhuān 喜歡(喜欢)
food	shíwù 食物; shípǐn 食品

food (Chinese)	zhōngcān 中餐
food (dish of)	cài 菜
food, grain	liángshi 糧食（粮食）
food (Western)	xīcān 西餐
food (whole meal)	fàncài 飯菜（饭菜）
fool	bèndàn 笨蛋
fool, fooling	kāiwánxiào 開玩笑（开玩笑）
foot	jiǎo 脚; zú 足
foot (British measure)	yīngchǐ 英尺; chǐ 呎
football	zúqiú 足球
forage, fodder	cǎoliào 草料
for a long time	cháng shíjiān 長時間（长时间）; hǎobàntiān 好半天
for a while, for the time being	yìshí 一時（一时）; zānshí 暫時（暂时）
force, compel	qiǎngpò 強迫（强迫）
force, physical strength	lì 力; lìliang 力量
forcibly, through compulsion	qiǎngpòde 強迫地
forecast	yùbào 預報（预报）
foreign	wàiguóde 外國的（外国的）
foreign country	wàiguó 外國（外国）
foreign language	wàiwén 外文; wàiyǔ 外語（外语）
foreigner	wàiguórén 外國人（外国人）
forenoon, morning	shàngwǔ 上午
foresight, prediction	yùjiàn 預見（预见）
foresee	yùjiàndào 預見到（预见到）
forest	shùlín 樹林（树林）
forestry	línyiè 林業（林业）; línxué 林學（林学）
for, for the sake of	wèile 爲了（为了）

forget	wàngjì 忘記(忘记); wàngle 忘了
forgetful, scatter-brained	shànwángde 善忘的
fork, table fork	chāzi 叉子
form, construct	gòuchéng 構成(构成)
form, style, pattern	yàngshì 樣式(样式)
formerly, in the past, before	cóngqián 從前(从前); yǐqián 以前
formidable, terrible	lìhaide 厲害的(厉害的)
forms (official)	biǎogé 表格
for nothing, in vain	báibái 白白
fortunate	xìngyùn 幸運(幸运)
fortunately	yǒuxìng 有幸; hěnzǒuyòu 很走運(很走运)
forty	sìshí 四十
forward	wǎngqián 往前
foster, nourish	péiyǎng 培養(培养)
foundation, basis	gēnjī 根基; jīchǔ 基礎(基础)
foundation, fund	jījīnhuì 基金會(基金会)
foundation (of a building)	dìjī 地基
foundation, root	gēnběn 根本
fountain	pēnquán 噴泉(喷泉)
fountain pen	gāngbǐ 鋼筆(钢笔)
four	sì 四
fourteen	shísì 十四
fourth	dìsì 第四
fragrant, nice-smelling	xiāng 香
frame (for a mirror or for eyeglasses)	jìngkuàng 鏡框(镜框)
framing	xiāng 鑲(镶)
France	Fǎguó 法國(法国)

free, freely	zìyóu 自由
free market	zìyóushìchǎng 自由市場(自由市场)
free of charge	búyàoqián 不要錢(不要钱); miǎnfèi 免費(免费)
free time	kòng 空; kòngyúshíjiān 空餘時間(空余时间)
freeze	dòng 凍(冻)
French (language)	Fǎyǔ 法語(法语); Fǎwén 法文
French (people)	Fǎguórén 法國人(法国人)
frequently	chángcháng 常常
fresh, new	xīnxiān 新鮮
fret, worry	guàxīn 掛心(挂心)
Friday	xīngqīwǔ 星期五
friend	péngyou 朋友
friendly, warmly	yǒuhǎo 友好; qīnqiè 親切(亲切)
friendship	yǒuyì 友誼(友谊)
frighten, scare, intimidate	xià 嚇(吓); xiàhu 嚇唬(吓唬); wēixié 威脅(威胁)
frightening	xiàrén 嚇人(吓人); kěpà 可怕
from	cóng 從(从)
from, at a distance from	jù 距; lí 離(离)
from, since	zìcóng 自從(自从)
from, starting from	cóng…qǐ 從…起(从…起)
from now on	jīnhòu 今後(今后)
front	qiánbian 前邊(前边)
in front of	zài…qiánmiàn 在…前面
frost	shuāng 霜
frown	zhòuméi 皺眉(皱眉)
frozen	dòngjié 凍結(冻结)
frozen food	lěngcáng shípǐn 冷藏食品

fruit	shuǐguǒr 水果兒(水果儿)
fruit juice	guǒzhī 果汁
fry	zhá 炸; jiān 煎; chǎo 炒
fulfil, complete, accomplish	wánchéng 完成
full, ample, abundant	chōngfèn 充分
full, filled	mǎnle 滿了
full (stomach)	bǎo 飽(饱)
full of, permeated with	chōngmǎn 充滿(充满)
fun	hǎowánr 好玩兒(好玩儿)
function, effect	zuòyòng 作用
fundamental, basic	gēnběnde 根本的
fungus	zhēnjūn 眞菌; mùěr 木耳
funny, ridiculous	kěxiàode 可笑的
fur	máo 毛; máopí 毛皮
furniture	jiāju 傢具(家具)
further, more	zài 再; háiyǒu 還有(还有)
future	jiānglái 將來(将来)

G

gain, obtain, achieve	huòdé 獲得(获得)
gambit, move	zhāofǎ 着法(着法)
gamble	dǔbuó 賭博(赌博)
gambling house	dǔchǎng 賭場(赌场)
game, recreation	yóuxì 遊戲(游戏)
gangway	tōnglù 通路; guòdào 過道(过道)
garbage	lājī 垃圾
garden	huāyuán 花園(花园)
gardener	huājiàng 花匠; yuándīng 園丁(园丁)

garlic	dàsuàn 大蒜
gasoline	qìyóu 汽油
gasoline station	jiāyóuzhàn 加油站
gate	mén 門(门); dàmén 大門(大门)
gate to a monastery	shānmén 山門(山门)
gathering of people	jíhuì 集會(集会)
gay, colorful	huálì 華麗(华丽)
gaze	zhùshì 注視(注视); dīng 盯
general, common	yìbānde 一般的
in general terms	lǒngtǒng 籠統(笼统)
general (in an army)	jiāngjūn 將軍(将军)
general aspect, situation	qíngjǐng 情景
general idea	dàyì 大意
gentle	wényǎde 文雅的

gentle, pleasantly affec-
   tionate
	wēnhéde 溫和的; wēnróude 溫
	   柔的

gentle (used only for people)	míngménde 名門的(名门的)
gentleman, Sir, Mr.	Xiānsheng 先生
gently, lightly	qīngqīng 輕輕(轻轻)
genuine, authentic	zhēnzhèngde 眞正的
genuine, real	zhēnshíde 眞實的(真实的)
geology	dìzhìxué 地質學(地质学)
German (language)	Déwén 德文; Déyǔ 德語(德语)
German (people)	Déguórén 德國人(德国人)
Germany	Déguó 德國(德国)
get, fetch	ná 拿
get, receive	dé 得; shōudào 收到; huòdé 獲 得(获得)
get a lift (in a car, cart, etc.)	dābiànchē 搭便車(搭便车)
get along	xiāngchǔ 相處(相处)

get in touch with	qǔdé liánluò 取得聯絡(取得联络)
get off	xià 下
get-together	liánhuān 聯歡(联欢)
get up	qǐchuáng 起床; qǐlái 起來(起来)
gift, present	lǐwù 禮物(礼物)
ginger	jiāng 薑(姜)
girl	nǚháir 女孩兒(女孩儿); nǚháizi 女孩子
girl, unmarried young woman	gūniang 姑娘
give	gěi 給(给)
give (as a present), send	sòng 送; sònggěi 送給(送给)
give back	huángěi 還給(还给)
give to	nágěi 拿給(拿给)
glad	gāoxìng 高興(高兴)
glaring, gaily-colored	xiānyàn 鮮艷(鲜艳)
glass	bōli 玻璃
glass (drinking)	bōli bēizi 玻璃杯子
glasses, spectacles	yǎnjìng 眼鏡(眼镜)
glaze (for porcelain)	yòumiàn 釉面
gloss, sheen	guāngzé 光澤(光泽)
gloves	shǒutào 手套
glue (n.)	jiāoshuǐ 膠水(胶水)
glue, paste (v.)	zhān 黏(粘)
go	qù 去; zǒudào 走到
go back	huíqù 回去
go back to	huídào 回到
go by, ride in	zuò⋯qù 坐⋯去
go directly to	zhídá 直達(直达)
go down	xià 下
go on, continue, resume	jìxù 繼續(继续)

go out	chū 出; chūqù 出去
go to bed	shuìjiào 睡覺(睡觉)
go to class	shàngkè 上課(上课)
go to meet, greet	yíng 迎; yíngjiē 迎接
go to school	shàngxué 上學(上学)
go towards	qiánwǎng 前往
go to work	shàngbān 上班
go up	shàng 上
goal, objective	mùbiāo 目標(目标)
goat	shānyáng 山羊
gold	jīn(zi) 金(子)
goldfish	jīnyú 金魚
golf	gāoěrfūqiú 高爾夫球(高尔夫球)
gong	luó 鑼(锣)
good, well	hǎo 好
better	bǐjiàohǎo 比較好(比较好); gèng-hǎo 更好
best	zuìhǎo 最好
not bad（ok）	búhuài 不壞(不坏); búcuò 不錯(不错)
not good	bùhǎo 不好
not so good	bùtàihǎo 不太好
good-bye	zàijiàn 再見(再见)
good day	nǐhǎo 你好
good-looking	hǎokàn 好看
good morning	zǎo 早
goods, commodity, mer-chandise	shāngpǐn 商品
goose	é 鵝(鹅)
gossip	liáotiānr 聊天兒(聊天儿)
govern	guǎn 管; guǎnxiá 管轄(管辖)
government	zhèngfǔ 政府

government offices	jīguān 機關(机关)
grab, take away by force	qiǎng 搶(抢)
grade (in quality)	děngji 等級(等级)
grade (in school)	niánjí 年級(年级)
grades, marks	fēnshù 分數(分数)
gradually, little by little	jiànjiàn 漸漸(渐渐)
graduate	bìyè 畢業(毕业)
graduate school	yánjiūyuàn 研究院
grain, food	liángshi 糧食(粮食)
gram (weight)	kè 克
grammar	yǔfǎ 語法(语法); wénfǎ 文法
grand, imposing, magnificent	xióngwei 雄偉(雄伟)
grandeur	zhuàngguān 壯觀(壮观)
grape	pútáo 葡萄
grape juice	pútáozhī 葡萄汁
grasp, hold	wò 握
grasp, seize	zhuā 抓
grass	cǎo 草
grateful	gǎnjīde 感激的
greasy	yóunì 油膩(油腻)
great (for people)	wěidà 偉大(伟大)
great, big, huge	dà 大
green	lǜ 綠(绿)
grill, barbecue (n.)	kǎoròujià 烤肉架
grill, barbecue (v.)	kǎoyìkǎo 烤一烤
grind	mó 磨
grope	mōsuǒ 摸索
ground, a field	chǎngdì 場地(场地)
ground, dirt	tǔdì 土地
ground meat	ròumò 肉末
group	tuántǐ 團體(团体)

group, crowd	qún 羣
group, (small)	xiǎozǔ 小組(小组)
grow	shēngzhǎng 生長(生长)
grow, plant	zhòng 種(种)
growing, rising (water level, prices, etc.)	shàngzhǎngde 上漲的(上涨的)
grown up	zhǎngdàde 長大的(长大的)
grueling, tiring	xīnkǔ 辛苦
guarantee	bǎozhèng 保證(保证)
guard (n.)	wèibīng 衞兵(卫兵)
guard (v.)	bǎowèi 保衞(保卫)
guess (n.)	cāicè 猜測(猜测)
guess (v.)	cāi 猜
guest	kèrén 客人
guest house	bīnguǎn 賓館(宾馆)
guide	xiàngdǎo 嚮導(向导)
guide, lead	dàilǐng 帶領(带领); yǐndǎo 引導(引导)
gun	qiāng 槍(枪)
gymnasium	tǐyùguǎn 體育館(体育馆)
gymnastics	tǐcāo 體操(体操)

H

habit	xíguàn 習慣(习惯)
hair (on one's head)	tóufa 頭髮(头发)
haircut	lǐfà 理髮(理发);
hairdresser, barber	lǐfàyuán 理髮員(理发员)
half	bàn 半; yíbàn 一半
halfday	bàntiān 半天
hall	guǎn 館(馆); tīng 廳(厅)
ham	huǒtuǐ 火腿

Han nationality	Hànzú 漢族(汉族)
hand	shǒu 手
hand-bag, bag	tíbāo 提包
hand over, hand in, deliver	jiāo 交
handsome	hěnjīngshen 很精神; piàoliàng 漂亮
hang	guà 挂
hanger (for clothes)	yījià 衣架
hangup	zhàng'ài 障礙(障碍)
happen, take place	fāshēng 發生(发生)
happiness	kuàilè 快樂(快乐)
happy	yúkuàide 愉快的; xìngfúde 幸福的; gāoxìngde 高興的(高兴的)
Happy Birthday	Shēngrìkuàilè 生日快樂(生日快乐)
harbor, port	gǎngkǒu 港口
hard, difficult	nán 難(难)
hard, tough, unyielding	yìng 硬
hard work, arduous struggle	nǔlìgōngzuò 努力工作; jiānkǔfèndòu 艱苦奮鬥(艰苦奋斗)
hard-working	nǔlìgōngzuòde 努力工作的
harm	shānghài 傷害(伤害); hàichù 害處(害处)
harm, injure	shānghài 傷害(伤害); sǔnhài 損害(损害)
harvest	fēngshōu 豐收(丰收)
harvest, yield	shōuhuò 收獲(收获)
haste	cōngmáng 匆忙
hat, cap	màozi 帽子
hate	hèn 恨

have	yǒu 有
have a joke, make fun of	kāiwánxiào 開玩笑(开玩笑)
have fun	wánr 玩兒(玩儿)
have not, did not, etc.	méi 沒
have only, only have	zhǐyǒu 只有
have to	búdèbú 不得不; zhǐhǎo 只好; bìxū 必須(必须)
he, him	tā 他
head	tóu 頭(头)
headache	tóuténg 頭疼(头疼)
head for	xiàng…kāiqù 向…開去; bēnxiàng 奔向
headline, title	biāotí 標題(标题)
headmaster	xiàozhǎng 校長(校长)
head of a delegation	tuánzhǎng 團長(团长)
head towards, leave for	wǎng 往
health	jiànkāng 健康
healthy	jiànkāngde 健康的
heap, pile	duī 堆
hear	tīng 聽(听)
heart	xīn 心
heater	jiārèqì 加熱器(加热器); nuǎnqì 暖氣(暖气)
electric heater	diànlú 電加熱器(电加热器)
coal heater	méilú 煤加熱器(煤加热器)
kerosene heater	méiyóulú 煤油加熱器(煤油加热器)
heavy	zòng 重
hectare	gōngqǐng 公頃(公顷)
heel (of a foot or a shoe)	gēn 跟
hello	nǐhǎo 你好; wèi 喂
help (with object)	bāngzhù 幫助(帮助)

help (without object)	bāngmáng 幫忙(帮忙)
hen	mǔjī 母鷄(母鸡)
hence, as a result, thus	yúshì 於是(于是); yīncǐ 因此
henceforth, from then on	cóngcǐ 從此(从此)
hen's egg	jīdàn 雞蛋(鸡蛋)
her	tā 她
here	zhèr 這兒(这儿); zhèlǐ 這裏(这里)
hero	yīngxióng 英雄
her	tāde 她的
hide	duǒ 躲; cáng 藏
high school (junior)	chūzhōng 初中
high school (senior)	gāozhōng 高中
high, tall	gāo 高
highway	gōnglù 公路
hill	shān 山
him	tā 他
hint	ànshì 暗示
hire, rent	zū 租
his	tāde 他的
historical site	gǔjī 古迹
history	lìshǐ 歷史(历史)
hold, contain	róngnà 容納(容纳)
hold (meeting, etc.)	jǔxíng 舉行(举行)
hold (something by hand)	ná 拿; duān 端
hold in one's arms	bào 抱
hole	dòng 洞
holiday	jiàrì 假日
home	jiā 家
home (courteous, never used for one's own)	fǔshàng 府上

home place	jiāxiāng 家鄉（家乡）
homework	zuòyè 作業（作业）
honest	lǎoshide 老實的（老实的）; chéngshíde 誠實的（诚实的）
Hong Kong	Xiānggǎng 香港
honor（n.）	róngyù 榮譽（荣誉）
honor（v.）	gěi…yǐróngyù 給…以榮譽（给…以荣誉）
hook, hanger	gōuzi 鉤子（钩子）
hope, wish	xīwàng 希望
horn（of a car）	lǎba 喇叭
horse	mǎ 馬（马）
horse carriage, cart	mǎchē 馬車（马车）
horse race	sàimǎ 賽馬（赛马）
hospital	yīyuàn 醫院（医院）
hospital bed	bìngchuáng 病牀（病床）
host, hostess, master, owner	zhǔrén 主人
hot	rè 熱（热）; tàng 燙（烫）
hot towel	rè máojīn 熱毛巾（热毛巾）
hour	xiǎoshí 小時（小时）; zhōngtóu 鐘頭（钟头）
house	fángzi 房子
household	hù 戶; rénjiā 人家
housewife	jiātíng fùnǔ 家庭婦女（家庭妇女）
how	rúhé 如何; zěnmeyàng 怎麼樣（怎么样）
how, to what extent	duō 多; duōme 多麼（多么）
how far	duōyuǎn 多遠（多远）
how long（length）	duōcháng 多長（多长）
how long（time）	duōcháng shíjiān 多長時間（多

長时间)

how many	jǐgè 幾個(几个)
how many, how much	duōshǎo 多少
how（was it）	zěnmeyàng 怎麼樣(怎么样)
however	kěshì 可是; búguò 不過(不过)
however, but, yet	dàn 但; dànshì 但是
humid, damp	cháoshī 潮濕(潮湿)
humidity	shīqì 濕氣(湿气)
hundred	bǎi 百
hungry, starving	è 餓(饿)
hunt, go hunting	dǎliè 打獵(打猎)
hunting gun	lièqiāng 獵槍(猎枪)
hurried, in a hurry	jímáng 急忙
hurried, rapid	jícù 急促
hurry	gǎnkuài 趕快(赶快)
hurry on（with）	gǎnjǐnbàn 趕緊辦(赶紧办)
hurt, ache	téng 疼
hurt, wound	shāng 傷(伤)

I

I, me	wǒ 我
ice	bīng 冰
ice cream	bīngqilín 冰淇淋
ice cube	bīngkuàir 冰塊兒(冰块儿)
ice-skating	huábīng 滑冰; liūbīng 溜冰
ice skating rink	liūbīngchǎng 溜冰場(溜冰场)
ice water	bīngshuǐ 冰水
idea	zhǔyì 主意
idea, thinking	xiǎngfǎ 想法; sīxiǎng 思想
ideal, idealistic	lǐxiǎngde 理想的
ideology, thought	sīxiǎng 思想

idiom, set phrase	chéngyǔ 成語(成语)
idle, slack	xián 閑(闲)
if	yàoshi 要是; rúguǒ 如果
if not	yàobù 要不
if only	zhǐyào 祇要(只要)
if, whether	shìfǒu 是否; shìbúshì 是不是
ill, illness, sick	yǒubìng 有病; bìngle 病了
illiterate	wénmáng 文盲
illustrated magazine	huàbào 畫報(画报)
illustration	chātú 插圖(插图); huà 畫;
imagine, consider	liàoxiǎng 料想
imitation	méfǎng 模仿
immediately, at once	lìkè 立刻; mǎshàng 馬上(马上)
immigrants, settlers	yímín 移民
impatient, short- tempered	xìngji 性急
import (n.)	jìnkǒu 進口(进口); jìnkǒuhuò 進口貨(进口货)
import (v.)	jìnkǒu 進口(进口)
important	zhòngyào 重要
important, urgent	yàojǐn 要緊(要紧)
impression	gǎnxiǎng 感想; yìnxiàng 印象
in, at, on	zài…shàng 在…上
in, between, among	zài…zhōng 在…中
in, inside	zài…nèi 在…內
in addition	háiyǒu 還有(还有); cǐwài 此外
in all	yígòng 一共
in a period of time	zàiyígèshíjīnèi 在一個時期內 (在一个时期内)
in order to	wèi 爲(为); wèile 爲了(为了)
inch (British measure)	yīngcùn 英寸; cùn 吋
include	bāokuò 包括

65

increase, raise	zēngjiā 增加
indeed, as predicted	guǒrán 果然
indeed, really	díquè 的確(的确); quèshí 確實 (确实)
indescribable	xíngróngbùchūde 形容不出的
India	Yìndù 印度
indicate	biǎoshì 表示
industry	gōngyè 工業(工业)
inevitable, bound to	bìrán 必然
inevitable, unavoidable	miǎnbùliǎo 免不了; nánmiǎn 難 免(难免)
inexpensive	piányi 便宜
inexpressible	shuō bu chūde 說不出的(说不 出的)
infant	yòu'ér 幼兒(幼儿)
infection	chuánrǎn 傳染(传染)
inferior grade	xiàděng 下等
inferior, poor	chà 差
inflamed, inflammation	fāyán 發炎(发炎)
inform, notify	gàosu 告訴(告诉); tōngzhī 通知
informally, without cere- mony	fēizhèngshìde 非正式地
injection	dǎzhēn 打針(打针)
injure, harm	sǔnhài 損害(损害); shānghài 伤 害(伤害)
ink	mòshuǐ 墨水
inlay, inset	xiāng 鑲(镶)
inquire about, ask about	xúnwèn 詢問(询问); dǎting 打 聽(打听)
inscribe	kè 刻; tíxiě 題寫(题写)
insect	kūnchóng 昆蟲(昆虫)
insert	chā 插

inside, within	lǐmiàn 裏面(里面); lǐtou 裏頭 (里头)
inside the city	shìnèi 市內
insist on, persist in	jiānchí 堅持(坚持)
institute	xuéyuàn (a university or college) 學院(学院); yánjiūsuǒ (a research institute) 研究所
instruct, direct	zhǐshì 指示
instrument, tool, utensil	gōngjù 工具
insult	wūrǔ 侮辱
insured mail	bǎojiàyóujiàn 保價郵件(保价邮件)
intact, perfect	wánzhěng 完整
intelligent	cōngming 聰明(聪明)
intend	dǎsuan 打算; xiǎng 想
intense, tense, nervous	jǐnzhāngde 緊張的(紧张的)
interest, liking	xìngqù 興趣(兴趣); àihào 愛好 (爱好)
interested in	duì…gǎnxìngqù 對…感興趣 (对…感兴趣)
interesting	yǒuqùde 有趣的; yǒuyìside 有意思的
international	guójìde 國際的(国际的)
International Labor Day, May Day (May 1)	"Wǔ—Yī" Guójì Láodòng Jié "五一"國際勞動節("五一"国际劳动节)
International Working Women's Day (March 8)	"Sān—Bā" Fùnǚ Jié "三八"婦女節("三八"妇女节)
interpret, interpreter	fānyì 翻譯(翻译)
intersection	shízì lùkǒur 十字路口兒(十字路口儿)

interview (for a job)	miànshì 面試
interview (by a reporter)	cǎifǎng 探訪(采访)
in that case	nàme 那麼(那么);jìránzhèyàng 既然這樣(既然这样)
into	jìnrù 進入(进入)
introduce, recommend	jièshào 介紹(介绍)
introduction (to a book)	xùyán 序言
introduction (to friends)	jièshào 介紹(介绍)
investigate	diàochá 調查(调查)
invitation	qǐngtiě 請帖(请帖); qǐngjiǎn 請柬(请柬)
invite	yāoqǐng 邀請(邀请)
invite guests	qǐngkè 請客(请客)
iron (metal)	tiě 鐵(铁)
iron, press (clothes)	yùn 熨; tàng 燙(烫)
irrigate	guàngài 灌溉
is	shì 是
it	ta 它; zhè 這(这)
Italian	Yìdàlìwén (the language) 意大利文; Yìdàlìyǔ (the language) 意大利語(意大利语); Yìdàlìrén (the people) 意大利人
Italy	Yìdàlì 意大利
itching	yǎng 癢(痒)
item, article	wùpǐn 物品
item (on a program)	jiémù 節目(节目)
item of business	xiàngmù 項目(项目)

J

jacket	wàitào 外套; shàngyī 上衣

Chinese closing jacket	dàjīnshàngyī 大襟上衣
center closing jacket	duìjīnshàngyī 對襟上衣（对襟上衣）
jail, imprison	jiānjìn 監禁（监禁）
jail, prison	jiānyù 監獄（监狱）
January	yīyuè 一月
Japan	Rìběn 日本
Japanese	Rìběnrén（the people）日本人; Rìwén（the language）日文; Rìyǔ（the language）日語（日语）
jasper（stone）	bìyù 碧玉
jealous	jídù 嫉妒（嫉妒）
Jeep（car）	jípǔchē 吉普車（吉普车）
jet, spurt	pēnshè 噴射（喷射）
jetty, wharf	mǎtou 碼頭（码头）
job	gōngzuò 工作
jogging suit	yùndòngyī 運動衣（运动衣）
join, take part in	cānjiā 參加（参加）
join, connect	liánjiē 連接（连接）
join forces	hélì 合力
joke	xiàohuà 笑話（笑话）
joke, crack a joke	shuōxiàohuà 說笑話（说笑话）
jolly	rènào 熱鬧（热闹）
jostle, crowd	jǐ 擠（挤）
journey	lǚxíng 旅行
joy	yúkuài 愉快
judge	fǎguān 法官
judge, assess, determine	pànduàn 判斷（判断）
juice	zhī 汁; shuǐguǒzhī 水果汁
July	qīyuè 七月

jump, spring	tiào 跳
jump on (upon)	pū 撲(扑)
juncture (in time)	shíhòu 時候(时候); guāntóu 關頭(关头)
juncture (place)	jiāojièchù 交界處(交界处)
June	liùyuè 六月
just, only, exactly	gānggāng 剛剛(刚刚)
just as, at the time of	zhèngdàng 正當(正当)
just like	zhèngxiàng 正像(正象)
just now, a moment ago	gāngcái 剛才(刚才)
justice	gōngzhèng 公正

K

keep, preserve, maintain	bǎochí 保持; bǎocún 保存
keep, retain	bǎoliú 保留
keep, save	shōuhǎo 收好
kerosene	méiyóu 煤油
kettle, pot	hú 壺(壶)
key	yàoshi 鑰匙(钥匙)
kick	tī 踢
kill	shā 殺(杀)
kilogram	gōngjīn 公斤
kilometer	gōnglǐ 公里
kind, good	héǎide 和藹的
kind, merciful	réncíde 仁慈的; héqìde 和氣的(和气的)
kind, sort, variety	zhǒng 種(种); zhǒnglèi 種類(种类)
kindergarten	yòu'éryuán 幼兒園(幼儿园)
king	guówáng 國王(国王)
kitchen	chúfáng 廚房

70

kite	fēngzheng 風箏(风筝)
kleenex	zhǐjīn 紙巾(纸巾)
knack	qiàomén 竅門(窍门)
knead	róu 揉; huómiàn 和麵(和面)
knee	xīgài 膝蓋(膝盖)
knife	dāozi 刀子
knit, knitting	zhēnzhī 針織(针织)
knock	qiāo 敲
know	zhīdao 知道
know (a language, a technique, etc.)	huì 會(会)
know (a person, a place, etc.)	rènshi 認識(认识)
know well, be familiar with	shúxī 熟悉
Korea	Cháoxiǎn 朝鮮(朝鲜)
Kowloon	Jiǔlóng 九龍(九龙)

L

Labor	láodòng 勞動(劳动); láogōng 勞工(劳工)
laborer	gōngrén 工人
lack	quēshǎo 缺少; chà 差
lacquer (carved)	diāoqī 雕漆
lacquerware	qīqì 漆器
ladder, steps	tī 梯; jiētī 階梯(阶梯)
lady	nǚshì 女士
lady (unmarried)	xiǎojiě 小姐
lake	hú 湖
lamb	gāoyáng (animal) 羔羊; yáng- ròu (meat) 羊肉

71

lamp	dēng 燈(灯)
land (as an airplane)	zhuólù 着陸(着陆)
land, field	dì 地; tǔdì 土地
landlord	dìzhǔ (owner of land) 地主; fángzhǔ (owner of house) 房主
landscape	fēngjǐng 風景(风景); shānshuǐ 山水
lane	hútòng 胡同
language	yǔyán 語言(语言)
lantern slides	huàndēng 幻燈(幻灯)
large	dà 大
last	zuìhòude 最後的(最后的)
last, at last	zuìhòu 最後(最后)
last time, final time	zuìhòu yícì 最後一次(最后一次)
lastingly, constantly	lǎoshì 老是; jīngchángshì 經常是(经常是); yǒngyuǎnshì 永遠是(永远是)
late	chí 遲(迟); wǎn 晚
later	yǐhòu 以後(以后); hòulái後來(后来)
later, after a short time	huítóu 回頭(回头)
Latin America	Lādīng Měizhōu 拉丁美洲
laugh	xiào 笑
laughable	hǎoxiào 好笑
laundry	xǐyīdiàn 洗衣店
lavatory	cèsuǒ 廁所(厕所)
law	fǎlǜ 法律
lawyer	lǜshī 律師(律师)
lay out, set (a table, etc.)	bǎi 擺(摆)
lay out, unfold	zhǎnkāi 展開(展开)

layer, level	céng 層(层)
lay down	fàngxià (to lay down something) 放下; guīdìng (to specify in a law) 規定(规定)
lazy	lǎn 懶(懒)
lead	dàilǐng 帶領(带领); lǐngdǎo 領導(领导)
leader	lǐngxiù 領袖(领袖); lǐngdǎo 領導(领导)
leadership	lǐngdǎo 領導(领导)
leader of a delegation	dàibiǎotuán tuánzhǎng 代表團團長(代表团团长)
leaf	shùyè 樹葉(树叶)
lean, thin	shòu 瘦
learn	xuéxí 學習(学习)
leather	pí 皮
leave	zǒu 走; dòngshēn 動身(动身)
leave, depart from, deviate from	líkāi 離開(离开)
leave, vacation	jià 假; jiàqī 假期
be on leave	dùjià 渡假
leave behind	shèngxià 剩下
leave for, go to	wǎng 往; qiánwǎng 前往
lecture	yǎnjiǎng 演講(演讲); jiǎngyǎn 講演(讲演)
lecture desk	jiǎngzhuō 講桌(讲桌)
left (direction)	zuǒ 左
left side	zuǒbiān 左邊(左边)
left over, surplus	shèngxiàde 剩下的; yú 餘(余)
leg	tuǐ 腿
leisure time	kòngxián shíjiān 空閒時間(空闲时间)

lemon	níngméng 檸檬(柠檬)
lend	jiè 借
length	chángdù 長度(长度)
length of time	qījiān 期間(期间); zhèn 陣(阵)
less than	bǐ…chà 比…差; bǐ…shǎo 比…少
lesson	kè (taught in a class) 課(课); jiàoxùn (drawn from experience) 教訓(教训)
let (someone do something)	ràng 讓(让)
let go, set free, release	fàng 放
letter	xìn 信
letter of an alphabet	zìmǔ 字母
level, flat, even	píng 平
level, standard	shuǐpíng 水平
lever, bar	gànggǎn 槓桿(杠杆)
liar	sāhuǎngderén 撒謊的人(撒谎的人)
liberal arts	wénkē 文科
liberate, liberation	jiěfàng 解放
liberated area	jiěfàngqū 解放區(解放区)
library	túshūguǎn 圖書館(图书馆)
lid, cover	gàir 蓋兒(盖儿)
lie (down)	tǎngxià 躺下
lie, tell an untruth	sāhuǎng 撒謊(撒谎)
lie, untruth	huǎnghuà 謊話(谎话)
life	shēnghuó (everyday life) 生活; shēngmìng (the state of being alive) 生命
life-like	bīzhēn 逼眞; xǔxǔrúshēng 栩栩如生

life time	yìshēng 一生; shēngqián (used for the deceased only) 生前
lift, elevator	diàntī 電梯(电梯)
light (for colors)	dàn 淡; qiǎn 淺(浅)
light, ignite, kindle	diǎnhuǒ 點火(点火); diǎnzháo 點着(点着); diǎnrán 點燃(点燃)
light, lamp	dēng 燈(灯)
light, lightweight	qīng 輕(轻)
light, ray of light	guāng 光; guāngmíng 光明
light a lamp	diǎndēng 點燈(点灯)
light (a stove), make (a fire)	shēnghuǒ 生火
lightning	shǎndiàn 閃電(闪电); dǎshǎn 打閃(打闪)
lightly, gently	qīngqīng 輕輕(轻轻)
like	xiàngsì 相似; lèisì 類似(类似)
like, be fond of	xǐài 喜愛(喜爱); xǐhuān 喜歡(喜欢)
like that, in that way	xiàngnàyàng 像那樣(象那样); nàme 那麼(那么)
like this, in this way	xiàngzhèyàng 像這樣(象这样); zhème 這麼(这么)
limp, walk lamely	guǎi 拐; yìquéyìguǎi 一瘸一拐
line, string	xiàn 綫(线)
line, place in or form a row	páichéngyīliè 排成一列; páiqí 排齊(排齐)
line the roads	jiādào 夾道(夹道)
link, join, connect	lián 連(连)
lion	shīzi 獅子(狮子)
liquid	yètǐ 液體(液体); yètài 液態(液态)

liquors	báijiǔ 白酒
list, contents, catalogue	mùlù 目錄(目录)
list	liè 列; lièjǔ 列舉(列举); biān 編 (编)
listen	tīng 聽(听)
literary composition, essay, article	wénzhāng 文章
literature	wénxué 文學(文学)
little, few	shǎo 少
little, little bit	yìdiǎn(r) 一點(兒)(一点(儿))
(a) little time	yíhuìr 一會兒(一会儿)
live (at), stay (at)	zhùzài 住在
live, be alive	huózhe 活着; shēngcún 生存
livelihood, living	shēnghuó 生活
lively	huópo 活潑(活泼)
lively, vividly	shēngdòng 生動(生动)
livestock	jiāchù 家畜; shēngchù 牲畜
living room	qǐjūshì 起居室
local	dìfāngde 地方的; dāngdìde 當地 的(当地的)
local products	tǔchǎn 土產(土产)
location, place	dìdiǎn 地點(地点); wèizhi 位置; chàngdì 場地(场地)
lock	suǒ 鎖(锁)
lonely	gūdú 孤獨(孤独)
long (with things and time)	cháng 長(长)
long (only with time)	jiǔ 久
long distance	chángtú 長途(长途)
long distance phone call	chángtú diànhuà 長途電話(长 途电话)
long life, longevity	chángshòu 長壽(长寿)

76

long live⋯	⋯wànsuì 萬歲(⋯万岁)
long since	zǎo 早; hěnjiǔ yǐ qián 很久以前
long time	jiǔ 久; hěnjiǔ 很久; bàntiān 半天
look, direct the eyes	kàn 看; wàng 望; qiáo 瞧
look, appear to be	xiǎnde 顯得(显得)
look, appearance	yàngzi 樣子(样子)
look afar, overlook	tiàowàng 眺望
look after, take care of	zhàoliào 照料
look closely at	zǐxìqiáo 仔細瞧(仔细瞧)
look down	xiàngxiàwàng 向下望; fǔshì 俯視(俯视)
look for, seek	zhǎo 找
look sideways	xiéshì 斜視(斜视)
look up (e.g. in a dictionary)	chá 查
look through, turn over	fānkàn 翻看; fān 翻
looks as if⋯	kànshàngqùxiàng⋯ 看上去像⋯(看上去象⋯)
looks like, seems	kànyàngzi 看樣子(看样子)
looks on, faces	miànduì 面對(面对)
loose, thin	xī 稀
loose fitting	tàiféi 太肥; shāodà 稍大
lorry, truck	kǎchē 卡車(卡车)
lose	diū 丟; diūshī 丟失
lose one's way	mílù 迷路
lose weight, reduce	jiǎnféi 減肥(减肥)
loss, losses	sǔnshī 損失(损失)
lost, defeated	shū 輸(输)
(a) lot of, lots of	hěnduō 很多
lotus root	ǒu 藕
loud, aloud	dàshēng 大聲(大声); xiǎng 響

77

(響)

loud and clear	xiǎngliàng 響亮(响亮)
loud, glaring (color)	guōfènxiānyànde 過份鮮艷的(过份鲜艳的)
lounge	xiūxīshí 休息室
lovable	kěàide 可愛的(可爱的)
love	ài 愛(爱); rè'ài 熱愛(热爱)
love to do something	àihào 愛好(爱好); hěnyuànyì 很願意(很愿意)
lovely	kěàide 可愛的(可爱的)
low (not high)	dī 低
lower, drop, reduce	jiàngdī 降低
luggage	xíngli 行李
luggage rack	xínglijià 行李架
lunar calendar	yīnlì 陰曆(阴历)
lunch	wǔfàn 午飯(午饭); zhōngfàn 中飯(中饭)
lyrics, words of a song	chàngcí 唱詞(唱词)

M

Macao	Àomén 澳門(澳门)
machine	jīqì 機器(机器)
magazine	zázhì 雜誌(杂志)
magnetic tape	cídài 磁帶(磁带)
magnificent, majestic	zhuànglì 壯麗(壮丽); zhuāngyán 莊嚴(庄严)
mail	jì 寄
mail, postal matter	yóujiàn 郵件(邮件)
mailman, postman	yóudìyuán 郵遞員(邮递员)
mainly, basically	zhǔyàode 主要地
main, principal, chief	zhǔyàode 主要的

maintain, keep, preserve	bǎochí 保持
maintenance	wéichí 維持(维持); wéixiū 維修(维修)
majestic	xióngwěide 雄偉的(雄伟的)
major, chief, principal	zhǔyàode 主要的
major, field of study	zhuānyè 專業(专业); zhuānxiū kèmù 專修科目(专修科目)
majority	duōshù 多數(多数)
make, cause	shǐ 使; lìng 令; jiào 叫
make, do	zuò 做; gàn 幹(干)
make, form into	zǔchéng 組成(组成)
make a fortune	fācái 發財(发财)
make a general investigation (survey)	pǔchá 普查
make a joke, make fun of	kāiwánxiào 開玩笑(开玩笑)
make inquiries	dǎtīng 打聽(打听)
make out, understand	lǐjiě 理解
make products	shēngchǎn 生產(生产)
make a telephone call	dǎdiànhuà 打電話(打电话)
make use of	lìyòng 利用
man, male	nánrén 男人
man-made	rénzào 人造
manage (certain affairs)	bànlǐ 辦理(办理)
manage, administer	guǎnlǐ 管理
manage, deal with	duìfu 對付(对付); rìngfu 應付(应付)
manage to, have time to	shèfǎ 設法(设法)
management	guǎnlǐ 管理
manager	jīnglǐ 經理(经理)
manpower (workforce)	rénlì 人力
manufactory	zhìzàochǎng 製造廠(制造厂)
manufacture	zhìzào 製造(制造)

manufactured goods	zhìpǐn 製品(制品)
many	duō 多; hěnduō 很多
map	dìtú 地圖(地图)
March	sānyuè 三月
march on, advance	qiánjìn 前進(前进); jìnjūn 進軍(进军)
mark, sign	jìhao 記號(记号)
mark, symbol	fúhào 符號(符号)
market, bazaar	shìchǎng 市場(市场)
marks, grades	fēngshù 分數(分数)
marry	jiéhūn 結婚(结婚)
martial arts	wǔshù 武術(武术)
marvellous	miào 妙; hǎojíle 好極了(好极了)
mask (for face)	miànjù 面具
mask (for mouth)	kǒuzhào 口罩
masses	qúnzhòng 羣眾(群众)
massive, fat	kuíwúde 魁梧的(魁梧的)
master, grasp, gain control of	zhǎngwò 掌握
master, learn (a skill, etc.)	xuéhuì 學會(学会)
master of the house	zhǔrén 主人
match, competition	sài 賽(赛); bǐsài 比賽(比赛)
matches (fire sticks)	huǒchái 火柴
material	cáiliào 材料
mathematics	shùxué 數學(数学)
matter (affair)	shìqing 事情
matter (substance)	wùzhì 物質(物质)
May	Wǔyuè 五月
may, can	kěyǐ 可以
maybe	yěxǔ 也許(也许); kěnéng 可能

80

maybe, perhaps	huòzhě 或者; yěxǔ 也許(也许)
me, I	wǒ 我
meal	fàn 飯(饭)
meal (as a whole, including staple food and dishes)	fàncài 飯菜(饭菜)
have a meal, take a meal	chīfàn 吃飯(吃饭)
mean, indicate, express	biǎoshì 表示
meaning, idea	yìsi 意思
meaning, significance	yìyì 意義(意义)
meaningful	yǒuyìyì 有意義(有意义)
meaningless	méiyǒu yìyì 沒有意義(没有意义)
meanwhile	yìbiān…yìbiān 一邊…一邊(一边…一边); tóngshí 同時(同时)
measure (n.)	chǐdù 尺度; jìliáng dānwèi 計量單位
measure (v.)	liáng 量
measurement	liángdù 量度; dàxiǎo 大小; chǐcùn 尺寸
meat	ròu 肉
mechanic	jīxièshī 機械師(机械师)
mechanics	lìxué 力學(力学)
mechanize, mechanization	jīxièhuà 機械化(机械化)
medical examination	yīxué jiǎnchá 醫學檢查(医学检查)
medicine (in general)	yào 藥(药); yàopǐn 藥品(药品)
medicine (liquid)	yàoshuǐ 藥水(药水)
medicine (medical	yīkē 醫科(医科)

81

courses in general)

medicine (pills)	yàopiàn 藥片(药片); yàowán 藥丸(药丸)
medium grade	zhōngděng 中等
meek, gentle	wēnshùnde 溫順的(温顺的)
meet, encounter	yùjiàn 遇見(遇见)
meet (friends or guests)	huìjiàn 會見(会见)
meet, make the acquaintance	rènshi 認識(认识)
meet, welcome	yíngjiē 迎接
meeting	huìyì 會議(会议)
have a meeting	kāihuì 開會(开会)
meeting, talks	huìtán 會談(会谈)
meeting-place, conference (assembly) hall	huìchǎng 會場(会场)
member	chéngyuán 成員(成员); huìyuán 會員(会员)
memorial	jìniàn 紀念(纪念)
memorial hall	jìniànguǎn 紀念館(纪念馆)
mend (clothes)	féngbǔ 縫補(缝补)
mention, refer to	tídào 提到
menu	càidān 菜單(菜单); càipǔ 菜譜(菜谱)
merchandise (n.)	huòwù 貨物(货物); shāngpǐn 商品
merchandise (v.)	mǎimài 買賣(买卖); tuīxiāo 推銷(推销); jīngshāng 經商(经商)
merely, only	zhǐbúguò 只不過(只不过)
merits, achievement	gōngjì 功績(功绩); gōngláo 功勞(功劳)
merry	yúkuài 愉快

message	xìnxī 信息; xiāoxī 消息
leave a message	liúyán 留言
metal	jīnshǔ 金屬(金属)
meteorology	qìxiàngxué 氣象學(气象学)
meter (unit of measure)	mǐ 米; gōngchǐ 公尺
method, way	bànfǎ 辦法(办法); fāngfǎ 方法
middle, center	zhōngyāng 中央
in the middle, in between	zàizhōngjiān 在中間(在中间)
middle school	zhōngxué 中學(中学)
midnight	bànyè 半夜; wǔyè 午夜
mild, plain, not spicy (food)	qīngdàn 清淡
mild, warm (weather)	wēnnuǎn 溫暖
mile	yīnglǐ 英里
military attache	wǔguān 武官
military expert	jūnshì zhuānjiā 軍事專家(军事专家)
milk	niúnǎi 牛奶
milkman	sòngnǎirén 送奶人
million	bǎiwàn 百萬(百万)
mind, care, take offence	jièyì 介意
mineral water	kuàngquánshuǐ 礦泉水(矿泉水)
minibus	xiǎoxíng gōnggòng qìchē 小型公共汽車; miànbāochē 麵包車(面包车)
minister (head of a ministry)	bùzhǎng 部長(部长)
vice-minister	fùbùzhǎng 副部長(副部长)
ministry	bù 部
mink fur	diāopí 貂皮

minority	shǎoshù 少數(少数)
minute (unit of time)	fēn 分
minute, tiny, fine	wēixiǎo 微小
mirror	jìngzi 鏡子(镜子)
mislay, lose	nòngdiūle 弄丢了
miss, unmarried woman	xiǎojiě 小姐; nǚshì 女士
mistake, error	cuòwù 錯誤(错误)
mister, gentleman	xiānsheng 先生
mix, confuse	hùnxiáo 混淆
mixed nuts	shíjǐnguǒrén 什錦果仁(什錦果仁)
model, fine example	mófàn 模範(模范)
modernize, modernization	xiàndàihuà 現代化(现代化)
modest	qiānxū 謙虛(谦虚)
modify, revise, correct	xiūgǎi 修改
moisture	shuǐfèn 水分
mold	múzi 模子
moment of time	yíhuìr 一會兒(一会儿)
momentarily	yíhuìr 一會兒(一会儿); zànshí 暫時(暂时)
Monday	xīngqīyī 星期一
money	qián 錢(钱)
monk, priest	sēng 僧; héshàng 和尚
month	yuè 月
this month	zhègèyuè 這個月(这个月)
last month	shàngyuè 上月
next month	xiàyuè 下月
early in the month	shàngxún 上旬
late in the month	xiàxún 下旬
middle of the month	zhōngxún 中旬
monument, stone	bēi 碑

84

mood, atmosphere	qìfèn 氣氛(气氛)
moon	yuèliàng 月亮
moonlight	yuèguāng 月光
moral education	déyù 德育
more and more	yuèláiyuè …越來越…(越来越…); yuèfā 越發(越发)
more, even more	gèngduō 更多; gèngjiā 更加; duō 多
more or less	huòduōhuòshǎo 或多或少
moreover	érqiě 而且
morning	shàngwǔ 上午; zǎochén 早晨
morning exercises	zǎocāo 早操
most	zuì 最
at the most	zuìduō 最多
most, mostly, largely	dàbùfen 大部分
mostly, chiefly	zhǔyào 主要; duōbàn 多半
mother	mǔqīn 母親(母亲); māma 媽媽(妈妈)
motherland	zǔguó 祖國(祖国)
motorcycle	mótuōchē 摩托車(摩托车)
mount, ascend, scale	dēng 登; dēngshàng 登上
mountain	shān 山
mountain area	shānqū 山區(山区)
mountain peak	shānfēng 山峯
mountain ridge	shānjǐ 山脊
mouth	zuǐ 嘴; kǒu 口
mouth, an entrance or exit	chūrùkǒu 出入口; kǒu 口
move, get moving	dòng 動(动)
move, remove	bān 搬
movement, motion	yùndòng 運動(运动)
movie	diànyīng 電影(电影)

TV movie	diànshìjù 電視劇(电视剧)
movie house	diànyǐngyuàn 電影院(电影院)
moving, touching	dòngrénde 動人的(动人的)
mow, cutdown	yì 刈; gé 割
mowing machine	yìcǎojī 刈草機(刈草机)
much, many	hěnduō 很多
muscle	jīròu 肌肉
muster, rally, assemble	jíhé 集合
mud	ní 泥
multicolour	duōsè 多色; cǎisè 彩色
multitudinous	zhòng duō 眾多(众多)
museum	bówùguǎn 博物館(博物馆)
music	yīnyuè 音樂(音乐)
musician	yīnyuèjiā 音樂家(音乐家)
musical instrument	yuèqì 樂器(乐器)
must	bìxū 必須(必须)
must, have to	děi 得; bìxū 必須(必须)
mustard	jièmò 芥末
mutton	yángròu 羊肉
mutually, one another	bǐcǐ 彼此; hùxiāng 互相
my, mine	wǒde 我的
myself	wǒzìjǐ 我自己

N

name (family and/or given)	xìngmíng 姓名; míngzi 名字
family name	xìng 姓
given name	míngzi 名字
name (v.)	mìngmíng 命名
nanny, nursery attendant	bǎomǔ 保姆
nap, siesta	xiǎoshuì 小睡

napkin	cānjīn 餐巾
narrow, cramped	xiázhǎi 狹窄(狭窄)
nation	guó 國(国)
nation, nationality	mínzú 民族
National Day	guóqìngrì 國慶日(国庆日)
native	běndìde 本地的
native dress	guófú 國服(国服)
native place	kùxiāng 故鄉(故乡)
natural	zìránde 自然的
nature character	běnxìng 本性
nature, natural world	zìránjiè 自然界; zìrán 自然
naughty	táoqìde 淘氣的(淘气的)
near	jìn 近
nearby	fùjìn 附近
nearly, about the same	chàbuduō 差不多
nearly, soon	kuài…le 快…了
neat	zhěngjié 整潔(整洁); gānjìng 乾淨(干净)
necessary	bìxūde 必須的(必须的)
necessities (articles)	rìchángyòngpǐn 日常用品
necktie	lǐngdài 領帶(领带)
need	xūyào 需要; yào 要
need, should, ought to	yīnggāi 應該(应该)
needle	zhēn 針(针)
needless, useless	búyòng 不用; méiyòng 沒用
neighbor	línjū 鄰居(邻居)
neighboring, adjacent	fùjìnde 附近的
neither…nor…	jìbù…yòubù… 既不…又不…
never	yǒngbù 永不; cóngbù 從不(从不); juébù 絕不(绝不)
new	xīn 新
new word	shēngcí 生詞(生词)

news	xiāoxi 消息
newspaper	bàozhǐ 報紙(报纸)
Newsweek	Xīnwénzhōukān《新聞周刊》 (《新闻周刊》)
New Year	xīnnián 新年
New Year (Chinese Spring Festival)	chūnjié 春節(春节)
New Zealand	Xīnxīlán 新西蘭(新西兰)
next, the following	xiàyígè 下一個(下一个)
nice	hǎo 好
night	yè 夜
night club	yèzǒnghuì 夜總會(夜总会)
nighttime	yèli 夜裏(夜里)
nine	jiǔ 九
nineteen	shíjiǔ 十九
ninety	jiǔshí 九十
ninth	dìjiǔ 第九
no, not	bù 不
no, not any	méiyǒu 沒有
no matter (what, who, where, when, and how)	búlùn 不論(不论)
nobody, no one	méirén 沒人
nod the head	diǎntóu 點頭(点头)
noise, din, hubbub	chǎonào 吵鬧(吵闹)
nonsense!	húshuō 胡說(胡说)!; huāngtáng 荒唐!; méiyǒudehuà 沒有的話(没有的话)!
noon	zhōngwǔ 中午
north	běi 北
North America	Běi Měizhōu 北美洲
Northeast China	Dōngběi 東北(东北)
Northern part	běifāng 北方; běibù 北部

nose	bízi 鼻子
not able to	bùnéng 不能
not as good as	bùrú 不如
not bad	búcuò 不錯(不错)
not only	búdàn 不但
not only…but also…	búdàn…érqiě… 不但…而且…
not well	bùshūfu 不舒服
notable, famous	zhùmíngde 著名的
note (brief, informal)	tiáozi 條子(条子)
notebook	běnzi 本子; bǐjìběn 筆記本(笔记本)
notes, explanations	zhùshì 註釋(注释)
notify, inform	tōngzhī 通知
novel, fiction	xiǎoshuō 小說(小说)
November	shíyīyuè 十一月
now	xiànzài 現在(现在)
nowadays	xiànzài 現在(现在); rújīn 如今
nuclear physics	héwùlǐ 核物理
number	shùmù 數目(数目)
number, figure	shùzì 數字(数字)
number (of persons)	(rén) shù 人數(人数)
number of times	cì 次
first time	dìyícì 第一次
second time	dìèrcì 第二次
numerous	xǔduō 許多(许多); hěnduō 很多
nurse	hùshì 護士(护士)
nurse (v.)	hùlǐ 護理(护理)
nursery	tuōérsuǒ 托兒所(托儿所)
nutrition	yíngyǎng 營養(营养)

89

O

oar	jiǎng 槳(桨)
obedient	fúcóng 服從(服从)
obey	tīnghuà 聽話(听话); fúcóng 服從(服从)
object	dōngxi 東西(东西)
objective	kèguān 客觀(客观)
objective, goal, aim	mùdì 目的
obstruct, block	dǎng 擋(挡); zǔsè 阻塞
obtain, achieve, get	qǔdé 取得; huòdé 獲得(获得)
obvious, quite clear	míngxiǎnde 明顯的(明显的)
occasional	ǒuěr 偶爾(偶尔)
occasionally, bits and pieces	ǒurán 偶然
occupy, take up	zhàn 佔(占)
occur, happen	fāshēng 發生(发生)
ocean	hǎiyáng 海洋
Oceania	Dàyángzhōu 大洋洲
o'clock	diǎnzhōng 點鐘(点钟)
October	shíyuè 十月
odorless, non-smelling	méiyǒuqìwèide 沒有氣味的(没有气味的); wénbúchūde 聞不出的(闻不出的)
of	…de …的; shǔyú…de 屬於…的(属于…的)
of course	dāngrán當然(当然); dāngránle 當然了(当然了)
occasion (formal)	chǎnghé 場合(场合)
occasion, time	cì 次
odd, strange	qíguài 奇怪

off, deviating from	líkāi 離開(离开)
office	bàngōngshì 辦公室(办公室)
office hours	bàngōngshíjiàn 辦公時間(办公时间)
office worker, clerk	zhíyuán 職員(职员)
official	guān 官
official business, public affairs	gōngwù 公務(公务)
often	chángcháng 常常
often, usually	tōngcháng 通常; wǎngwǎng 往往
oil	yóu 油
oilfield	yóutián 油田
okay	hǎoba 好吧
old	lǎo (of people) 老; jiù (of things) 舊(旧)
old (used for age)	suì 歲(岁)
How old are you?	nín duōdà suìshù?您多大歲數? (您多大岁数?); Nǐ jǐsuìle? 你幾歲了?(你几岁了?)
old, veteran	lǎozīgéde 老資格的(老资格的); lǎo 老
old-fashioned	gǔlǎo 古老
old man	lǎorén 老人; lǎotóur 老頭兒(老头儿)
old people	lǎorén 老人
old woman	lǎotàitài 老太太
oleander	jiāzhútáo 夾竹桃(夹竹桃)
on, at, in	zài 在; zài…shàng 在…上
on foot	zǒuzhē 走着
on top of	zài…dǐngshàng 在…頂上(在…顶上)

91

once, at one time	yícì 一次; céngjīng 曾經(曾经)
once, on one occasion, for a time	yídù 一度
once a day	yītiānyícì 一天一次
once again	zàiyíbiàn 再一遍
one	yī 一
one hundred	yìbǎi 一百
one of	zhīyī 之一
only, alone	zhǐyǒu 祇有(只有)
only, merely	zhǐ 祇(只)
only if…	zhǐyào… 祇要…(只要…)
open	kāi 開(开); zhāngkāi 張開(张开); dǎkāi 打開(打开)
open (offices, etc.)	kāimén 開門(开门)
opening, mouth (of street, etc.)	kǒu 口; kǒur 口兒(口儿)
opening ceremony	kāimùshì 開幕式(开幕式)
open up land for cultivation	kāihuāng 開荒(开荒)
opera	gējù 歌劇(歌剧)
Peking opera	jīngjù 京劇(京剧)
opera costumes	xìzhuāng 戲裝(戏装)
operate, manage, run	bàn 辦(办); jīngyíng 經營(经营)
operation	xíngdòng 行動(行动); huódòng 活動(活动)
operation (surgical)	shǒushú 手術(手术)
operator (telephone)	jiēxiànshēng 接綫生(接线生); huàwùyuán 話務員(话务员)
opinion	yìjiàn 意見(意见)
opportunely, coincidentally	qiǎohé 巧合

opportunity, chance	jīhuì 機會(机会)
opposite, facing	duìmiànde 對面的(对面的)
opposite side	duìfāng 對方(对方)
optimism	lèguānzhǔyì 樂觀主義(乐观主义)
optimist	lèguānzhǔyìzhě 樂觀主義者(乐观主义者)
optimistic	lèguānde 樂觀的(乐观的)
or (as a question)	háishì 還是(还是)
or (in an affirmative sentence)	huò 或; huòzhě 或者
either…or…	búshì…jiùshì… 不是…就是…
order, command	mìnglìng 命令
order (the way things are arranged)	shùnxù 順序(顺序); zhìxù 秩序
order, instruction to produce, etc.	dìnggòu 訂購(订购)
order, order form	dìngdān 訂單(订单)
order, give a command	mìnglìng 命令
order, request to be supplied	dìnggòu 訂購(订购)
order food	diǎncài 點菜(点菜); yàocài 要菜
ordinarily	tōngcháng 通常
ordinary	pǔtōngde 普通的 (普通的); píngchángde 平常的
ordinary times	píngshí 平時(平时)
organize	zhěnglǐ 整理; zǔzhī 組織(组织)
original, former	yuánláide 原來的(原来的)
originally, at first	zhuìchū 最初; běnlái 本來(本来)
ornaments, fittings	zhuāngshìpǐn 裝飾品(装饰品);

	bǎishè 擺設(摆设)
orphan	gūér 孤兒(孤儿)
other	qítā 其他的; biéde 別的; lìng wàide 另外的
others, the rest, the remainder	qīyú 其餘(其余)
other people, others	biérén 別人
otherwise	bùrán 不然; fǒuzé 否則(否则)
ought to, should	yīngdāng 應當(应当); yīnggāi 應該(应该)
our	wǒménde 我們的(我们的)
out	zàiwài 在外; xiàngwài 向外
out of order, broken	huàile 壞了(坏了)
outdated, used	jiùde 舊的(旧的); guòshíle 過時了(过时了)
outlet	chūlù 出路
outline	dàgàng 大綱(大纲); gěnggài 梗概
outside	wàitou 外頭(外头); wàibian 外邊(外边)
outside line	wàixiàn 外綫(外线)
over (used for temperature, age, etc.)	…duō …多
over a period of time	zài…qījiān 在…期間(在…期间)
overload	chāozài 超載(超载); guòzhòng 過重(过重)
over, exceeding (quantity)	chāo 超; chāoguò 超過(超过)
over, above, on top of	zài…zhīshàng 在…之上
overcoat, topcoat	dàyī 大衣
overcome	kèfú 克服
over-crowded	jǐmǎn 擠滿(挤满)

94

overflow	mànchūlái 漫出來(漫出来)
overnight	tōngxiāo 通宵; guòyè 過夜(过夜)
overview	zǒngdekànfǎ 總的看法(总的看法)
overall situation	zǒngde xíngshì 總的形勢(总的形势)
owe	qiàn 欠
owner	zhǔrén 主人; suǒyǒurén 所有人
ox	gōngniú 公牛

P

pack	zhuāng 裝(装); dǎbāo 打包
pack and transport	zhuāngyùn 裝運(装运)
package	bāoguǒ 包裹
paddle a boat (row a boat)	huáchuán 划船
page (in a book)	yè 頁(页)
pagoda	tǎ 塔
pain	téng 疼
paint (for paintings)	yánliào 顏料(颜料)
paint (heavy duty)	yóuqī 油漆
paint, draw	huà 畫(画)
painting	huàr 畫兒(画儿)
pair, couple	duì 對(对)
pant, breath hard	chuǎn 喘
pants	chángkù 長褲(长裤); kùzi 褲子(裤子)
pantyhose	liánkùwà 連褲襪(连裤袜)
paper	zhǐ 紙(纸)
paradise	tiāntáng 天堂

parcel	bāoguǒ 包裹
pardon, excuse	yuánliàng 原諒(原谅)
pare, slice	xiāo 削
parents	fùmǔ 父母; shuāngqīn 雙親(双亲)
park	gōngyuán 公園(公园)
park (a car)	tíngchē 停車(停车)
parking lot	tíngchēchǎng 停車場(停车场)
part, a part of	bùfen 部分; yíbùfen 一部分
participate, take part in	cānjiā 參加(参加)
partner	hézuòzhě 合作者; hégǔrén 合股人
party, meet together	jùhuì 聚會(聚会)
party, entertainment	zhāodàihuì 招待會(招待会)
pass, ticket	tōngxíngzhèng 通行證(通行证)
pass (v.)	jīngguò 經過(经过); guò 過(过)
pass by (on one's way)	cōng…pángbiān guòqù 從…旁邊過去(从…旁边过去); lùguò 路過(路过)
pass away, die	shìshì 逝世
pass on, transfer	chuán 傳(传)
pass through, pass by	chuānguò 穿過(穿过); tōngguò 通過(通过); jīngguò 經過(经过)
passenger	lǚkè 旅客
passport	hùzhào 護照(护照)
past, previous	cóngqián 從前(从前); guòqù 過去(过去)
path	xiǎolù 小路
patient, sick person	bìngrén 病人
patience, patient	nàixīn 耐心

96

pattern, sample, shape	yàngzi 樣子(样子)
pause	zàntíng 暫停(暂停)
pause mark	dùnhào 頓號(顿号)
pavement	rénxíngdào 人行道
pay, earnings	gōngzī 工資(工资)
pay attention	zhùyì 注意
pay for	fùqián 付…錢(付…钱)
pay back, give back, return	huán 還(还)
peace	hépíng 和平; píng'ān 平安
peaceful, quiet	ānjìng 安靜
peak (of hill)	shāndǐng 山頂(山顶)
peasant	nóngmín 農民(农民)
pedal (n.)	jiǎodēngzi 腳蹬子
pedal (v.)	dēng 蹬
pedestrian	xíngrén 行人
Peking Opera	Jīngjù 京劇(京剧)
pen	gāngbǐ 鋼筆(钢笔)
pen, ball point	yuánzhūbǐ 圓珠筆(圆珠笔)
pencil	qiānbǐ 鉛筆(铅笔)
penny, cent	fēn 分
people	rénmín 人民
People's Daily	Rénmín Rìbào《人民日報》(《人民日报》)
People's Republic of China	Zhōnghuá Rénmín Gònghéguó 中華人民共和國(中华人民共和国)
pep up, cheer (players) on	jiào…jiāyóu 叫…加油 on
perceive, sense, feel	gǎnjué 感覺(感觉); chájué 察覺(察觉)
percent	bǎifēnzhī… 百分之…

97

perfect, complete	wánshàn 完善
perfect, intact	wánzhěng 完整
perfect order	yǒutiáo bù wěn 有條不紊(有条不紊)
perform, performance	biǎoyǎn 表演
performance (of machinery)	xìngnéng 性能
performance (theater)	yǎnchū 演出
perhaps, maybe	yěxǔ 也許(也许); huòxǔ 或許(或许)
period, decimal point	diǎn 點(点)
period, full stop	jùhào 句號(句号)
period, stage, phase	jiēduàn 階段(阶段)
periodical	qīkān 期刊; zázhì 雜誌(杂志)
period of time	shíqī 時期(时期)
permission	xǔkě 許可(许可)
permit, allow	yǔnxǔ 允許(允许)
perplexed	míhuòbùjiě 迷惑不解
persist	jiānchí 堅持(坚持)
person	rén 人
personnel	rényuán 人員(人员)
personally, in person	qīnzì 親自(亲自)
perspiration in sleep	dàohàn 盜汗
petroleum	shíyóu 石油
pharmacy	yàodiàn 藥店(药店)
phenomenon	xiànxiàng 現象(现象)
phoenix	fènghuáng 鳳凰(凤凰)
phone call	diànhuà 電話(电话)
long distance call	chángtú diànhuà 長途電話(长途电话)
phonetic order, sound order	yīnxù 音序

phonetic transcription	yīnbiāo 音標(音标)
photograph (n.)	zhàopiàn 照片
photograph (v.)	pāizhào 拍照; zhàoxiàng 照相
phrase	duǎnyǔ 短語(短语); cízǔ 詞組(词组)
physical culture, physical education	tǐyù 體育(体育)
physical examination	tǐjiǎn 體檢(体检)
physical training	duànliàn 鍛煉(锻炼)
physical strength, force	lì 力; tǐlì 體力(体力)
physics	wùlǐxué 物理學(物理学)
physique, stature	tǐgé 體格(体格); shēncái 身材
piano	gāngqín 鋼琴(钢琴)
pick, select	tiāoxuǎn 挑選(挑选)
pick up	jiǎnqǐlái 揀起來(拣起来)
picnic	yěcān 野餐
picnic basket	yěcān shílán 野餐食籃(野餐食篮)
pictorial	huàbào 畫報(画报)
picture, painting	huàr 畫兒(画儿)
piece	kuài 塊(块); piàn 片
pig	zhū 豬
pile up, heap	duīqǐ 堆起
pill	yàowán 藥丸(药丸)
pillow	zhěntou 枕頭(枕头)
pin (n.)	biézhēn 別針(别针)
pin (v.)	biéshàng 別上
pingpong	pīngpāngqiú 乒乓球
pinnacle	zuìgāofēng 最高峯
pitiful	kěliánde 可憐的(可怜的)
pity	liánmǐn (sympathy) 憐憫(怜悯); tóngqíng (sympathy) 同

	情; hànshì (something causing regret) 憾事
place, location	dìdiǎn 地點; dìfāng 地方
place, put	fàng 放; fàngzài 放在
places, various places	gèdì 各地
plain, flat land	píngyuán 平原
plain and neat	zhěngjié 整潔(整洁)
plan	jìhuà 計劃(计划)
plan, intend, intention	dǎsuàn 打算
plant (as a tree)	zhíwù 植物
plant, grow (a tree, etc.)	zhòng 種(种)
plate	pánzi 盤子(盘子)
platform, stand	táizi 臺子(台子); píngtái 平臺(平台)
play (script)	jùběn 劇本(剧本)
play, modern drama	huàjù 話劇(话剧)
play	wán 玩; yóuxì 遊戲(游戏)
play (ball)	dǎ (qiú) 打(球)
play (chess)	xià (qí) 下(棋)
play (football)	tī (zúqiú) 踢(足球)
play the role of, act the part of	bànyǎn 扮演
plaything, toy	wánjù 玩具; wányìr 玩意兒(玩意儿)
player, athelete	bǐsàizhě 比賽者(比赛者); yùndòngyuán 運動員(运动员)
playground	cāochǎng 操場(操场)
please	qǐng 請(请)
pleased, happy	gāoxìng 高興(高兴)
pleasure	yúkuài 愉快
plentiful	duō 多; fēngfùde 豐富的(丰富的)

pliable, yielding, soft	ruǎn 軟(软)
plot (of a play)	jùqíng 劇情(剧情)
plot (of land)	kuài 塊(块)
plug	sāizi 塞子; chātóu (electrical appliance) 插頭(插头)
plug in, insert	chā 插
plus, added to	jiā 加
pocket, pouch	kǒudàir 口袋兒(口袋儿)
poem	shī 詩(诗)
poet	shīrén 詩人(诗人)
poetic feeling	shīyì 詩意(诗意)
poetry	shīgē 詩歌(诗歌); shīcí 詩詞(诗词)
point, dot	diǎn 點(点)
point at, point to, show	zhǐ 指
poisoned	zhòngdú 中毒
police	jǐngchá 警察
police headquarters	gōngānjú 公安局; jǐngchájú 警察局
policy, guiding principle	fāngzhēn 方針(方针); zhèngcè 政策
polish	cāliàng 擦亮; móguāng 磨光
polite, courteous	yǒulǐmào 有禮貌(有礼貌); kèqì 客氣(客气)
politics, political affairs	zhèngzhì 政治
pollution	wūrǎn 污染
pond, pool	chí 池
pool, pod	yóuyǒngchí 游泳池
poor	qióng 窮(穷)
poor in oil	pínyóu 貧油(贫油)
poor, not up to standard	chà 差
population	rénkǒu 人口

porcelain wares	cíqì 瓷器
pork	zhūròu 猪肉
portrait	xiàng 像
position, status	dìwèi 地位
position, location	wèizhì 位置
possible	kěnéngde 可能的
possibility	kěnéngxìng 可能性
post office	yóujú 郵局(邮局)
postage	yóuzī 郵資(邮资)
postal parcel (packet)	bāoguǒ 包裹
postcard	míngxìnpiàn 明信片
poster, advertisement	guǎnggào 廣告(广告); hǎibǎo 海報(海报)
poster, placard	zhāotiē 招貼(招贴)
postpone, delay	tuīchí 推遲(推迟)
pot (for cooking)	guō 鍋(锅)
pot (for flowers)	pén 盆
pot, kettle	hú 壺(壶)
pottery	táoqì 陶器
pound	bàng 磅
pound, sterling	bàng 鎊(镑)
pour (out), dump, empty	dǎodiào 倒掉
pour, tip	dào 倒
power, strength	lìliàng 力量
practice	liànxí 練習(练习)
practice economy	jiéyuē 節約(节约)
practiced, expert	shúliàn 熟練(熟练)
praise, commend	biǎoyáng 表揚(表扬)
precipitate a disaster, get into trouble	chuǎnghuò 闖禍(闯祸)
precious, valuable	bǎoguì 寶貴(宝贵); zhēnguì 珍貴(珍贵)

precise, exact	zhǔnquè 準確(准确)
precisely, exactly	wánquánduì 完全對(完全对)
(as) predicted (as) expected	guǒrán 果然
predict	yùyán 預言(预言)
prefer, would rather	nìngyuàn 寧願(宁愿); nìngkě 寧可(宁可)
pregnant	huáiyùn 懷孕(怀孕)
premier	zǒnglǐ 總理(总理)
prepare	yùbèi 預備(预备); zhǔnbèi 準備(准备)
present, gift	lǐwù 禮物(礼物)
preserve, maintain	wéihù 維護(维护); bǎochí 保持
preserve, retain	bǎoliú 保留
press, push down	yā 壓(压)
press (clothes)	tàng (yīfú) 燙(衣服)(烫(衣服))
press with hand or fingers	àn 按; èn 摁
pretty, attractive	hǎokàn 好看; piàoliàng 漂亮
previous, past	guòqù 過去(过去)
previously	céngjīng 曾經(曾经)
previously (indefinite past)	yǐqián 以前
price	jiàqián 價錢(价钱); jiàgé 價格(价格)
primary school	xiǎoxué 小學(小学)
principally	zhǔyào 主要
principle, fundamental rule	yuánzé 原則(原则)
principle, theory	yuánlǐ 原理
printing factory	yìnshuāchǎng 印刷廠(印刷厂)

103

prison	jiānyù 監獄(监狱)
probably	duōbàn 多半; dàgài 大概
problem, question	wèntí 問題(问题)
procedure	chéngxù 程序; shǒuxù 手續(手续)
proceed, advance	jiánjìn 前進(前进); jìnxing 進行(进行)
proceed to	kāishǐ 開始(开始); zhóushǒu 着手
proclaim	xuāngào 宣告
produce, generate	chǎnshēng 產生(产生)
produce, manufacture	shēngchǎn 生產(生产); zhìzào 製造(制造)
product	chǎnpǐn 產品(产品)
production	shēngchǎn 生產(生产)
professor	jiàoshòu 教授
program	jiémù (of TV, etc.) 節目(节目); chéngxù (of computers) 程序
progress, make progress	jìnbù 進步(进步)
progressively, more and more	zhújiàn 逐漸(逐渐); yuèláiyuè 越來越(越来越)
prohibit, ban, forbid	jìnzhì 禁止
prolific	duōchǎnde 多產的(多产的)
promote, accelerate	cù 促; cùjìn 促進(促进)
promise	xǔnuò 許諾(许诺); dāying 答應(答应)
promise	nuòyán 諾言(诺言)
promptly, at once, immediately	liánmáng 連忙(连忙); mǎshàng 馬上(马上)
pronunciation	fāyīn 發音(发音)
proper, formal	shìdàngde 適當的(适当的);

	zhèngguīde 正規的（正规的）
properly	shìdàngde 適當地（适当地）
property rights	chǎnquán 產權（产权）
propose, suggest	tíyì 提議（提议）; jiànyì 建議（建议）
prospect, future	qiántú 前途
prosperous, thriving	fánhuá 繁華（繁华）; fánróng 繁榮（繁荣）
protect	bǎohù 保護（保护）
prove, confirm, proof	zhèngmíng 證明（证明）
provide, supply	tígōng 提供; gōngjǐ 供給（供给）
province (equivalent to a state in the United States)	shěng 省
prudent, careful	jǐnshèn 謹慎（谨慎）
public, common, communal	gōnggòng 公共
public affairs, official business	gōngwù 公務（公务）
publish	chūbǎn 出版
puff, blow	chuī 吹
pull, drag, haul	tuō 拖; lā 拉
pull, pluck	bá 拔
pulse	màibó 脈搏（脉搏）
punctual	ànshí 按時（按时）
punctuation	biāodiǎn 標點（标点）
pupil	xuéshēng 學生
purchase (n.)	gòumǎi 購買（购买）; gòudéwù 購得物（购得物）
purchase, buy	gòumǎi 購買（购买）
purport, significance	yìyì 意義（意义）
purse	qiánbāo 錢包（钱包）

purse, handbag	shǒutíbāo 手提包
pursue, chase	zhuī 追; gǎn 趕(赶)
push, shove	tuī 推
put, place	bǎi 擺(摆)
put in	fàngjìn 放進(放进)
put into practice	shíjiàn 實踐(实践)
put off	tuīchí 推遲(推迟)
put on	fàngzài…shàng 放在…上
put on (clothes)	chuān 穿; chuānshàng 穿上
put on (the cover)	gàishàng 蓋上(盖上)

Q

quality	zhìliàng 質量(质量)
quantity	shùliàng 數量(数量)
quarter	sìfēnzhīyī 四分之一
quarter of an hour	kè 刻
question	wèntí 問題(问题)
question mark	wènhào 問號(问号)
queue	chángduì 長隊(长队); páiduì 排隊(排队)
quick, fast	kuài 快
quiet, peaceful	ānjìng 安靜
quiet, tranquil	píngjìng 平靜
quit	tíngzhǐ 停止; líkāi 離開(离开)
quite	xiāngdāng 相當(相当)
quite clear, obvious	míngxiǎn 明顯(明显)
quiz, test, exam	kǎoshì 考試(考试)
quotation mark	yǐhào 引號(引号)

R

radio	shōuyīnjī 收音機(收音机)
railway	tiělù 鐵路(铁路)
railway station	huǒchēzhàn 火車站(火车站)
rain (n.)	yǔ 雨; yǔshuǐ 雨水
rain (v.)	xiàyǔ 下雨
heavy rain	dàyǔ 大雨
rainbow	cǎihóng 彩虹
rain-drenched	bèiyǔlíntòu 被雨淋透
raindrop	yǔdiǎn 雨點(雨点)
rainstorm, storm	bàofēngyǔ 暴風雨
raise, improve, increase	tígāo 提高
raise, lift up	jǔ 舉(举)
raise, promote to a high-er post	tíshēng 提升
raise, put up	jiànlì 建立
raise curtain (in a theater)	kāimù 開幕(开幕)
raise money	chóukuǎn 籌歀(筹款)
rarely	hěnshǎo 很少
rascal	wúlài 無賴(无赖); liúmáng 流氓
rather, preferring to	nìngkě 寧可(宁可); nìngyuàn 寧願(宁愿)
rather (good, bad, etc.)	xiāngdāng 相當(相当); pō 頗(颇)
ravine	gōu 溝(沟)
raw materials	yuánliào 原料
razor	tìdāo 剃刀
read (visually)	kàn 看
read (aloud)	dú 讀(读); niàn 唸(念)
read a book	kànshū 看書(看书)
reading room	yuèlǎnshì 閱覽室(阅览室)

ready	zhǔnbèihǎode 準備好的(准备好的)
real, genuine, true	zhēnzhèngde 眞正的
real, really	zhēnde 眞的
realistic	shíjìde 實際的(实际的); xiànshíde 現實的(现实的)
reality	shíjì 實際(实际); xiànshí 現實(现实)
realize, come to see	rènshí 認識(认识)
really	zhēnde 眞的; fēicháng 非常
really, honestly	shízài 實在(实在)
reason (n.)	lǐyóu 理由; yuányīn 原因
reason (v.)	jiǎnglǐ 講理(讲理)
reason, hows and whys	dàolǐ 道理
reasonable	hélǐde 合理的
receipt	shōujù 收據(收据)
receive, get, accept	shōudào 收到; dédào 得到
receive, grant an interview to	jiējiàn 接見(接见)
receive (guests)	jiēdài (kèren) 接待(客人)
recent	zuìjìnde 最近的
recently	jìnlái 近來(近来)
reception	zhāodàihuì 招待會
receptionist	jiēdàiyuán 接待員(接待员)
reception room	huìkèshì 會客室(会客室)
reckon, compute	suàn 算
recognize, know, be familar with	rènshi 認識(认识)
recommend, introduce	jièshào 介紹(介绍); tuījiàn 推薦(推荐)
reconstruct	chóngjiàn 重建
record, make a tape	lùyīn 錄音(录音)

recording of	
record, take notes	jìlù 記錄
record, result	chéngjī 成績(成绩)
record disc	chàngpiān 唱片
record player	chàngjī 唱機(唱机)
recording tape	lùyīncídài 錄音磁帶(录音磁带)
recover	huīfù 恢復(恢复)
recreation, games	xiāoqiǎn 消遣; yúlè 娛樂(娱乐)
reduce, curtail	xiāojiǎn 削減
referee, judge, umpire	cáipànyuán 裁判員(裁判员)
refined, elegant	wényǎ 文雅
reflect, cast an image of	fǎnyìng 反映; biǎoxiàn 表現(表现)
refresh oneself	jiěfá 解乏
refreshing, cool	liángshuǎng 涼爽
refrigerator	diànbīngxiāng 電冰箱(电冰箱)
refugee	nànmín 難民(难民)
regarding, concerning	guānyú 關於(关于)
region, district	dìqū 地區(地区)
register (for postal matter)	guàhào 掛號(挂号)
register, registry	dēngjì 登記(登记)
registration desk	dēngjìchù 登記處(登记处)
regularly, all the time	jīngcháng 經常(经常)
regulate	guǎnlǐ 管理; tiáozhěng 調整(调整)
related to	yǒuguān 有關(有关)
relation, relationship	guānxi 關係(关系)
relatively	bǐjiào 比較(比较); xiāngduì 相對(相对)
relatives	qīnqī 親戚(亲戚)
relax	fàngsōng 放鬆(放松)

relevance, connection	guānxì 關係(关系)
reliable	kěkàode 可靠的
rely on, depend on	yīkào 依靠
remain, stay	shèngxià 剩下; liúxià 留下
remainder, surplus	shèngyú 剩餘(剩余); shèng-xiàde 剩下的
remember	jìde 記得(记得)
remind	tíxīng 提醒
remote, far away	yáoyuǎn 遙遠(遥远)
remove, move	bān 搬; yí 移
remove, take away	chè 撤
rent, hire	zū 租
rent	zūjīn 租金
repair	xiūlǐ 修理
repeat	chóngfù 重複(重复)
repeatedly, in succession	fǎnfù 反覆(反复); zàisān 再三
repertoire	jùmù 劇目(剧目)
reply	huídá 回答
report	bàogào (an official one) 報告 (报告); bàodǎo (made in a paper) 報導(报导)
reporter	jìzhě 記者(记者)
represent, show, express	biǎoxiàn 表現(表现)
representative, delegate	dàibiǎo 代表
representative (of someone's work)	dàibiǎozuò 代表作
reproduction	fùzhìpǐn 複製品(复制品)
republic	gònghéguó 共和國(共和国)
request, ask for	qǐng 請(请); yāoqiú 要求
require	xūyào 需要; yāoqiú 要求
rescue, save	jiù 救
research	yánjiū 研究

resemble, be like, take after	xiàng 像(象)
reservation, reserve	yùdìng 預訂(预订); dìng 訂(订)
reside	zhùzài 住在; zhù 住
residence	fǔshang 府上; zhùchù 住處(住处)
resist, parry	dǐdǎng 抵擋(抵挡); dǐknàg 抵抗
resources	zīyuán 資源(资源)
respect	zūnjìng 尊敬
respond, answer	xiǎngyìng 響應(响应); huídá 回答
responsibility	zérèn 責任(责任)
take responsibility	fùzé 負責(负责)
rest, the	qíyú 其餘(其余)
rest, relax	xiūxi 休息; xiē 歇
restaurant	fànguǎn (Chinese style) 飯館(饭馆); cāntīng (Western style) 餐廳(餐厅)
result, consequence	jiéguǒ 結果(结果)
resume, continue	jìxù 繼續(继续)
retell, repeat	fùshù 複述(复述)
retreat	tuì 退; hòutuì 後退(后退)
return, go back	huí 回; guī 歸(归)
return, give back	huán 還(还)
revenge, avenge	bàochóu 報仇(报仇); bàofù 報復(报复)
review	fùxí 複習(复习)
revise, modify	xiūgǎi 修改
revolt against	fǎnkàng 反抗
revolution	gémìng 革命

revolutionary	gémìngde (adj.) 革命的; gémìngjiā (n.) 革命家
revolve, turn	zhuàn 轉(转)
revolve around, center on	wéirǎo 圍繞(围绕)
rewarded amply	yǒuhǎobào 有好報(有好报); zhòngchóu 重酬
rewrite	gǎixiě 改寫(改写)
rice, cooked rice	mǐfàn 米飯(米饭)
rice plant	dàozi 稻子
rice paddy	dàotián 稻田
rice-flour meat	mǐfěnròu 米粉肉
rich	fùyǒu 富有; fēngfù 豐富(丰富)
ride (a horse, a bike, etc.)	qí 騎(骑)
ride in, to go by	chéng 乘; zuò 坐
riddle	míyǔ 謎語(谜语)
right, correct	duì 對(对)
right, exactly	shuōdéduì 說得對(说得对)
right (side or direction)	yòu 右
right after, in close succession	jiēzhe 接着
right away, immediately	mǎshàng 馬上(马上); zhèjiù 這就(这就)
right side	yòubiān 右邊(右边)
ripe	shú 熟
rise, ascend	shēng 升; shēnggāo 升高
rise, stand up	qǐlái 起來(起来)
rising, growing	zhàng 漲(涨)
river	jiāng 江; hé 河
road	lù 路
road surface	lùmiàn 路面
roast	kǎo 烤

rob, steal	dàoqiè 盜竊（盜窃）
rock	yánshí 岩石
rock (v.)	yáobǎi 搖擺（搖擺）
roll, wind	juǎn 捲
roll of film	jiāojuǎn 膠捲（胶卷）
Romanization	Luómǎhuà 羅馬化（罗马化）
roof (of a house)	wūdǐng 屋頂（屋顶）
roof beam	fángliáng 房樑（房梁）
room	fángjiān 房間（房间）; wūzi 屋子
room, enough space	kōngjiān 空間（空间）
room number	fánghào 房號（房号）
root of plant	gēn 根
rostrum	jiǎngtái 講臺（讲台）; zhǔxítái 主席臺（主席台）
rotten	fǔlànde 腐爛的（腐烂的）
rough (surface, etc.)	cūcāode 粗糙的
roughly, presumably	dàgài 大概
round, circular, spherical	yuánxíngde 圓形的（圆形的）; yuánde 圓的（圆的）
row (a boat)	huá 划; huáchuán 划船
row, line, queue	háng 行; pái 排
rub, feel	mócā 摩擦; róu 揉
ruin, spoil	huǐhuài 毀壞（毁坏）
ruined	huàile 壞了（坏了）; huǐle 毀了
ruler (person in power)	tǒngzhìzhě 統治者（统治者）
ruler (measure)	chǐ 尺
rumbling sound	hōnglōngshēng 轟隆聲（轰隆声）
run, flow	liú 流
run, go swiftly	pǎo 跑
run, have a run, do some running	pǎobù 跑步
run a fever	fāshāo 發燒

run a race, race	sàipǎo 賽跑(赛跑)
run after, pursue	zhuī 追
run into, come across, encounter, meet	pèngjiàn 碰見(碰见); yùjiàn 遇見(遇见)
rush	chōng 衝(冲); chuǎng 闖(闯)
rush in	chuǎngjìn 闖進(闯进)
rush out of	chuǎngchū 闖出(闯出)
Russia	Éguó 俄國(俄国)
Russian	Éguórén (people) 俄國人(俄国人); Éwén (language) 俄文
rust (n.)	xiù 銹(锈)
rust (v.)	shēngxiù 生銹(生锈)
rustling sound	shāshāshēng 沙沙聲(沙沙声)

S

sack, bag	kǒudài 口袋
sacrifice	xīshēng 犧牲(牺牲)
sad	bēishāng 悲傷(悲伤)
safe	ānquán 安全
sail	fān 帆
salad	shālà 沙拉
salary	gōngzī 工資(工资); xīnshuǐ 薪水
salesman, salesperson, shop assistant	diànyuán 店員(店员); shòuhuòyuán 售貨員(售货员); huǒjì 夥計(伙计)
salt	yán 鹽(盐)
salute	xínglǐ 行禮(行礼)
same	yíyàng 一樣(一样); tóngyàng 同樣(同样)
sample, pattern	yàngpǐn 樣品(样品)
sandwich	jiáxīnmiànbāo 夾心麵包(夹心面

包); sānmíngzhì 三明治

satchel, schoolbag	shūbāo 書包(书包)
satisfactory	mǎnyìde 滿意的(满意的)
Saturday	xīngqīliù 星期六
sausage	xiāngcháng 香腸(香肠)
save	shěng 省
save effort	shěnglì 省力
save money	shěngqián 省錢(省钱)
save trouble	shěngshì 省事
save worry	shěngxīn 省心
save, avoid	shěngde 省得
save, economize	jiéshěng 節省
save, rescue	jiù 救; qiǎngjiù 搶救(抢救)
savings, deposits	cúnkuǎn 存欵
savor, taste (n.)	wèi 味
savor, taste (v.)	cháng 嚐(尝)
say	shuō 說(说)
say good-bye	gàobié 告別; zàijiàn 再見(再见)
scale	chèng 稱(称)
scale, scope, dimension	guīmó 規模(规模)
scarce	quēfá 缺乏; shǎo 少
scary	kěpà 可怕
scene	chǎngmiàn 場面(场面); bùjǐng (theatrical) 布景
scene (in play)	chǎng 場(场)
scenery, landscape, view	fēngjǐng 風景(风景)
scenic spot	míngshèng 名勝(名胜)
schedule (n.)	rìchéngbiǎo 日程表
schedule (v.)	páidìng 排定
scholar	xuézhě 學者(学者)
school	xuéxiào 學校(学校)
primary school	xiǎoxué 小學(小学)

middle (high) school	zhōngxué 中學(中学)
university, college	dàxué 大學(大学)
schoolmate	tóngxué 同學(同学)
science	kēxué 科學(科学)
science (as a school subject)	lǐkē 理科
science and technology	kēxué jìshù 科學技術(科学技术)
scissors	jiǎndāo 剪刀
scold	zémà 責罵(责骂)
scope, scale, dimension	guīmó 規模(规模)
scroll	huàzhóu 畫軸(画轴)
sculpture	diāosù (the art) 雕塑; diāoxiàng (statue) 雕像
sea	hǎi 海
seafood	hǎiwèi 海味
seaman	hǎiyuán 海員(海员)
seashore, beach	hǎibīn 海濱(海滨); hǎitān 海灘(海滩)
season	jìjié 季節(季节)
spring	chūntiān 春天
summer	xiàntiān 夏天
autumn, fall	qiūtiān 秋天
winter	dōngtiān 冬天
seasoning	tiáowèipǐn 調味品(调味品); zuóliào 作料
seat	zuòwèi 座位
secondhand goods	jiùhuò 舊貨(旧货)
secret	mìmì 秘密
secretary in an office	mìshū 秘書(秘书)
secretary in a Party	shūjì 書記(书记)
section (in an office)	chù 處(处); kē 科

section, part	bùfen 部分
see	kàn 看; kànjiàn 看見(看见)
see, view	guānkàn 觀看(观看)
see off	sòng 送; sòngxíng 送行
see to	zhùyì 注意; liúxīn 留心
seedling, sprout	miáo 苗
seek, look for	zhǎo 找
seek shelter (from a rain)	bìyǔ 避雨
seem	hǎoxiàng 好像(好象)
seemingly, it seems as if	sìhū 似乎
seize, catch, capture	zhuō 捉
seldom	hěnshǎo 很少
select	tiāoxuǎn 挑選(挑选)
self	zìjǐ 自己
sell	mài 賣(卖)
seller	màifāng 賣方(卖方)
selling price	màijià 賣價(卖价)
send	sòng 送
send, dispatch (a messenger, troops, etc.)	pài 派
send, post, mail (a letter)	jì 寄
sense, perceive, feel	gǎnjué 感覺(感觉)
sentence (in grammar)	jùzi 句子
sentence (in court)	pànjué 判決; pànxíng 判刑
separate (v.)	gékāi 隔開(隔开)
separate (adj.)	fēnkāide 分開的(分开的)
September	jiǔyuè 九月
serious	yánzhòng (critical) 嚴重(严重); rènzhēn (conscientious) 認真(认真); yánsù (serious in manner or expressing) 嚴

117

肅(严肃)

serve	fúwù 服務(服务)
serve at table	shìyìng…chīfàn 侍應…吃飯(侍应…吃饭)
service	fúwù 服務(服务)
service, agency	shè 社
set forth one's views	fābiǎo yìjiàn 發表意見(发表意见)
set free, let go	fàng 放
set one's mind at rest	fàngxīn 放心
set out, display	chénliè 陳列(陈列)
set out, start a journey	chūfā 出發(出发)
set up, establish	chuànglì 創立(创立); jiànlì 建立
settlers, immigrants	yímín 移民
seven	qī 七
seventeen	shíqī 十七
seventh	dìqī 第七
seventy	qīshí 七十
several, a few	jǐ 幾(几)
several kinds	jǐzhǒng 幾種(几种)
severe	yánzhòng 嚴重(严重)
sex	xìngbié 性別
shadow	yǐngzi 影子
shake	yáo 搖
shake hand	wòshǒu 握手
shall, will	jiāngyào 將要(将要)
shallow	qiǎn 淺(浅)
shape	yàngzi 樣子(样子); xíngzhuàng 形狀(形状)
sharp	fēnglì 鋒利(锋利); kuài 快
shave	guāhúzi 刮鬍子(刮胡子)

118

she, her	tā 她
shed, shack	péngzi 棚子
sheep	yáng 羊
shift, move	yídòng 移動(移动)
ship	chuán 船
shirt	chènshān 襯衫(衬衫); chènyī 襯衣(衬衣)
shoes	xié 鞋
shop	shāngdiàn 商店
shop window	chúchuāng 橱窗
short (of stature)	ǎi 矮
short (length)	duǎn 短
short of	chà 差; quē 缺
should	jiāng 將(将); huì 會(会)
should, ought to	yīnggāi 應該(应该)
shoulder (n.)	jiān 肩
shoulder (v.)	dānfù 擔負(担负); káng 扛
shout, yell	hǎn 喊
show, express	biǎoshì 表示
show, performance	biǎoyǎn 表演
show (movies, etc.)	fàngyìng 放映
show, teach	jiāo 教
show, concern for, be concerned about	guānxīn 關心(关心)
shower, take a shower	xǐlínyù 洗淋浴
shrimp	xiǎoxiā 小蝦(小虾)
shrink	suō 縮(缩)
shut	guān 關(关)
shutters	bǎiyèchuāng 百葉窗(百叶窗)
shy	rènshēng 認生(认生); hàixiū 害羞
sick	bìng 病

side	biān 邊(边)
siesta, nap	wǔshuì 午睡; wǔxiū 午休
sightseeing	yóulǎn 遊覽(游览)
sign, affix signature	qiānzì 簽字(签字)
signboard	zhāopái 招牌; guǎnggàopái 廣告牌(广告牌)
significance	yìyì 意義(意义)
sign, omen	zhàotou 兆頭(兆头)
sign, placard	biāoyǔpái 標語牌(标语牌)
signpost	lùbiāo 路標(路标)
silent	ānjìng 安靜
silk	sīchóu 絲綢(丝绸)
similar	xiāngsì 相似
simple	róngyì 容易; jiǎndān 簡單(简单)
simplify	jiǎnhuà 簡化(简化); jīngjiǎn 精簡(精简)
simply, only	jǐn 僅(仅); zhǐ 祇(只)
since, as, now that	jìrán 既然
since, from	zìcóng…yǐlái 自從…以來(自從…以来)
sing	chànggē 唱歌(唱歌)
Singapore	Xīnjiāpō 新加坡
singer, vocalist	gēshǒu 歌手; gēchàngjiā 歌唱家
singles (for games)	dāndǎ 單打(单打)
Sinkiang	Xīnjiāng 新疆
sister, elder	jiějie 姐姐
sister, younger	mèimei 妹妹
sit	zuò 坐
Sit down, please.	qǐngzuò 請坐(请坐)
sit for examination	cānjiā kǎoshì 參加考試(参加考試)

sitting room	kètīng 客廳(客厅); tángwū 堂屋
six	liù 六
sixteen	shíliù 十六
sixth	dìliù 第六
sixty	liùshí 六十
size (dress, etc.)	hào 號(号); mǎ 碼(码)
size, measurement	dàxiǎo 大小
skating	liūbīng 溜冰; huábīng 滑冰
skating rink	liūbīngchǎng 溜冰場(溜冰场)
sketch, sketch map	lüètú 略圖(略图)
sketchy, brief, simple	cūlüè 粗略; dàgài 大概
ski (on snow)	huáxuě 滑雪
ski (on water)	huáshuǐ 滑水
skill	jìshù 技術(技术); shǒuyì 手藝 (手艺)
skilled	shúliànde 熟練的(熟练的)
skin, wrapping	pí 皮; pír 皮兒(皮儿)
skirt	qúnzi 裙子
sky	tiān 天
slack, idle	lǎnsǎn 懶散(懒散); xián 閑(闲)
sled	xuěqiāo 雪撬
sleep	shuìjiào 睡覺(睡觉)
sleeping berth	wòpù 臥舖(卧铺)
sleeping car	wòchē 臥車(卧车)
sleeping	shuìjiào 睡覺(睡觉); shuìzháode 睡着的
sleeves	xiùzi 袖子
slice (n.)	piàn 片
slice (v.)	qiēpiàn 切片
slides (lantern)	huàndēng 幻燈(幻灯)
slipcover	tàozi 套子(套子)

slogan	biāoyǔ 標語(标语)
slow	màn 慢
small	xiǎo 小
small food, tidbits	diǎnxīn 點心(点心); língshí 零食
smart	cōngmíng 聰明(聪明); nénggàn 能幹(能干)
smash, break (a record)	dǎpò 打破
smash, break, destory	jīhuǐ 擊毀(击毁)
smash, drive (a tennis ball, etc.)	chōu 抽; shāqiú 殺球
smell, scent (n.)	wèi 味; wèir 味兒(味儿)
smell (v.)	wén 聞(闻)
smelly, stinking	chòu 臭
smile	wēixiào 微笑
smoke (n.)	yān 烟
smoke (v.)	chōuyān 抽烟
smoothly, successfully	shùnlì 順利(顺利)
snack	xiǎochī 小吃
snake	shé 蛇
sniff	xiù 嗅; wén 聞(闻)
snow (n.)	xuě 雪
snow (v.)	xiàxuě 下雪
snow plow	sǎoxuějī 掃雪機(扫雪机)
so	rúcǐ 如此; zhème 這麼(这么)
so, thus	zhèyàng 這樣(这样)
so, therefore	yīncǐ 因此
so long as	zhǐyào 衹要(只要)
soap	féizào 肥皂
soccer	zúqiú 足球
social get together	liánhuānhuì 聯歡會(联欢会)
socialism	shèhuìzhǔyì 社會主義(社会主

	义)
society	shèhuì 社會(社会)
socks, stockings	wàzi 襪子(袜子)
soda water	qìshuǐ 汽水
sofa	shāfā 沙發(沙发)
soft drink	qīngliáng yǐnliào 清涼飲料(清涼飲料)
soft, pliable, yielding	róuruǎn 柔軟(柔软)
soil	tǔrǎng 土壤
soldier	bīng 兵; zhànshì 戰士(战士)
solely, only	dāndúde 單獨的(单独地); wéiyīde 唯一地
solid, firm	jiāngùde 堅固的(坚固的)
solve	jiějué 解決
some	yìxiē 一些
some, somewhat	yǒuyìdiǎnr 有一點兒(有一点儿)
someday	yǒuyìtiān 有一天
sometimes	yǒushíhòu 有時候(有时候)
son	érzi 兒子(儿子)
son-in-law	nǚxu 女婿
song	gē 歌
song words	gēcí 歌詞(歌词)
soon, before long, soon after	bùjiǔ 不久; kuài 快
soon, shortly, at an early date	zǎorì 早日
sorry	duìbùqǐ 對不起(对不起)
sort, kind of	zhǒng 種(种)
sound	shēngyīn 聲音
sound (of something astir), happenings	dòngjìng 動靜(动静)

123

sound, give out a sound	fāchū shēngyīn 發出聲音(发出声音)
sound, give an impression	tīngqǐlái 聽起來(听起来)
soup	tāng 湯(汤)
sour	suān 酸
south	nán 南
southern part	nánfāng 南方
Soviet Union	Sūlián 蘇聯(苏联)
sow (seeds)	bōzhǒng 播種(播种)
soy sauce	jiàngyóu 醬油(酱油)
spacious	kuānchǎng 寬敞(宽敞)
Spain	Xībānyá 西班牙
Spaniard	Xībānyárén 西班牙人
Spanish (language)	Xībānyáwén 西班牙文; xībānyáyǔ 西班牙語(西班牙语)
spare ribs	páigǔ 排骨
spare time, leisure time	yèyú shíjiān 業餘時間(业余时间)
speak	shuōhuà 說話(说话)
special	tèbié 特別
specialist	zhuānjiā 專家(专家)
speciality, profession	zhuānyè 專業(专业)
specially, particularly	tèdì 特地
species	zhǒnglèi 種類(种类)
specify	zhǐdìng 指定
spectacular, splendid	jīngcǎi 精彩
spectator	guānzhòng 觀眾(观众)
speedy	xùnsù 迅速
spend	huāfèi 花費(花费)
spend money	huāqián 花錢(花钱)

124

spend time	xiāomó shíjiān 消磨時間(消磨时间); guòrìzi 過日子(过日子)
spending money	língyòngqián 零用錢(零用钱)
sphere, area	lǐngyù 領域(领域); fāngmiàn 方面
sphere, a three dimensional surface	qiú 球; qiúmiàn 球面
spherical, circular	yuánde 圓的(圆的)
spicy	làde 辣的
spinning top	tuóluó 陀螺
spiral spring	tánhuáng 彈簧(弹簧)
spirited, lively	jīngshén bǎomǎn 精神飽滿(精神饱满)
spirits, spirituous liquors	lièjiǔ 烈酒
splendid	jīngcǎi 精彩
spoil	sǔnhuài 損壞(损坏); zāotà 糟蹋
spoon	sháo 勺
sports	tǐyù 體育(体育); yùndòng 運動(运动)
sportsfield	yùndòngchǎng 運動場(运动场)
sports (athletic) ground	yùndòngchǎng 運動場(运动场)
sportsman, sportswoman	yùndòngyuán 運動員(运动员)
sports meeting	yùndònghuì 運動會(运动会)
spray	pēn 噴(喷)
spread, circulate	chuánbō 傳播(传播)
spread, cover	pū 鋪(铺)
spring (season)	chūntiān 春天
spring, metal spiral	tánhuáng 彈簧(弹簧)
Spring Festival	chūnjié 春節(春节)
spring flowers	yíngchūnhuā 迎春花
spring-stream	quánshuǐ 泉水

squander	làngfèi 浪費(浪费); huīhuò 揮霍(挥霍)
square	fāngxíng (a plane figure) 方形; guǎngchǎng (an open area) 廣場(广场)
stadium	tǐyùchǎng 體育場(体育场)
staff member, functionary	zhíyuán 職員(职员)
stage	tái 臺(台); wǔtái 舞臺(舞台)
staircase	lóutī 樓梯(楼梯)
stamp	yóupiào 郵票(邮票)
stand (n.)	tái 臺(台); jià 架
stand (v.)	zhàn 站; lì 立
stand up	zhànqǐlái 站起來(站起来)
standard, level	biāozhǔn 標準(标准)
star	xīng 星
start doing something, proceed to do some- thing	dòngshǒu 動手(动手)
start off	dòngshēn 動身(动身)
state, condition	qíngxíng 情形; zhuàngtài 狀態 (状态)
state, country	guójiā 國家(国家)
state (in U.S.)	zhōu 州
State Department (U.S.)	Guówùyuàn 國務院(国务院)
State Council (China)	Guówùyuàn 國務院(国务院)
station	zhàn 站
stationery	wénjù 文具
statue	diāoxiàng 雕像
status, condition	qíngkuàng 情況(情况); zhuàng- tài 狀態(状态)
status, position	dìwèi 地位; shēnfèn 身分
staunch	jiānqiáng 堅强(坚强)

126

stay	dòuliú 逗留(逗留); zhù 住
stay overnight, stay for the night	guòyè 過夜(过夜)
steady, sure, calm	wěn 穩(稳)
steak	niúpái 牛排
steal	tōu 偷
steam (n.)	zhēngqì 蒸氣(蒸气)
steam (v.)	zhēng 蒸
steam boat	lúnchuán 輪船(轮船)
steamed bread	mántou 饅頭(馒头)
steel	gāng 鋼(钢)
steel (stainless)	búxiùgāng 不銹鋼(不锈钢)
steep	dǒu 陡
stench	chòu 臭
step	bùfá 步伐; bùzi 步子
steps, ladder	jiētī 階梯(阶梯)
stew	dùn 燉(炖)
beef stew	dùnniúròu 燉牛肉(炖牛肉)
chicken stew	dùnjī 燉鷄(炖鸡)
stick	gùnzi 棍子
stick (on)	tiē 貼(贴)
stick, insert	cì 刺; zhā 扎; chā 插
stifle	mēnsǐ 悶死(闷死); zhìxī 窒息
still, as before	hái 還(还)
stimulate, arouse, stir	cìjī 刺激
stockings	wàzi 襪子(袜子); chángwà 長襪(长袜)
stomach	wèi 胃
stone, rock	shítou 石頭(石头)
stone monument	bēi 碑
stop	tíng 停
stop, station	zhàn 站

127

store, pack away	cún 存
store, shop	diàn 店
storehouse, storeroom	kùfáng 庫房(库房)
storm	bàofēngyǔ 暴風雨(暴风雨)
story	gùshì 故事
stove	lúzi 爐子(炉子)
straight	zhí 直
straight ahead	yìzhízǒu 一直走
straighten	shēnzhí 伸直
strange, queer, odd	qíguài 奇怪
stranger	mòshēngrén 陌生人
straw (for drinking)	xīguǎnr 吸管兒(吸管儿)
straw shed	cǎowū 草屋
streaks, stripes	tiáowén 條紋(条纹)
street	jiē 街
strength	lìliàng 力量
strenghten	jiānqiáng 加强
strenuously	yònglì de 用力地
stretch, extend	shēn 伸
strict, tight	yán 嚴(严)
strike, knock	qiāo 敲
string, cord	shéngzi 繩子(绳子)
string, line	xiàn 綫(线)
stripes, streaks	tiáowén 條紋(条纹)
strive	nǔlì 努力
strokes (of a Chinese character)	bǐhuà 筆劃(笔划)
stroll	sànbù 散步; guàng 逛
strong	qiángliè 强烈
strong, powerful	qiáng 强; qiángdà 强大
strong, sturdy	jiēshi 結實(结实)
structure	gòuzào 構造(构造)

128

struggle against	dòuzhēng 鬥爭(斗争)
student	xuésheng 學生(学生)
student studying abroad	liúxuéshēng 留學生(留学生)
study	xuéxí 學習(学习)
study abroad	liúxué 留學(留学)
study on one's own	zìxué 自學(自学)
stuffing, filling (in a dumpling, etc.)	xiànr 餡兒(馅儿)
stupid	bèn 笨
stupid fellow, fool	chǔnrén 蠢人; bèndàn 笨蛋
sturdy, strong	jiēshi 結實(结实)
style, appearance	yàngzi 樣子(样子); yàngshì 樣式(样式)
subject to approval	yǒudàipīzhǔn 有待批准
subjective, subjectivity	zhǔguān 主觀(主观)
submerge, flood	yān 淹; yānmò 淹沒
substance, content	nèiróng 內容
suburbs	jiāoqū 郊區(郊区)
succeed	chénggōng 成功
successful	chénggōngde 成功的
successfully, smoothly, without a hitch	shùnlì 順利(顺利)
succession, in	jiēlián 接連(接连)
such	zhème 這麼(这么); zhèyàng 這樣(这样)
suddenly, all of a sudden	tūrán 突然; hūrán 忽然
suffer	zāoshòu 遭受
sufficient	zúgòu 足夠
sugar	táng 糖
suggest, propose	jiànyì 建議(建议)
suit (Western)	xīfú 西服
suit, conform with	shìhé 適合(适合)

suitable	héshì 合適(合适)
suitcase	xiāngzi 箱子
sultry	mēnrè 悶熱(闷热)
summer	xiàtiān 夏天
summer vacation	shǔjià 暑假
sun	tàiyáng 太陽(太阳)
Sunday	xīngqīrì 星期日; xīngqītiān 星期天
sunny, fine	qínglǎng 晴朗
sunrise	rìchū 日出
sunset	rìluò 日落
superior grade, first class	shàngděng 上等
supermarket	chāojí shìchǎng 超級市場(超级市场)
supper	wǎnfàn 晚飯(晚饭)
supplementary	bǔchōngde 補充的(补充的)
supply, provide	tígòng 提供
support	zhīchí 支持
suppose, consider, think of a way	xiǎng 想
sure	yídìng 一定
be sure of, believe	quèxìn 確信(确信)
surgery	wàikē 外科
surgical operation	shǒushù 手術(手术)
surname and first name, full name	xìngmíng 姓名
surplus	shèngyú 剩餘(剩余); duōyú 多餘(多余)
surprise	jīngqí 驚奇(惊奇)
surround	bāowéi 包圍(包围)
surrounding	huánjìng 環境(环境)
swallow	yàn 咽; tūn 吞

130

sway	yáohuàng 搖晃
sweat, perspiration	hàn 汗
sweater	máoyī 毛衣
sweep, clean away	sǎo 掃(扫); dǎsǎo 打掃(打扫)
sweep (the floor, etc.)	sǎodì 掃地(扫地)
sweet	tián 甜
sweets	tángguǒ 糖果
swift, rapid	xùnsù 迅速; kuài 快
swim	yóuyǒng 游泳
swimming pool	yóuyǒngchí 游泳池
switch (electrical)	kāiguān 開關(开关)
switch, transfer	zhuǎnhuàn 轉換(转换)
switch off	guāndiào 關掉(关掉)
switch on	dǎkāi 打開(打开)
switchboard	zǒngjī 總機(总机)
Switzerland	Ruìshì 瑞士
swollen	zhǒng 腫(肿)
sword	jiàn 劍(剑)
symbol	xiàngzhēng 象徵(象征)
symphony	jiāoxiǎngyuè 交響樂(交响乐)
symptoms (of a disease)	zhèngzhuàng 症狀(症状)
symptoms (patient's)	bìngzhuàng 病狀(病状)
system	tǐxì 體系(体系); zhìdù 制度

T

table (for meals, etc.)	zhuōzi 桌子
table (of figures, times, etc.)	biǎo 表; biǎogé 表格
table cloth	zhuōbù 桌布
table lamp	táidēng 檯燈(台灯)
table salt	shíyán 食鹽(食盐)

tablet	bēi 碑; biǎn'é 匾額(匾额)
tablet (medicine)	yàopiàn 藥片(药片)
table tennis	pīngpāngqiú 乒乓球
tail	wěiba 尾巴
tailor	cáifeng 裁縫(裁缝)
take, hold	ná 拿; wò 握
take (a car, a bus, etc.)	chéng 乘; zuò 坐
take a bath	xǐzǎo 洗澡
take a rest	xiūxi 休息
take a seat	zuò 坐
take away	názǒu 拿走
take back	náhuí 拿回
take care, careful	xiǎoxīn 小心
take care of, look after	zhàogù 照顧(照顾)
take offence	shēngqì 生氣(生气)
take shape, form, become	xíngchéng 形成
talent, ability	cáinéng 才能
talk	tánhuà 談話(谈话); shuōhuà 說話(说话)
talk freely, chat	xiántán 閑談(闲谈); liáotiān 聊天
talk silly	xiāshuō 瞎說(瞎说)
talks, meeting	huìtán 會談(会谈)
tall	gāo 高
tape (cassette)	lùyīndài 錄音帶(录音带)
tape recorder	lùyīnjī 錄音機(录音机)
task	rènwù 任務(任务)
taste, likes	àihào 愛好(爱好); xìngqù 興趣(兴趣)
taste, flavor	wèi 味; zīwèi 滋味
taste (v.)	chángchàng 嚐嚐(尝尝)

tasty	hǎochī 好吃; kěkǒu 可口
tax	shuì 税
tax free	miǎnshuì 免税
taxi	chūzū qìchē 出租汽車(出租汽車)
tea	chá 茶
tea bowl	cháwǎn 茶碗
tea cup	chábēi 茶杯
tea house	cháguǎn 茶館(茶馆)
tea leaves	cháyè 茶葉(茶叶)
tea pot	cháhú 茶壺(茶壶)
teach	jiāo 教
teacher	lǎoshī 老師(老师); jiàoshī 教師(教师)
teach in a class	shàngkè 上課(上课)
teaching faculty	jiàozhíyuán 教職員(教职员)
team, unit	zǔ 組(组); duì 隊(队)
teapot, kettle	cháhú 茶壺(茶壶)
technical transfer	jìshù zhuǎnràng 技術轉讓(技術转让)
technique	jìshù 技術(技术)
technology	jìshù 技術(技术); gōngyì 工藝(工艺)
teeth	yáchǐ 牙齒(牙齿)
telegram	diànbào 電報(电报)
telegraph charge	diànbàofèi 電報費(电报费)
telegraphy form	diànbàozhǐ 電報紙(电报纸)
telephone	diànhuà 電話(电话)
telephone, long distance	chángtú diànhuà 長途電話(长途电话)
telephone set	diànhuàjī 電話機(电话机)
television (TV)	diànshì 電視(电视)

tell·	gàosu 告訴(告诉)
tell, describe	jiǎngyìjiǎng 講一講(讲一讲)
temper	píqì 脾氣(脾气)
temper, strengthen, toughen	duànliàn 鍛煉(锻炼)
temper, mood	qíngxù 情緒(情绪); xīnqíng 心情
temperature	wēndù 溫度; tǐwēn (body) 體溫(体温); qìwēn (weather) 氣溫(气温)
fahrenheit	huáshì 華氏(华氏)
centigrade	shèshì 攝氏(摄氏)
temple	miào 廟(庙); sìyuàn 寺院
Temple of Heaven	Tiāntán 天壇(天坛)
ten	shí 十
tender	róuruǎn 柔軟(柔软)
tennis	wǎngqiú 網球(网球)
play tennis	dǎ wǎngqiú 打網球(打网球)
tense, taut	jǐnzhāngde 緊張的(紧张的)
ten thousand	wàn 萬(万)
terminal	zhōngdiǎn 終點(终点)
terrible	kěpàde 可怕的
terribly, severely	lìhài 厲害(厉害)
test	kǎoshì 考試(考试); cèyàn 測驗(测验)
text	kèwén 課文(课文)
textile mill	fǎngzhīchǎng 紡織廠(纺织厂)
textiles	fǎngzhīpǐn 紡織品(纺织品)
Thailand	Tàiguó 泰國(泰国)
than (in "more than" "less than" etc.)	bǐ 比
thank	gǎnxiè 感謝(感谢)

134

thanks	xièxie 謝謝(谢谢); duōxiè 多謝(多谢)
that	nà 那; nèi 那
That is so.	shìde 是的
That's all.	wánle 完了
that very day, on the same day	dàngtiān 當天(当天)
that way, in such a manner, thus	nàyàng 那樣(那样)
theater	jùyuàn 劇院(剧院)
theater ticket	xìpiào 戲票(戏票)
their	tāménde (males) 他們的 (他们的); tāménde (females) 她們的(她们的)
the more…the more	yuè…yuè… 越…越…
then	nàme 那麼(那么)
then, afterwards	ránhòu 然後(然后); hòulái 後來(后来)
theory	lǐlùn 理論(理论)
there	nǎr 哪兒(哪儿); nàr 那兒(那儿)
therefore	suǒyǐ 所以; yīncǐ 因此
there is (there are)	yǒu 有
there is (there are) not	méiyǒu 沒有
thereupon, following that	gēnzhe 跟着
thereupon, hence, consequently, as a result	yúshì 於是(于是)
thermometer	wēndùbiǎo 溫度表
thermos	nuǎnshuǐpíng 暖水瓶
these	zhèxiē 這些(这些)
they, them	tāmén (males) 他們(他们); tāmén (females) 她們(她们); tāmén (plural for "it") 它們

（它们）

thick	hòu 厚
thief, pilferer	xiǎotōu 小偷
thin	shòu (lean) 瘦; bó (not thick) 薄; xī (of low density, etc.) 稀; xì (fine) 細(细)
thing	dōngxī 東西(东西)
think	xiǎng 想
think, consider	yǐwéi 以爲(以为); rènwéi 認爲 (认为)
think over, ponder over	kǎolǜ 考慮(考虑)
thinker	sīxiǎngjiā 思想家
third	dìsān 第三
Third World	Dìsānshìjiè 第三世界
thirsty	kě 渴
thirteen	shísān 十三
thirteenth	dìshísān 第十三
thirty	sānshí 三十
this	zhè 這(这)
this day, today	jīntiān 今天
this way, in such a manner, thus	zhèyàng 這樣(这样)
this year	jīnnián 今年
thorough	chèdǐ 徹底(彻底); tòudǐng 透頂 (透顶)
those	něixiē 哪些
thought, thinking, idea	sīxiǎng 思想
thoughtful, attentive, satisfactory	zhōudào 周到
thousand	qiān 千; yìqiān 一千
ten thousand	yíwàn 一萬(一万)
hundred thousand	shíwàn 十萬(十万)

136

thread (n.)	xiàn 綫(线)
thread (v.)	chuānxiàn 穿綫(穿线)
three	sān 三
thrifty	jiéyuē 節約(节约)
thriving, prosperous	fánróngde 繁榮的(繁荣的)
throat	hóulóng 喉嚨(喉咙)
throng, crowd, jostle	jǐ 擠(挤)
throng	rénqún 人羣
throw, cast	rēng 扔
thumb	dàmǔzhǐ 大拇指
thumb pin, thumb tack	túdīng 圖釘(图钉)
thunder (n.)	léi 雷
thunder (v.)	dǎléi 打雷
thunderstorm	léiyǔ 雷雨
Thursday	xīngqīsì 星期四
thus, so	nàme 那麽(那么); zhème 這麽 (这么)
Tiananmen (Gate of Heavenly Peace)	Tiān'ānmén 天安門(天安门)
Tibet	xīzàng 西藏
ticket	piào 票
ticket office	shòupiàochù 售票處(售票处)
ticket seller	shòupiàoyuán 售票員(售票员)
tidy, neat	zhěngqí 整齊(整齐)
tidy up	shōushi 收拾
tie, necktie	lǐngdài 領帶(领带)
tie up	kǔnqǐlái 捆起來(捆起来)
tiger	lǎohǔ 老虎
tight, close	jǐn 緊(紧)
till, until	zhídào 直到
time	shíjiān 時間(时间); shíhòu 時候 (时候); gōngfu 工夫

137

all the time	yìzhí 一直
at that time	nàshíhòu 那時候（那时候）
at the same time	tóngshí 同時（同时）
first time	chūcì 初次
in a little time	yíhuìr 一會兒（一会儿）
lots of time	hěndōu shíjiān 很多時間（很多时间）
next time	xiàyícì 下一次
times, number of times	cì 次; cìshù 次數（次数）
times, era	shídài 時代（时代）
tiny, minute, fine	wēixiǎo 微小
tire (for car)	lúntāi 輪胎（轮胎）
tired	lèi 累
tiring, gruelling	xīnkǔ 辛苦
title, headline	biāotí 標題（标题）
toast	kǎomiànbāo 烤麵包
tobacco	yān 烟; yāncǎo 烟草
tobacco leaves	yānyè 烟葉（烟叶）
today	jīntiān 今天
toe	jiǎozhǐtóu 腳指頭（脚指头）
together	yìqǐ 一起
together with	gēn 跟; hé 和
toilet	cèsuǒ 廁所（厕所）; wèishēngjiān 衛生間（卫生间）
toilet paper	shǒuzhǐ 手紙（手纸）
toilsome, hard, strenuous	xīnkǔ 辛苦
Tokyo	Dōngjīng 東京（东京）
tolerate	kuānróng 寬容（宽容）
tomato	xīhóngshì 西紅柿（西红柿）
tomb	língmù 陵墓
tomorrow	míngtiān 明天
tone	shēngdiào 聲調（声调）

tone, manner of speaking	yǔqì 語氣(语气)
tongue	shétou 舌頭(舌头)
tonsil	biǎntáoxiàn 扁桃腺
too, also	yě 也
too, excessively	tài 太
tool, instrument	gōngjù 工具
tooth	yá 牙
toothache	yátòng 牙痛
tooth-brush	yáshuā 牙刷
tooth-paste	yágāo 牙膏
toothpick	yáqiānr 牙簽兒(牙签儿)
top	dǐng 頂(顶); tóu 頭(头)
topsy-turry, at sixes and sevens	luànqībāzāo 亂七八糟(乱七八糟)
tortoise	wūguī 烏龜(乌龟)
total, overall, general	zǒng 總(总)
total, whole, complete	quán 全
to, towards	qù 去; wàng 往
touch	pèng 碰; jiēchù 接觸(接触); mō 摸
tour	yóulǎn 遊覽(游览); lǚxíng 旅行
tour group	lǚyóutuán 旅遊團(旅游团)
toward (a direction)	wǎng 往; xiàngzhe 向着
toward, regarding	guānyú 關於(关于)
towel	máojīn 毛巾
town	zhèn 鎮(镇); chéngshì 城市
toy, plaything	wánjù 玩具; wányìr 玩意兒(玩意儿)
tractor	tuōlājī 拖拉機(拖拉机)
trade, line of business	hángyè 行業(行业)
trade, commerce	màoyì 貿易(贸易)
trade fair	jiāoyìhuì 交易會(交易会)

trademark, brand	shāngbiāo 商標(商标)
traditional Chinese medicine	zhōngyī 中醫(中医)
traffic	jiāotōng 交通
traffic light	jiāotōng zhǐhuīdēng 交通指揮燈(交通指挥灯)
train	huǒchē 火車(火车)
train, training	xùnliàn 訓練(训练)
train station	huǒchēzhàn 火車站(火车站)
transfer, pass on	chuán 傳(传); zhuǎn 轉(转)
transform	zhuǎnhuà 轉化(转化); zhuǎnbiàn 轉變(转变)
translate	fānyì 翻譯(翻译)
translator	fānyì 翻譯(翻译)
travel, trip, journey	lǚxíng 旅行
travel agency	lǚxíngshè 旅行社
traveller's check	lǚxíng zhīpiào 旅行支票
treasure	zhēnpǐn 珍品
treasure, value, cherish	zhēnxī 珍惜
treatment (medical)	zhìliáo 治療(治疗)
tree	shù 樹(树)
triangle	sānjiǎoxíng 三角形
trifle	xiǎoshì 小事
trolley	diànchē 電車(电车)
trouble	máfan 麻煩(麻烦)
trousers	kùzi 褲子(裤子)
truck, lorry	kǎchē 卡車(卡车)
true	zhēnde 真的
trunk of the body	shēnqū 身軀(身躯)
trunk of a tree	shùgàn 樹幹(树干)
trust, believe	xìnrèn 信任
trustworthiness	xìnyòng 信用; kěkào 可靠

truth	zhēnlǐ 眞理
try	shìyíshì 試一試(试一试)
try to find time	chōushíjiān 抽時間(抽时间)
tub, barrel, keg	tǒng 桶
tub, bowl, pot	pén 盆
Tuesday	xīngqīèr 星期二
tuition	xuéfèi 學費(学费)
tumor	liú 瘤
tunnel	suìdào 隧道
turn, a shift in direction	guǎiwān 拐彎(拐弯)
turn, revolve, rotate	zhuàn 轉(转)
turn off	guāndiào 關掉(关掉)
turn on (the switch)	dǎkāi 打開(打开)
turn one's head	huítóu 回頭(回头)
turn over	fān 翻
turn round, face about	zhuǎnshēn 轉身(转身)
turnip	luóbo 蘿蔔(萝卜)
tutor	jiātíngjiàoshī 家庭教師(家庭教师); dǎoshī 導師(导师)
TV movie	diànshìjù 電視劇(电视剧)
TV set	diànshìjī 電視機(电视机)
twelve	shíèr 十二
twenty	èrshí 二十
twig, tree branch	shùzhī 樹枝
two	èr 二; liǎng 兩(两)
type, kind, variety	lèixíng 類型(类型)
type, typewrite	dǎzì 打字
typewriter	dǎzìjī 打字機(打字机)
typhoon	táifēng 颱風(台风)
typist	dǎzìyuán 打字員(打字员)

U

ugly	bùhǎokàn 不好看; chǒu 醜(丑)
umbrella	yǔsǎn 雨傘(雨伞)
unable to…	búhuì 不會(不会); bùnéng 不能
unacceptable	bùxíng 不行
unbutton	jiěkāi kòuzi 解開扣子(解开扣子)
unceasing	búduàn 不斷(不断); bùtíng 不停
uncertain	búdìngde 不定的
uncle	bófu (elder brother of one's father) 伯父; shūfu (younger brother of one's father) 叔父; jiùjiu (brother of one's mother) 舅舅; yífu (husband of one's aunt) 姨夫; 姨父; shūshu (a male friend of one's parents) 叔叔
under	zài…xiàbiān 在…下邊(在…下边)
undergo	jīnglì 經歷(经历)
underneath	dǐxia 底下
unfasten, let go	fàng 放
understand	dǒng 懂; liáojiě 瞭解(了解)
unfold	tānkāi 攤開(摊开); zhǎnkāi 展開(展开)
unfortunately	búxìng 不幸; kěxī 可惜
unit	dānwèi 單位(单位)
unit, team	duì 隊
unite, unity	tuánjié 團結(团结)

142

United Nations	Liánhéguó 聯合國(联合国)
United States (of America)	Měiguó 美國(美国)
U.S. dollars	Měiyuán 美元
universal	pǔbiànde 普遍的
universe	yǔzhòu 宇宙
university	dàxué 大學(大学)
unless, only if	chúfēi 除非
unload, discharge	xiè 卸; xièxià 卸下
unnecessary	fèi bíyàode 非必要的; duōyúde 多餘的(多余的)
unoccupied	kòngzhe 空着; wúrén 無人(无人)
unreasonably	wúlǐde 無理地(无理地)
until	zhídào 直到
unyielding, dauntless	bùqūde 不屈的
up	wǎngshàng 往上
upon	zài…shàngmiàn 在…上面
upright, straight	zhí 直; zhílì 直立
upstairs	lóushàng 樓上(楼上)
urge, try to persuade	quàn 勸(劝)
urgent, express	jǐnjí 緊急(紧急)
urgent matter	jíshì 急事
us	wǒmen 我們(我们)
use	yòng 用
used up	yòngguāng 用光
useful	yǒuyòng 有用
useless	méiyòng 沒用
usually	tōngcháng 通常
utensil	yòngjù 用具
utilize	lìyòng 利用

143

V

vacation	fàngjià 放假; xiūjià 休假
vacuum cleaner	xīchénqì 吸塵器(吸尘器)
vaguely	móhude 模糊地(模胡地)
valley	shāngǔ 山谷
valuable, precious	zhēnguì 珍貴(珍贵)
value	jiàzhi 價值(价值)
vapor, gas, steam	qì 汽
variety, kind, class	zhǒnglèi 種類(种类)
various	gèzhǒng gèyàng de 各種各樣的 (各种各样的)
vary, change	biànhuà 變化(变化)
vase	huāpíng 花瓶
vat, jar	gāng 缸
vegetable, dish	cài 菜
vegetables	cài 菜; shūcài 蔬菜
vehicles	chēliàng 車輛(车辆)
venue	chǎngdì 場地(场地)
very, extremely, highly	fēicháng 非常; hěn 很
vest	bèixīn 背心
victory	shènglì 勝利(胜利)
Vietnam	Yuènán 越南
view, scenery, landscape	fēngjǐng 風景(风景)
village	cūnzi 村子; cūnzhuāng 村莊(村庄)
vinegar	cù 醋
violent, fierce	jīliè 激烈
violet (color)	zǐsè 紫色
virtually, simply	shízhìshàng 實質上(实质上)
visa	qiānzhèng 簽證(签证)
vision	xiǎngxiànglì 想像力(想象力)

visit (a person)	bàifǎng 拜訪(拜访); bàihuì 拜會(拜会)
visit (a place)	cānguān 參觀(参观); fǎngwèn 訪問(访问)
visitor, guest	kèrén 客人
visitor, tourist	yóukè 遊客(游客); yóulǎnzhě 遊覽者(游览者)
vivid, lively	shēngdòngde 生動的(生动的)
vocabulary	cíhuì 詞滙(词汇)
vocalist	gēshǒu 歌手
Vodka	Fútèjiā 伏特加
voice, sound	shēngyīn 聲音(声音)
volley ball	páiqiú 排球
voltage	diànyā 電壓(电压)
volt	fútè 伏特
volume (of books)	běn 本; cè 冊
volume, cubical content	tǐjī 體積(体积)
volume of production, output	chǎnliàng 產量(产量)

W

wagon, cart	chē 車(车); huòchē 貨車(货车)
waist	yāo 腰
wait	děng 等
wait a moment	děngyìhuǐr 等一會兒(等一会儿)
wait on (upon)	fúshì 服侍
waiter, waitress	fúwùyuán 服務員(服务员)
wake up	xǐng 醒
walk	zǒu 走
wall	qiáng 牆(墙)

wall poster (at schools, factories, etc.)	qiángbào 牆報(墙报)
Wall Street Journal	Huáěrjiē rìbào 華爾街日報(华尔街日报)
wallet	píjiār 皮夾兒(皮夹儿); qiánbāor 錢包兒(钱包儿)
walnut	hétao 核桃
want	yào 要; xiǎngyào 想要
war	zhànzhēng 戰爭(战争)
ward	bìngfáng 病房
wardrobe	yīchú 衣櫥
warehouse	cāngkù 倉庫(仓库)
warm	nuǎnhuo 暖和; rèhūhū 熱呼呼(热呼呼)
warmly	rèliè 熱烈(热烈); rèqíng 熱情(热情)
warmly welcome	rèliè huānyíng 熱烈歡迎(热烈欢迎)
warn, caution against	gàojiè 告誡(告诫); jǐnggào 警告
wash	xǐ 洗
washable	kěxǐde 可洗的
washing machine	xǐyījī 洗衣機(洗衣机)
waste	làngfèi 浪費(浪费)
waste paper	fèizhǐ 廢紙(废纸)
watch (timepiece)	biǎo 錶(表)
watch (wrist)	shǒubiǎo 手錶(手表)
watch, look at	kàn 看
watch a contest	guānzhàn 觀戰(观战)
water (n.)	shuǐ 水
water (v.)	jiāo 澆(浇)
water and soil	shuǐtǔ 水土

waterfall	pùbù 瀑布
waterfront	hǎibīn 海濱(海滨); jiāngbiān 江邊(江边)
watermelon	xīguā 西瓜
waterproof	fángshuǐde 防水的
water-ski	huáshuǐ 滑水
wave (of sea)	làng 浪
wave, sway	yáohuang 搖撼(摇晃)
wave the hand	huīshǒu 揮手(挥手)
way, method	fāngfǎ 方法
way, lane	lù 路
way out	chūlù 出路
we, us	wǒmen 我們(我们); zánmen 咱們(咱们)
weak, feeble	ruò 弱
wear (clothes, stockings, etc.)	chuān 穿
wear (glasses, hat, tie, etc.)	dài 戴
weather	tiānqì 天氣(天气)
Wednesday	xīngqīsān 星期三
week	xīngqī 星期; lǐbài 禮拜(礼拜)
last week	shàngxīngqī 上星期; shànglǐbài 上禮拜(上礼拜)
next week	xiàxīngqī 下星期; xiàlǐbài 下禮拜(下礼拜)
weekend	zhōumò 周末
weekly magazine	zhōukān 周刊
weigh	chēng 稱(称)
weigh and consider, ponder	tuīqiāo 推敲
weight	zhòngliàng 重量

welcome	huānyíng 歡迎（欢迎）
well	hǎo 好
well（water or oil）	jǐng 井
well off, rich	fùyǒu 富有
west	xī 西
west end	xītou 西頭（西头）
Western food	Xīcài 西菜; Xīcān 西餐
Western medicine	Xīyào 西藥（西药）
wet	cháoshī 潮濕（潮湿）
wharf, jetty	mǎtou 碼頭（码头）
what	shénme 什麼（什么）
What for?	gànma？幹嗎?（干吗?）
wheat	xiǎomài 小麥（小麦）; màizi 麥子（麦子）
wheat, winter	dōngxiǎomài 冬小麥（冬小麦）
wheat flour	miànfěn 麵粉（面粉）
wheel	lúnzi 輪子（轮子）
when（at a time which）	dāng…de shíhòu 當…的時候（当…的时候）
when（at what time）	shénme shíhòu 什麼時候（什么·时候）
where	nǎr 哪兒（哪儿）
wherefore, therefore	yīncǐ 因此; suǒyǐ 所以
whether…or…	huòzhě…hòuzhě… 或者…或者…; shì…háishì… 是…還是…（是…还是…）
whether…or not	shìfǒu 是否
which	něi 哪; nà 那
whichever	wúlùnnǎgè 無論哪個（无论哪个）; wúlùnnǎxiē 無論哪些（无论哪些）
which kind	nǎyàng 哪樣（哪样）

148

which one	nǎge 哪個(哪个)
whiff	yízhèn 一陣(一阵)
while (conj.)	dāng…de shíhòu 當…的時候 (当…的时候)
while (n.)	yìhuìr 一會兒(一会儿)
Whisky	Wēishìjì 威士忌
white	bái 白; báide 白的
who	shuí 誰(谁)
who's	shuíde 誰的(谁的)
whole	quán 全; quánde 全的; zhěng- gède 整個的(整个的)
the whole family	quánjiā 全家
the whole way	yílù 一路
whom	shuí 誰(谁)
whose	shuíde 誰的(谁的)
why	wèishénme 爲什麼(为什么)
wide, broad	kuān 寬(宽)
widespread, universal	pǔbiàn 普遍
wife	qīzi 妻子; tàitài 太太; fūren 夫人
will	yìzhì 意志; yìzhìlì 意志力
will	yào 要; jiāngyào 將要(将要)
willing	yuànyì 願意(愿意)
will not	búhuì 不會(不会); búyuànyì 不 願意(不愿意)
will soon	kuài…le 快…了
willow	liǔ 柳; liǔshù 柳樹(柳树)
win, victory, triumph	shènglì 勝利(胜利)
win (v.)	yíng 贏(赢); shèng 勝(胜)
wind	fēng 風(风)
wind (a spring, a clock, etc.)	shàngfātiáo 上(發條)(上(发 条))
windmill	fēngchē 風車(风车)

window	chuāngzi 窗子
windy	guāfēngde 颶風的(刮风的)
wine	jiǔ 酒; pútáojiǔ 葡萄酒
wineshop, public house	jiǔbā 酒吧
winter	dōngtiān 冬天
winter vacation	hánjià 寒假
wipe	cā 擦 ·
wire	diànxiàn 電綫(电线)
wisdom	zhìhuì 智慧
wish (well)	zhù 祝
wish, hope	xīwàng 希望
with	hé 和; gēn 跟
with, by	yǐ 以
withdrawal	tuìchù 退出
witness	mùjizhě 目擊者(目击者); zhèng-rén 證人(证人)
wolf	láng 狼
woman	nǚrén 女人; fùnǚ 婦女(妇女)
wood	mù 木
woods, forest	shùlín 樹林(树林)
wool	yángmáo 羊毛
wool cloth	máoliào 毛料
woollen sweater, woolly	máoyī 毛衣
word	zì 字
word, new	shēngcí 生詞(生词)
words	cíhuì 詞彙(词汇)
work	gōngzuò 工作
go to work	shàngbān 上班
work hard	kǔgàn 苦幹(苦干)
work steps	gōngxù 工序
worker	gōngrén 工人
workshop	chējiān 車間(车间)

world	shìjiè 世界
worn out	yònghuài 用壞(用坏); pò 破
worry about, be anxious about	dānxīn 擔心(担心); zhāojí 着急
worship	chóngbài 崇拜
worth	zhíde 值得…
wound	shāng 傷(伤); dǎshāng 打傷(打伤)
wrap	bāozhuāng 包裝(包装)
wrapping	pí 皮
wrist watch	shǒubiǎo 手錶(手表)
write	xiě 寫(写)
write (a book)	xiězuò 寫作(写作)
write (a check)	kāi zhīpiào 開支票(开支票)
write (a letter)	xiěxìn 寫信(写信)
write down, record	jì 記(记)
writer	zuòzhě 作者; zuòjiā 作家
writing	xiězuò 寫作(写作)
writing brush	máobǐ 毛筆(毛笔)
written language, characters	wénzì 文字
wrong	cuòle 錯(错)

X

xerox	fùyìn 複印(复印)
Xinhua Dictionary	XīnhuáZìdiǎn 新華字典(新华字典)
x-ray	àikèsīguāng 愛克斯光(爱克斯光)

Y

Yangtse River	Chángjiāng 長江(长江)
yard, courtyard	yuànzi 院子
yard (=3feet)	mǎ 碼(码)
year	nián 年
this year	jīnnián 今年
last year	qùnián 去年
the year before last	qiánnián 前年
next year	míngnián 明年
early next year	míngnián niánchū 明年年初
late next year	míngnián niándǐ 明年年底
the whole year	quánnián 全年
year, grade (in a school)	niánjí 年級(年级)
yearly, from year to year	niánnián 年年
years	niánjì 年紀(年纪); suì 歲(岁)
years (historical dates)	niándài 年代
yell, shout	jiào 叫; hǎn 喊
yellow	huáng(de) 黃(的)
Yellow River	Huánghé 黃河
yes	shìde 是的
yesterday	zuótiān 昨天
yet, but, however	dànshì 但是; kěshì 可是
yet, still	hái 還(还)
yielding, weak	ruǎn 軟(软)
yogurt	suānniúnǎi 酸牛奶
you	nǐ (singular) 你; nǐmen (plural) 你們(你们)
young	niánqīng 年輕(年轻)
younger brother	dìdi 弟弟
your	nǐde (singular) 你的; nǐmende

　　　　　　　　　　（plural）你們的（你们的）

You're welcome　　búkèqì 不客氣（不客气）
yourself　　　　　nǐzìjǐ 你自己
yourselves　　　　nǐmenzìjǐ 你們自己（你们自己）
youth　　　　　　qīngnián 青年

Z

zero　　　　　　　líng 零
zipper　　　　　　lāliàn 拉鏈（拉链）
zoo　　　　　　　dòngwùyuán 動物園（动物园）

Part Two

Specialized Glossaries

1. *Nuclear Power Generation*

absorber	xīshōujì 吸收劑（吸收剂）
absorption	xīshōu 吸收
activation	huóhuà 活化
active fuel length	yǒuxiào ránliào chángdù 有效燃料長度（有效燃料长度）
attenuation	suāijiǎn 衰減
availability factor	kěliyònglǜ 可利用率
axial offset	zhóuxiàngpiānchà fēnshù 軸向偏差分數（轴向偏差分数）
axial power distribution	zhóuxiànggōnglǜ fēnbù 軸向功率分佈（轴向功率分布）
background radiation	běndìfúshè 本底輻射（本底辐射）
barn	bǎ 靶
base load	jīběn fùhè 基本負荷（基本负荷）
beginning-of-life	shòuqī kāiduān 壽期開端（寿期开端）
binary fission	èrfēn lièbiàn 二分裂變（二分裂变）
biological shield	shēngwùpíngbì 生物屏蔽
blanket	zhàishēngqū 再生區（再生区）
bleed	xièfàn 泄放
blowdown	páifàn 排放
boiling crisis	fèiténg línjiè 沸騰臨界（沸腾临界）
boiling-water reactor	fèishuǐduī 沸水堆
Breakdown orifice	jiǎnyākǒngbǎn 減壓孔板（减压孔板）

breeder reactor	zēngzí fǎnyìngduī 增殖反應堆 (增殖反应堆)
breeding gain	zēngzí zēngyì 增殖增益
bulk boiling	zhěngtǐ fèiténg 整體沸騰(整体沸腾)
burnable poison	kěrán dúwù 可燃毒物
burner reactor	ránshāoduī 燃燒堆(燃烧堆)
burnout	shāohuǐ 燒毀(烧毁)
burnup	ránhào 燃耗
capacity factor	róngliàng xìshù 容量系數(容量系数)
capital costs	zīběnfèi 資本費(资本费); zhǒngtóuzī 總投資(总投资)
caustic corrosion	jiǎnxìng fǔshí 碱性腐蝕(碱性腐蚀)
chain reaction, nuclear	liànshì fǎnyìng 鏈式反應(链式反应)
charging flow	bǔjǐshuǐ liúliàng 補給水流量(补给水流量)
channel	dào 道; fǎnyìngdào 反應道(反应道)
chemical shim	huàxué bǔcháng 化學補償(化学补偿)
cladding	bāoké 包壳
clean	jìng (duīxīn) 淨 (堆芯)
closed-cycle reactor system	bìhé xúnhuán fǎnyìngduī xìtǒng 閉合循環反應堆系統(闭合循环反应堆系统)
coastdown	zhújiàn jiàngdī fùhè huáxíng 逐漸降低負荷滑行(逐渐降低负荷滑行)
cold leg	lěngduàn 冷段

cold-reactor	lěngduī 冷堆
cold shutdown	lěngtíngduī 冷停堆
cold-water accident	lěngshuǐ shìgù 冷水事故
colloids	jiāotǐ 膠體(胶体)
containment	ānquánké 安全壳
contamination	wūrǎn 污染
conversion ratio	zhuǎnhuànbǐ 轉換比(转换比)
converter reactor	zhuǎnhuàn fǎnyìngduī 轉換反應堆(转换反应堆)
coolant	lěngquèjì 冷却劑(冷却剂)
core	héxīn 核心; duīxīn 堆芯
creep	rúbiàn 蠕變(蠕变)
crevice corrosion	fèngxì fǔshí 縫隙腐蝕(缝隙腐蚀)
critical heat flux	línjiè rètōngliàng 臨界熱通量(临界热通量)
criticality	línjiè zhuàngtài 臨界狀態(临界状态)
cross-section	jiémiàn 截面
crud	zázhì 雜質(杂质); jīgòu 積垢(积垢)
curie	jūlǐ 居里
damping	zǔní 阻尼
daughter	zǐtǐ 子體(子体)
deadband	sǐqū 死區(死区)
decay	shuāibiàn 衰變(衰变)
decay heat	shuāibiànrè 衰變熱(衰变热)
decontamination factor	qùwū yīnzǐ 去污因子
degassing	tuōqì 脱氣(脱气)
delayed neutrons	huǎnfa zhōngzǐ 緩發中子(缓发中子)
demand factor	xūqiú yīnshù 需求因數(需求

因数）

departure from nucleate boiling	piānlípàohé fèiténg 偏離泡核沸騰（偏离泡核沸腾）
depleted uranium	pínhuàyóu 貧化鈾（贫化铀）
design basis accident	shèjì yījù shìgù 設計依據事故（设计依据事故）
design safe shutdown earthquake	shèjì ānquántíngduī dìzhèn 設計安全停堆地震（设计安全停堆地震）
deuterium	dāo 氘; zhòngqīng 重氫（重氢）
direct-cycle reactor system	zhíjiē xúnhuán fǎnyìng duī xìtǒng 直接循環反應堆系統（直接循环反应堆系统）
disadvantage factor	búlìyīnzǐ 不利因子
doppler effect	duōpǔlèxiàoyìng 多普勒效應（多普勒效应）
dose	jìliàng 劑量（剂量）
dose rate	jìliànglǜ 劑量率（剂量率）
doubling time	jiābèi shíjiān 加倍時間（加倍时间）
downcomer	xiàjiàngduàn 下降段
drift	piāoyí 漂移
dryout	shāogān 燒乾（烧干）
dual-cycle reactor system	shuāngxúnhuán fǎnyìngduī xìtǒng 雙循環反應堆系統（双循环反应堆系统）
dynamic（core）measurements	dòngtài cèdìng 動態測定（动态测定）
effective multiplication factor	yǒuxiào bèizēng yīnshù 有效倍增因數（有效倍增因数）
elevation head	shuǐtóu 水頭（水头）
end-of-life	shòuqí zhōngduān 壽期終端（寿

158

期终端）

endothermic	xīrède 吸熱的（吸热的）
enthalpy	hán 焓
entrophy	shāng 熵
epithermal flux	chāorè zhōngzǐ tōngliàng 超熱中子通量（超热中子通量）
equilibrium fuel cycle	pínghéng ránliào xúnhuán 平衡燃料循環（平衡燃料循环）
excess reactivity	hòubèi fǎnyìngxìng 後備反應性（后备反应性）
excursion	gōnglǜjùzēng 功率驟增（功率骤增）
exoenergetic	fàngnéngde 放能的
fast breeder reactor	kuàizhòngzǐ zēngzhíduī 快中子增殖堆
fertile	kězhuǎnhuànde 可轉換的（可转换的）; néngzēngzhíde 能增殖的
fissile	yìlièbiànde 易裂變的（易裂变的）
fission	lièbiàn 裂變（裂变）; fēnliè 分裂（分裂）
fissionable	kělièbiànde 可裂變的（可裂变的）
fission products	lièbiàn chǎnwù 裂變產物（裂变产物）
fission yield	lièbiàn chǎn'é 裂變產額（裂变产额）
flow coastdown accident	shīliú shìgù 失流事故
fluence	zhùliàng 注量
flux	tōngliàng 通量
fouling	jiégòu 結垢（结垢）
fuel cycle	ránliào xúnhuán 燃料循環（燃料

159

fuel economy	ránliào ránshāo xiàolǜ 燃料燃燒效率(燃料燃烧效率); ránliào jīngjì 燃料經濟(燃料经济)
fuel management	ránliào guǎnlǐ 燃料管理
fuel matrix	ránliào jītǐ 燃料基體(燃料基体)
fuel pattern	ránliào ānpái shìyàng 燃料安排式樣(燃料安排式样)
galvanic corrosion	diànǒu fǔshí 電偶腐蝕(电偶腐蚀)
generation time	měidài shíjiān 每代時間(每代时间)
half-life	bànshuāiqī 半衰期
heat sink	rèhuò 熱壑(热壑); lěngyuán 冷源(冷源)
heat tracing	guǎndào jiārè bǎowēn 管道加熱保溫(管道加热保温)
heavy-water	zhòngshuǐ 重水
heterogeneous reactor	fēijūnyún (fǎnyìng) duī 非均匀(反應)堆(非均匀(反应)堆)
hideout	(péng)chénjī (硼)沉積((硼)沉积)
homogeneous reactor	jūnyún (fǎnyìng)duī 均匀(反應)堆(均匀(反应)堆)
hot channel	règuǎn 熱管(热管)
hot channel factor (engineering)	règuǎn yīnzǐ (gōngchéng) 熱管因子(工程)(热管因子(工程))
hot channel factor (nuclear)	règuǎn yīnzǐ (hé) 熱管因子(核)(热管因子(核))
hot channel factor (total)	règuǎn yīnzǐ (zǒng) 熱管因子(總)(热管因子(总))

hot reactor	rètài (fǎnyìng) duī 熱態(反應)堆(热态(反应)堆)
hot spot	rèdiǎn 熱點(热点)
hot-to-cold reactivity change	rèdàolěng fǎnyìngxìng biàngēng 熱到冷反應性變更(热到冷反应性变更)
hydrazine	liánān 聯氨(联氨)
hydriding	qīnghuà 氫化(氢化)
importance factor	zhòngyàoxìng yīnzǐ 重要性因子
indirect-cycle reactor system	jiànjiēxúnhuán fǎnyìng duī xìtǒng 間接循環反應堆系統(间接循环反应堆系统)
integrated flux	jīfēn tōngliàng 積分通量(积分通量)
interlock	hùsuǒ 互鎖(互锁)
ion exchange	lízǐ jiāohuàn 離子交換(离子交换)
ionization chamber	diànlíshì 電離室(电离室)
irradiation	fúzhào 輻照(辐照)
isotope	tóngwèisù 同位素
kinetic (core) measurements	dòngtài cèdìng 動態測定(动态测定)
lag	chíyán 遲延(迟延)
lattice	gézi 格子; diǎnzhèn 點陣(点阵)
leakage	xièlòu 泄漏
leadage bypass	xièlòu pánglù 泄漏旁路
letdown flow	xiàxièliú 下泄流
light-water	qīngshuǐ 輕水(轻水)
linear power density	xiàngōnglǜ mìdù 綫功率密度(线功率密度)
load cycling	fùhè zhōuqīxìng biàngēng 負荷周期性變更(负荷周期性变更)

load factor	fùhè yīnshù 負荷因數(负荷因数)
load follow	fùhè gēnzōng 負荷跟踪(负荷跟踪)
load swing	fùhè bǎifú 負荷擺幅(负荷摆幅)
local boiling	júbù fèiténg 局部沸騰(局部沸腾)
local corrosion	júbù fūshí 局部腐蝕(局部腐蚀)
loss-of-coolant accident	shīshuǐ shìgù 失水事故
loss-of-flow accident	duànliú shìgù 斷流事故(断流事故)
loss-of-load transient	shuǎifùhè shùnbiàn guòchéng 甩負荷瞬變過程(甩负荷瞬变过程)
magnetite	sānyǎnghuàsìtiě 三氧化四鐵(三氧化四铁); cítiěkuàng 磁鐵礦(磁铁矿)
maximum credible accident	zuìdà kěxìn shìgù 最大可信事故
maximum permissible concentration	zuìdà róngxǔ nóngdù 最大容許濃度(最大容许浓度)
maximum permissible dose	zuìbà róngxǔ jìliàng 最大容許劑量(最大容许剂量)
megawatt day per metric ton	MWD/MT(U) zhàowǎrì/gōngdūnyóu 兆瓦日/公噸鈾(兆瓦日/公吨铀)
mil	mǐ'ěr 密耳(千分之一英寸)
mixed-bed demineralization	hǔnhéchuáng tuōyánqì 混合床脫鹽器(混合床脱盐器)
moderator	mànhuàjì 慢化劑(慢化剂)
moderator coefficient	mànhuàjì xìshù 慢化劑係數(慢化剂系数)

moderator/fuel ratio	mànhuàjì yú ránliàobǐ 慢化劑與燃料比(慢化剂与燃料比)
multiplication factor	bèizēng xìshù 倍增係數(倍增系数)
MWD/MT(U)	zhàowǎrì/gōngdūnyóu兆瓦日/公噸鈾(兆瓦日/公吨铀)
natural circulation reactor	zìrán xúnhuán fǎnyìngduī 自然循環反應堆(自然循环反应堆)
natural uranium	tiānrán, yóu 天然鈾(天然铀)
neutron	zhōngzǐ 中子
neutron (number)density	zhōngzǐ mìdù 中子密度
neutron economy	zhōngzǐde yǒuxiào lìyòng 中子的有效利用
neutron flux	zhōngzǐ tōngliàng 中子通量
neutron lifetime	zhōngzǐ shòuqī 中子壽期(中子寿期)
neutrons, delayed	huǎnfā zhōngzǐ 緩發中子(缓发中子)
neutrons, fast	kuài zhōngzǐ 快中子
nil-ductility transition temperature	wúyánxìng zhuǎnbiàn wēndù 無延性轉變溫度(无延性转变温度)
noble fission gases	xīyǒu lièbiàn qìtǐ 稀有裂變氣體(稀有裂变气体)
no-source accident	wúyuán shìgù 無源事故(无源事故)
nuclear reaction	héfǎnyìng 核反應(核反应)
nuclear steam supply system	hézhēngqì gōngjǐ xìtǒng 核蒸氣供給系統(核蒸气供给系统)
nuclear superheating	héguòrè 核過熱(核过热)
nucleate boiling	pàohé fèiténg 泡核沸騰(泡核沸腾)

nuclide	hésù 核素
offset (error)	piānzhì wùchā 偏置(誤差)(偏置(误差))
operating base earthquake	yùnxíng yījù dìzhèn 運行依據地震(运行依据地震)
override	qǔdài 取代
overshoot	guòtiáoliàng 過調量(过调量); gòuchōng 過衝(过冲)
parastitic capture	jìshēng fúhuò 寄生俘獲(寄生俘获)
partial nucleate boiling	bùfen pàohé fèiténg 部分泡核沸騰(部分泡核沸腾)
percent mille (pcm)	shíwànfēnzhīyī 十万分之一
period	zhōuqī 周期
pitch	jiéjù 節距(节距)
plutonium cycle	bùxúnhuán 鈈循環(钚循环)
poison	dúwù 毒物
power coefficient of reactivity	fǎnyìngxìng gōnglǜ xìshù 反應性功率係數(反应性功率系数)
power defect	gōnglǜ quēshī 功率缺失
power demand coefficient	gōnglǜ xūqiú xìshù 功率需求係數(功率需求系数)
power density	gōnglǜ mìdù 功率密度
power reactor	dònglì fǎnyìngduī 動力(反應)堆(动力(反应)堆)
precursor	xiānqū hésù 先驅核素(先驱核素); mǔtǐ 母體(母体)
pressure vessel	yālì róngqì 壓力容器(压力容器)
pressurized-water reactor	yāshuǐ fǎnyìngduī 壓水(反應)堆(压水(反应)堆)
prompt criticality	shùnfā línjiè 瞬發臨界(瞬发临

prompt jump	shùntiàobiàn 瞬跳變(瞬跳变)
prompt neutron fraction	shùnfā zhōngzǐ fèn'é 瞬發中子份額(瞬发中子份额)
prompt neutrons	shùnfā zhōngzǐ 瞬發中子(瞬发中子)
quality	pǐnzhì 品質(品质)
radioactive equilibrium	fàngshèxìng pínghéng 放射性平衡
radioactive tracing	fàngshèxìng shìzōngfǎ 放射性示踪法
radioactivity	fàngshèxìng 放射性
radioisotope	fàngshèxìng tóngwèisù 放射性同位素
radiolysis	fúzhào fēnjiě 輻照分解(辐照分解)
radionuclide	fàngshèxìng hésù 放射性核素(放射性核素)
ramp power change	xiézēnggōnglǜ biàngēng 斜增功率變更(斜增功率变更)
ramp rate	xiézēnglǜ 斜增率
rated load	édìng fùhè 額定負荷(额定负荷)
reactivity	fǎnyìngxìng 反應性(反应性)
reactivity balance	fǎnyìngxìng qīngdān 反應性清單(反应性清单)
reactivity feedback	fǎnyìngxìng huíshū 反應性回輸(反应性回输)
reactor trip	shìgùbǎohù tíngduī 事故保護停堆(事故保获停堆)
recycling	zàixúnhuán 再循環(再循环)
reflector	fǎnshècéng 反射層(反射层)
reflood	huíguàn 回灌

refueling interval	huànliào jiāngé 換料間隔(换料间隔)
regenerative cycle	huírè xúnhuán 回熱循環(回热循环)
reheat (ing)	zàirè 再熱(再热)
REM	léimǔ 雷姆
resins	shùzhī 樹脂(树脂)
resonance absorption	gòngzhèn xīshōu 共振吸收
roentgen	lúnqín 倫琴(伦琴)
runback (turbine)	jiǎnsù (wōlúnjī)(渦輪機)減速;((涡轮机)减速)
saturated (steam)	bǎohé (zhēngqì)飽和(蒸氣);(饱和(蒸气))
saturation	bǎohé 飽和(饱和)
scram	jǐnjí tíngduī 緊急停堆(紧急停堆)
seed (and blanket). core	diǎnhuǒqū (—zàishēngqū) duīxīn 點火區(一再生區)堆芯;(点火区(一再生区)堆芯)
self-shielding	zìpíngbì 自屏蔽
self-shielding factor	zìpíng yīnzǐ 自屏因子
shadowing	yīnbì 蔭蔽(荫蔽)
shield	píngbì 屏蔽
shrinking	shōusuō 收縮(收缩)
shutdown	tíngduī 停堆
shutdown margin	tíngduī yùdù 停堆裕度
sinter	shāojié 燒結(烧结)
source neutron	yuán zhōngzǐ 源中子
span	kuàjù 跨距
specific activity	fàngshèxìng bǐdù 放射性比度; bǐ fàngshèxìng (qiángdù) 比放射性(强度)

放射性(强度)

specific heat	bǐrè 比熱(比热)
specific inventory	bǐ tóuliàoliàng 比投料量
specific power	bǐ gōnglǜ 比功率
spectral shift reactor	pǔyí fǎnyìngduī 譜移反應堆(谱移反应堆)
spent fuel	shāoguòde ránliào 燒過的燃料(烧过的燃料)
spider	xīngzhuàng jiētóu 星狀接頭(星状接头)
spontaneous fission	zìfā lièbiàn 自發裂變(自发裂变)
stability	wěndìngxìng 穩定性(稳定性)
stable film boiling	wěndìng mótài fèiténg 穩定膜態沸騰(稳定膜态沸腾)
stable isotope	wěndìng tóngwèisù 穩定同位素(稳定同位素)
start-up accident	qǐdòng shìgù 起動事故(起动事故)
static (core) measure-ments	jìngtài cèdìng 靜態測定(静态测定)
steady state	wěntài 穩態(稳态)
steady-state operation	wěntài yùnxíng 穩態運行(稳态运行)
steam break	zhēngqì (guǎndào) pòliè (shìgù) 蒸氣(管道)破裂(事故)(蒸气(管道)破裂(事故))
steam dump	zhēngqì páifàng 蒸氣排放(蒸气排放)
step change	jiēyuè biànhuà 階躍變化(阶跃变化)
step power change	jiēyuè gōnglǜ biàngēng 階躍功率變更(阶跃功率变更)

stoichimometric	huàxuéjìliàngde 化學計量的（化学计量的）
stress corrosion	yìnglì fǔshí 應力腐蝕（应力腐蚀）
streaming	gōudàoxiàoyìng 溝道效應（沟道效应）
stretch-out	shòuqī yánshēn（壽期）延伸（（寿期）延伸）
subcooled	guòlěngde 過冷的（过冷的）
subcritical multiplication	cìlínjiè péizēng 次臨界培增（次臨界培增）
subcritical state	cìlínjiè zhuàngtài 次臨界狀態（次臨界状态）
supercritical state	chāolínjiè zhuàngtài 超臨界狀態（超临界状态）
superheat(ing)	guòrè 過熱（过热）
superheated	guòrède 過熱的（过热的）
swelling	péngzhàng 膨脹（膨胀）
tavg	píngjūn wēndù 平均溫度
temperature coefficient of reactivity	fǎnyìngxìng wēndù xìshù 反應性溫度係數（反应性温度系数）
ternary fission	sānfēn lièbiàn 三分裂變（三分裂变）
thermal breeder reactor	rèzhōngzǐ zēngzhí fǎnyìngduī 熱中子增殖反應堆（热中子增殖反应堆）
thermal efficiency	rèxiàolǜ 熱效率（热效率）
thermal neutron	rèzhōngzǐ 熱中子（热中子）
thermal shield	rèpíngbì 熱屏蔽（热屏蔽）
thorium	tǔ 釷（钍）
threshold	yùzhí 閾值（阈值）
tilting factor	qīngxié yīnshù 傾斜因數（倾斜

	因数)
transient	shùntài 瞬態(瞬态)
transients	zàntài guòchéng 暫態過程(暫态过程)
trip	tiàozhá 跳閘(跳闸); shìgù tingduī 事故停堆
tritium	chuān 氚
turbine trip	wōlúnjī zìdòngtíngjī 渦輪機自動停機(涡轮机自动停机)
unit net efficiency	jīzǔ jìngxiàolǜ 機組淨效率(机组净效率)
void coefficient (of reactivity)	kōngpào xìshù (fǎnyìngxìng)空泡係數((反应性)空泡系数)
void (fraction)	kōngpào fèné 空泡份額(空泡份额)
water dissociation	shuǐfēnjiě 水分解
withdrawal accident	(kòngzhìbàng) tíchū shìgù (控制棒)提出事故
worth	(fǎnyìngxìng) jiàzhí (反應性)價值((反应性)价值)
xenon	xiān 氙
xenon-effect	xiānxiàoyìng 氙效應(氙效应)
yield point	qūfúdiǎn 屈服點(屈服点)
zircaloy	gàohéjīn 鋯合金(锆合金)
zirconium	gào 鋯(锆)

2. Electrical Engineering

adaptor plug
zhuǎnjiē chātóu 轉接插頭(转接插头)

aggregate capacity
zǒngróngliàng 總容量(总容量);
zǒnggōnglǜ 總功率(总功率)

air compressor
kōngqì yāsuōjī 空氣壓縮機(空气压缩机)

alternating current
jiāoliúdiàn 交流電(交流电)

ampere
ānpéi 安培

analogue computer
mónǐ jìsuànjī 模擬計算機(模拟计算机)

antenna
tiānxiàn 天綫(天线)

atomic (nuclear)power station
yuánzǐnéng diànzhàn 原子能電站(原子能电站)

automatic control
zìdòng kòngzhì 自動控制(自动控制)

automatic frequency control (AFC)
zìdòng pínlǜ kòngzhì 自動頻率控制(自动频率控制)

automatic on-load tap-changer
dàifùhé zìdòng fēnjiē kāiguān 帶負荷自動分接開關(带负荷自动分接开关)

automation
zìdònghuà 自動化(自动化)

automation equipment
zìdònghuà shèbèi 自動化設備(自动化设备)

automation of electric-power system
diànlì xìtǒng zìdònghuà 電力系統自動化(电力系统自动化)

automation of thermal power station
huǒlì fādiànzhàn zìdònghuà 火力發電站自動化(火力发电站自动化)

auto transformer	zìǒu biànyāqì 自耦變壓器（自耦變壓器)
axial compressor	zhóuliúshì yāsùjī 軸流式壓縮機（軸流式压缩机)
axial flow water turbin	zhóuliúshì shuǐlúnjī 軸流式水輪機（軸流式水轮机)
azimuth angle extraction	fāngwèijiǎo lùqǔ 方位角錄取（方位角录取)
basic load	jīběn fùhè 基本負荷（基本负荷)
belt conveyor	pídài yùnshūjī 皮帶運輸機（皮帶运输机)
bit (binary digit)	(èrjìnzhìde) wèi（二進制的)位; bǐtè 比特
blip	(yíngguāngpíngshàngde) jiāntóu xìnhào（荧光屏上的)尖頭信號（(荧光屏上的)尖头信号)
boiler	guōlú 鍋爐（锅炉)
breadboard	mónǐbǎn 模擬板（模拟板);shìyànbǎn 試驗板（试验板)
breadboard design	mónǐbǎn shèjì 模擬板設計（模拟板设计)
capacitance	diànróng 電容（电容)
capacity	diànróng 電容（电容); gōnglǜ 功率
central control room	zhōngyāng kòngzhìshì 中央控制室
centrifugal compressor	líxīnshì yāqìjī 離心式壓氣機（离心式压气机)
ceramic substrate	táocí jīdǐ 陶瓷基底
chimney	yāncōng 烟囱
circuit	diànlù 電路（电路)

circuit-breaker	duànlùqì 斷路器(断路器)
closed cycle	bìlù xúnhuán 閉路循環(闭路循环)
coal	méi 煤
coal grinder, pulverizer	móméijī 磨煤機(磨煤机)
combustion	ránshāo 燃燒(燃烧)
combustion chamber	ránshāoshì 燃燒室(燃烧室)
component design	zǔjiàn shèjì 組件設計(组件设计)
compressor	yāqìjī 壓氣機(压气机)
computer	jìsuànjī 計算機(计算机)
computer control system	jìsuànjī kòngzhì xìtǒng 計算機控制系統(计算机控制系统)
condensate	lěngníng 冷凝; lěngníngshuǐ 冷凝水
condensate pump	lěngníngshuǐbèng 冷凝水泵
condenser	lěngníngqì 冷凝器
conductive pattern	dǎodiàn túxíng 導電圖形(导电图形)
conductor	dǎotǐ 導體(导体)
control	kòngzhì 控制
control desk, control board	kòngzhìtái 控制臺(控制台)
control rod	kòngzhìgān 控制桿(控制杆); kòngzhìbàng 控制棒
control system	kòngzhì xìtǒng 控制系統
cooling tower	lěngquètǎ 冷卻塔(冷却塔)
cooling water	lěngquèshuǐ 冷卻水(冷却水)
critical speed	línjiè zhuànsù 臨界轉速(临界转速)
current	diànliú 電流(电流)
cycle	xúnhuán 循環(循环)

data logger	shùjù zìdòng jìlùqì 數據記錄器（数据记录器）
data processing	shùjù chǔlǐ 數據處理（数据处理）
deaerator	chúqìqì 除氣器（除气器）
detailed survey	xiángcè 詳測（详测）
detector	jiǎnbōqì 檢波器（检波器）
digital computer	shùzì jìsuànjī 數字計算機（数字计示机）
digital process control	shùzì chéngxù kòngzhì 數字程序控制（数字程序控制）
direct current	zhíliú 直流; zhíliúdiàn 直流電（直流电）
direct current motor	zhílǜ diàndòngjī 直流電動機（直流电动机）
discrete element	fēnlì yuánjiàn 分立元件
effective head	yǒuxiào shuǐtóu 有效水頭（有效水头）; yǒuxiào luòchā 有效落差
efficiency	xiàolǜ 效率
electric machinery	diànjī 電機（电机）
electric motor	diàndòngjī 電動機（电动机）
electric power generation	fādiàn 發電（发电）
electronic computer	diànzǐ jìsuànjī 電子計算機（电子计算机）; diànnǎo 電腦（电脑）
electronic digital computer	diànzǐ shùzì jìsuànjī 電子數字計算機（电子数字计算机）
electronic equipment	diànzǐ shèbèi 電子設備（电子设备）
electronic instrument	diànzǐ yíbiǎo 電子儀表（电子仪表）
electronics	diànzǐxué 電子學（电子学）

emergency stop protection	jǐnjí tíngjī bǎohùzhuangzhì 緊急停機保護裝置(紧急停机保护装置)
encapsulation	mìfēng 密封
etchant	fǔshíjì 腐蝕劑(腐蚀剂)
etching	shíkè 蝕刻(蚀刻); fǔshí jiāgōng 腐蝕加工(腐蚀加工)
evaporation	zhēngfā 蒸發(蒸发)
evaporation	zhēngtú 蒸塗(蒸涂)
extraction of radar information	léidá xìnxī lùqǔ 雷達信息錄取(雷达信息录取)
firing	diǎnrán 點燃(点燃); qǐdòng 起動(起动)
flame spraying	huǒyán pēntú 火焰噴塗(火焰喷涂)
flashing	shǎnhú 閃弧(闪弧); shǎnzhēng 閃蒸(闪蒸)
flow discharge	liúliàng 流量
frequency	pínlǜ 頻率(频率)
fuse	bǎoxiǎnsī 保險絲(保险丝)
gas-turbo generator	ránqìlún fādiànjī 燃氣輪發電機(燃气轮发电机)
generation, total	zǒngfādiànliàng 總發電量(总发电量)
generator	fādiànjī 發電機(发电机)
generator main circuit breaker	fādiànjī zhǔduànlùqì 發電機主斷路器(发电机主断路器)
geothermal power station	dìrè fādiànzhàn 地熱發電站(地热发电站)
governor	tiáosùqì 調速器(调速器)
grid	gāoyā diànwǎng 高壓電網(高压电网)

ground surveillance radar	dìmiàn jiānshì léidá 地面監視雷達（地面监视雷达）
grounding transformer, earthing transformer	jiēdì biànyāqì 接地變壓器（接地变压器）
guidance radar	zhìdǎo léidá 制導雷達（制导雷达）
head	shuǐtóu 水頭（水头）
heat exchange	rèjiāohuàn 熱交換（热交换）
heat exchanger	huànrèqì 換熱器（换热器）
heat transfer	rèchuándǎo 熱傳導（热传导）
heat transfer equipment	chuánrè shèbèi 傳熱設備（传热设备）
high head	gāoshuǐtóu 高水頭（高水头）
high pressure cylinder	gāoyā qìgāng 高壓氣缸（高压气缸）
high tension line	gāoyā xiànlù 高壓綫路（高压线路）
horizontal type motor	wòshì diàndòngjī 臥式電動機（卧式电动机）
horsepower	mǎlì 馬力（马力）
hydroelectric generation	shuǐlì fādiàn 水力發電（水力发电）
hydroelectric power station	shuǐlì fādiànzhàn 水力發電站（水力发电站）
hydropower station	shuǐdiànzhàn 水電站（水电站）
impulse water turbin	chōngjīxíng shuǐlúnjī 衝擊型水輪機（冲击型水轮机）
increasing the reliability of equipment	tígāo shèbèide kěkàoxìng 提高設備的可靠性（提高设备的可靠性）
induced-draft fan	chōufēngjī 抽風機（抽风机）
induction motor	gǎnyìng diàndòngjī 感應電動機

	（感应电动机）; yìbù diàn dòngjī 異步電動機（异步电动机）
installed capacity	zhuāngjī róngliàng 裝機容量（装机容量）
insulating base	juéyuán 絕緣板（绝缘板）
integrated circuit	jíchéng diànlù 集成電路（集成电路）
intermediate pressure cylinder	zhōngyā qìgāng 中壓氣缸（中压气缸）
interrupting capacity-kva	duànkāiróngliàng—qiānfúān 斷開容量—千伏安（断开容量—千伏安）
intraconnection element	nèijiē yuánjiàn 內接元件
kilowatt（KW）	qiānwǎ 千瓦
kilowatt-hour（kwh）	qiānwǎ（xiǎo）shí 千瓦（小）時（千瓦（小）时）; dù 度
load shedding	shuǎi fùzài 甩負載（甩负载）
low head	dīshuǐtóu 低水頭（低水头）
low pressure cylinder	dīyā qìgāng 低壓氣缸（低压气缸）
low tension line	dīyā xiànlù 低壓綫路（低压线路）
machinery	jīqì 機器（机器）; jīxiè 機械（机械）
mask	yǎnmó 掩模
microcircuit	wēixíng diànlù 微型電路（微型电路）
microelectronic element	wēidiànzǐ yuánjiàn 微電子元件（微电子元件）
microelement	wēixíng yuánjiàn 微型元件
micrologic	wēixíng luójì 微邏輯（微逻辑）

micromanipulator	wēixíng cāozòng shèbèi 微型操縱設備(微型操纵设备)
micromatrix	wēijǔzhèn 微矩陣(微矩阵)
micromodule	wēixíng zǔjiàn 微型組件(微型组件)
microprogram	wēichéngxù 微程序
microprogramming	wēichéngxù shèjì 微程序設計(微程序设计)
milligal	háojiā 毫伽
miniaturization	xiǎoxínghuà 小型化
mixed flow water turbin	hùliúshì shuǐlúnjī 混流式水輪機(混流式水轮机)
motor	diàndòngjī 電動機(电动机)
multilayer wiring	duōcéng bùxiàn 多層布綫(多层布线)
navigation radar	dǎoháng léidá 導航雷達(导航雷达)
network protector	wǎngluò bǎohùzhuāngzhì 網絡保護裝置(网络保护装置)
nuclear-generated electrical power	hé diànlì 核電力(核电力)
nuclear reactor	(yuánzǐ)hé fǎnyìngduī (原子)核反應堆((原子)核反应堆)
numerical control	shùzì kòngzhì 數字控制(数字控制)
off peak hours	zhèngcháng fùhè shíjiān 正常負荷時間(正常负荷时间)
off peak period	zhèngcháng fùhè qī jiān 正常負荷期間(正常负荷期间)
open cycle	kāishì xúnhuán 開式循環(开式循环)
outward element	wàijiē yuánjiàn 外接元件

overflow	yìliú 溢流
package	zǔhéjiàn 組合件; fēngzhuāng 封裝(封装)
packaged circuit	zǔzhuāng diànlù 組裝電路(组装电路)
parabolic antenna	pāowùmiàn tiānxiàn 拋物面天線(抛物面天线)
peak hours	gāofēng fùhè shíjiān 高峯負荷時間(高峰负荷时间)
peak load period	gāofēng fùhè qíjiān 高峯負荷期間(高峰负荷期间)
penstock	jìnshuǐguǎn 進水管(进水管)
photoetching	guāngkè 光刻
photoresist	guāngmǐn kàngshíjì 光敏抗蝕劑(光敏抗蚀剂); guāngzhì kàngshíjì 光致抗蝕劑(光致抗蚀剂)
potted microelement	fēng zhuāng wēixíng yuánjiàn 封裝微型元件(封装微型元件); máirùde wēixíng yuánjiàn 埋入的微型元件
potting	fēngzhuāng 封裝(封装); máirù 埋入
power	diànlì 電力(电力)
power equipment plant	fādiàn shèbèi zhìzàochǎng 發電設備製造廠(发电设备制造厂)
power factor	gōnglǜ yīnshù 功率因數(功率因数)
power house	fādiàn chǎng 發電廠(发电厂); dònglì shì 動力室(动力室)
power line	shūdiànxiàn 輸電綫(输电线); diànyuánxiàn 電源綫(电源

線)

power plant	fādiànchǎng 發電廠(发电厂)
power transformation and transmission	biàndiàn shūdiàn 變電輸電(变电输电)
preparing a budget	biānzhì yùsuàn 編製預算(编制预算)
pressure	diànyā 電壓(电压); yālì 壓力(压力)
pressure cylinder	yālì qìgāng 壓力氣缸(压力气缸)
primary plant	yīhuílù zhuāngzhì 一回路裝置(一回路装置); (Zhēngqì fāshēng zhuāngzhì)(蒸氣發生裝置)(蒸气发生装置)
printed circuit	yìnshuā diànlù 印刷電路(印刷电路)
printed wiring board	yìnshuā xiànlùbǎn 印刷綫路板(印刷线路板)
pulverizer, coal grinder	mómÉijī 磨煤機(磨煤机)
pump storage power station	chōushuǐ xùnéng diànzhàn 抽水蓄能電站(抽水蓄能电站)
radar	léidá 雷達(雷达)
rated capacity	édìng gōnglǜ 額定功率(额定功率)
rate of flow-cubic meters per second	liúliànglǜ—lìfāngmǐ/miǎo 流量率—立方米/秒
reactance	diànkàng 電抗(电抗)
reaction water turbin	fǎnjīxíng shuǐlúnjī 反擊型水輪機(反击型水轮机)
rectifier	zhěngliúqì 整流器
reducing power consumption	jiǎnshǎo hào diàn liàng 減少耗電量(减少耗电量)

reducing the number of components	jiǎnshǎo yuánjiàn shùmù 減少元件數目(减少元件数目)
reducing the number of soldered connections	jiǎnshǎo hànjiēchù 減少焊接處(减少焊接处)
reducing the volume	jiǎnxiǎo tǐjī 減少體積(减少体积)
reducing the weight	jiǎnqīng zhòngliàng 減輕重量(减轻重量)
reflector antenna	fǎnshèqì tiānxiàn 反射器天綫(反射器天线)
reheating	zàirè 再熱(再热)
remote control	yáokòng 遙控
repair shop	xiūpèi chējiān 修配車間(修配车间)
resistance	diànzǔ 電阻(电阻)
resistivity prospecting (survey)	diànzǔlüfǎ kāntàn 電阻率法勘探(电阻率法勘探)
rotating antenna	xuánzhuǎn tiānxiàn 旋轉天綫(旋转天线)
safety regulations	ānquán shǒuzé 安全守則(安全守则)
satellite surveillance radar	wèixīng jiānshì léidá 衛星監視雷達(卫星监视雷达)
scanner	sǎomiáo tiānxiàn 掃描天綫(扫描天线); sǎomiáoqì 掃描器(扫描器)
secondary plant	èrhuílù (qìlúnjī)dònglì zhuāngzhì 二回路(汽輪機)動力裝置(二回路(汽轮机)动力装置)
screen printing	wǎngbǎn yìnshuā 網板印刷(网板印刷); sīmù yìnshuā 絲幕印刷(丝幕印刷)

English	Chinese
semi-conductor component	bàndǎotǐ yuánjiàn 半導體元件（半导体元件）
shaft	zhǔzhóu 主軸（主轴）
shut down	tíngjī 停機（停机）
single phase motor	dānxiàng diàndòngjī 單相電動機（单相电动机）
solar power station	tàiyángnéng diànzhàn 太陽能電站（太阳能电站）
solid circuit	gùtǐ diànlù 固體電路（固体电路）
solid state circuit	gùtài diànlù 固態電路（固态电路）
space-borne radar	hángtiān léidá 航天雷達（航天雷达）
speed-governing system	tiáosù xìtǒng 調速系統（调速系统）
spraying	pēntú 噴塗（喷涂）
squirrel-cage type motor	shǔlóngshì diàndòngjī 鼠籠式電動機（鼠笼式电动机）
starting up	kāidòng 開動（开动）
station service system	chǎngyòngdiàn xìtǒng 廠用電系統（厂用电系统）
steam main	zhǔ zhēngqìguǎn 主蒸氣管（主蒸气管）
steam raising capacity (live steam rate)-tons per hour	zhēngqì fāshēng nénglì (zhēngqì fāshēng lǜ)— měi yi xiǎo shí dūnshù 蒸氣發生能力（蒸氣發生率）—每一小時噸數（蒸气发生能力（蒸气发生率）—每一小时吨数）
steam turbine	qìlúnjī 汽輪機（汽轮机）
step-down transformer	jiàngyā biànyāqì 降壓變壓器

181

	（降壓變壓器）（降压变压器）
step-up transformer	shēngyā biànyāqì 升壓變壓器（升压变压器）
stop valve	zhǔqìmén 主汽門（主汽门）
substation	biàndiànzhàn 變電站（变电站）
substrate	jípiàn 基片; chèndǐ 襯底（衬底）
supervisory panel	jiānshì xìnhàopán 監視信號盤（监视信号盘）
surface condenser	biǎomiàn lěngníngqì 表面冷凝器
surge arrester	bìléiqì 避雷器（避雷器）; fáng-zhǐ guòzàide fàngdiànqì 防止過載的放電器（防止过载的放电器）
survey	cèliáng 測量（测量）; diàochá 調查（调查）
switchboard	pèidiànpán 配電盤（配电盘）
switchgear	kāiguān shèbèi 開關設備（开关设备）
switchroom	pèidiànshì 配電室（配电室）
synchronous motor	tóngbù diàndòngjī 同步電動機（同步电动机）
tail race	wěishuǐqú 尾水渠
target acquisition	mùbiāo tàncè 目標探測（目标测探）
temperature	wēndù 溫度
thermal power generation	huǒlì fādiàn 火力發電（火力发电）
thermal power station	huǒlì fādiànzhàn 火力發電站（火力发电站）
thermosetting compound	règù huàhéwù 熱固化合物（热固化合物）

thick-film circuit	hòumó diànlù 厚膜電路(厚膜电路)
thick-film hybrid integrated circuit	hòumó hùnhé jíchéngdiànlù 厚膜混合集成電路(厚膜混合集成电路)
thin film	bómó 薄膜
thin film microcircuit	bómó wēixíngdiànlù 薄膜微型電路(薄膜微型电路)
three-dimensional radar (space radar)	sānzuòbiāo léidá 三座標雷達(三座标雷达); kōngjiān léidá 空間雷達(空间雷达)
three phase motor	sānxiàng diàndòngjī 三相電動機(三相电动机)
thrust bearing	tuīlì zhóuchéng 推力軸承(推力轴承)
thyristor	bàndǎotǐ kāiguān yuánjiàn 半導體開關元件(半导体开关元件)
tidal power station	cháoxī diànzhàn 潮汐電站(潮汐电站)
tinkertoy module	duīdiéshì wēixíng zǔjiàn 堆叠式微型組件(堆迭式微型组件)
transformer	biànyāqì 變壓器(变压器)
transformer (main)	zhǔbiànyāqì 主變壓器(主变压器)
transformer station, sub-station	biàndiànsuǒ 變電所(变电所)
transmission transformer	shūdiàn biànyāqì 輸電變壓器(输电变压器)
turbine	wōlúnjī 渦輪機(涡轮机); tòupíng 透平
turbine rotor	wōlúnjī zhuànlún 渦輪機轉輪

	（涡轮机转轮）
turbogenerator	wōlún fādiànjī 渦輪發電機（涡轮发电机）
turbogenerator unit	wōlún fādiànjīzǔ 渦輪發電機組（涡轮发电机组）
types of power stations	fādiànzhàn lèixíng 發電站類型（发电站类型）
unit capacity	dānwèi róngliàng 單位容量（单位容量）; dānjī gōnglǜ 單機功率（单机功率）
uranium rod	yóubàng 鈾棒（铀棒）
vertical type motor	lìshì diàndòngjī 立式電動機（立式电动机）
voltage	diànyā 電壓（电压）
water (hydraulic) turbin	shuǐlúnjī 水輪機（水轮机）
water-jet air ejector	pēnshuǐ chōuqìjī 噴水抽氣機（喷水抽气机）
wave	bō 波
wind power station	fēnglì fādiànzhàn 風力發電站（风力发电站）
zone of radar coverage	léidá fùgài kōngyù 雷達覆蓋空域（雷达复盖空域）

3. Petroleum

absorbent oil	xīshōuyóu 吸收油
aero-magnetic prospecting (survey)	hángkōng cílì kāntàn 航空磁力勘探; hángkōng cícè 航空磁測(航空磁测)
air sac	qìnáng 氣囊(气囊)
anthracite	wúyānméi 無烟煤(无烟煤)
aviation gasoline	hángkōng qìyóu 航空汽油
barrel type core bit	tǒngshì qǔxīnzuàntóu 筒式取心鑽頭(筒式取心钻头)
barrels per day (pd)	tǒng/tiān 桶/天
base of operation on land	lùshàng hòuqín jīdì 陸上後勤基地(陆上后勤基地)
bit	zuàntóu 鑽頭(钻头)
bitumen	lìqīng 瀝青(沥青)
bituminous coal	yānméi 烟煤
blow-off preventer	fángpēnqì 防噴器(防喷器)
bore hole	zuānkǒng 鑽孔(钻孔)
carbon black	tànhēi 炭黑
carbonate content	tànsuānyán hánliàng 碳酸鹽含量(碳酸盐含量)
casting resin	zhùmó shùzhī 鑄模樹脂(铸模树脂)
combination gas	yóujǐngqì 油井氣(油井气)
compactness of rocks	yánshíde zhìmìxìng 岩石的致密性
conductivity of rocks	yánshíde diàndǎoxìng 岩石的電導性(岩石的电导性)
core	yánxīn 岩心

core analysis	yánxīn fēnxī 岩心分析
core barrel	yánxīntǒng 岩心筒
coring	qǔyánxīn 取岩心
crown block	tiānchē 天車 (天车)
crude oil production	cǎiyóu 採油 (采油)
crude oil products	yuányóu chǎnpǐn 原油產品 (原油产品)
deposition	diànjī 澱積 (淀积)
derrick	jǐngjià 井架
detonation	bàozhà 爆炸; bàopò 爆破
diamond bit	jīngāngshí zuàntóu 金鋼石鑽頭 (金钢石钻头)
diesel oil	cháiyóu 柴油
directional drilling	dìngxiàng zuānjǐng 定向鑽井 (定向钻井)
drill	zuànjī 鑽機 (钻机)
drill stem	zuàngǎn 鑽桿 (钻杆)
driller's log	zuānjǐng jìlù 鑽井記錄 (钻井记录)
drilling cuttings	zuānxiè 鑽屑 (钻屑)
drilling direction	dìngxiàng zuānjǐng 鑽井方位 (钻井方位)
drilling fluid	zuānyòng chōngxǐyè 鑽用沖洗液 (钻用冲洗液)
drilling mud	zuānjia 鑽渣 (钻渣); zuāntàn níjiāng 鑽探泥漿 (钻探泥浆)
drill rod	zuàngǎn 鑽桿 (钻杆)
drive	chuándòng 傳動 (传动); dazhuāng 打樁 (打桩)
earth wax	dìlà 地蠟 (地蜡)
electrical bit	diànzuàntóu 電鑽頭 (电钻头)
electrical geophysical	diàndìqiú wùlǐfǎ 電地球物理法

method	（电地球物理法）
electrical logging	diàncèjǐng 電測井（电测井）
electromagnetic pros-pecting（survey）	diàncífǎ kāntàn 電磁法勘探（电磁法勘探）
exciter	lìcíjī 礪磁機（砺磁机）
explosion	bàozhà 爆炸
feul oil	ránliàoyóu 燃料油; zhòngyóu 重油
fixed platform	gùdìngshì píngtái 固定式平臺（固定式平台）
floating type platform	fúzhōushì píngtái 浮舟式平臺（浮舟式平台）
flush production	shuǐlì tiánchōng cǎiyóu 水力填充採油（水力填充采油）
gas	qì 氣（气）; qìmiáo 氣苗（气苗）
gas-cap drive	qìmào qūdòng 氣帽驅動（气帽驱动）
gas compressor	qìtǐ yāsuōjī 氣體壓縮機（气体压缩机）; yāqìjī 壓氣機（压气机）
gas field	qìtián 氣田（气田）
gas lift production	qìtǐ qū yóu cǎiyóu 氣體驅油採油（气体驱油采油）
gas oil	cū cháiyóu 粗柴油; wǎsīyóu 瓦斯油; qìyóu 氣油（气油）
gas-oil ratio	qìyóubǐ 氣油比（气油比）
general valve	zǒngzhámén 總閘門（总闸门）
geochemical prospecting（survey）	dìqiú huàxué kāntàn 地球化學勘探（地球化学勘探）
geological map	dìzhìtú 地質圖（地质图）
geological survey	dìzhì diàochá 地質調查（地质调查）
geophysical prospecting	dìqiú wùlǐ kāntàn 地球物理勘

(survey)	探
gravimeter	bǐzhòngjì 比重計(比重计); zhònglìyí 重力儀(重力仪)
gravimeter method	zhòng liáng fēnxī fǎ 重量分析法
gravity anomaly	zhònglì yìcháng 重力異常(重力异常)
gravity drainage	zìliu páishuǐ自流排水;zìzhòng páishuǐ 自重排水
gusher	zìpēn yóujǐng 自噴油井(自喷油井)
hydrocarbon gas	tīngqì 烴氣(烃气)
improvement of permeability of the reservoir	yóucéng shèntòuxìng de gǎishàn 油層滲透性的改善（油层渗透性的改善）
induction logging	gǎnyìng cèjǐng 感應測井(感应测井)
injection	zhù 注
injection of gas	zhùqì 注氣(注气)
injection of water	zhùshuǐ 注水
jack-up type platform	shēngjiàngshì píngtái 升降式平臺(升降式平台)
liquefied petroleum gas	yèhuà shíyóuqì 液化石油氣(液化石油气)
location of well	jǐngwèi xuǎndìng 井位選定(井位选定)
logging	cèjǐng 測井(测井)
loose pulley	yóudòng huáchē 游動滑車(游动滑车)
lubricating oil	rùnhuáyóu 潤滑油(润滑油)
magnetic change of rocks	yánshíde cíxìng biànhuà 岩石的磁性變化(岩石的磁性变化)
magnetic prospecting	cílì kāntàn 磁力勘探

（survey）

magnetic tape seismo- graph	cídài dìzhènyí 磁帶地震儀(磁带 地震仪)
magnetometer	cílìyí 磁力儀(磁力仪)
magnifier	fàngdàqì 放大器
maintenance of oil pipe pressure	bǎochí yóucéng yālì 保持油管 壓力(保持油管压力)
mechanical production	jīxiè cǎiyóu 機械採油(机械采 油)
mobile device	kěyídòngde zhuāngzhì 可移動 的裝置(可移动的装置)
mooring equipment	xìbó shèbèi 繫泊設備(系泊设 备)
motor gasoline（U.S.）	chēyòng qìyóu 車用氣油(车用 气油)
motor petrol（U.K.）	chēyòng qìyóu 車用氣油(车用 气油)
motor spirit	chēyòng qìyóu 車用氣油(车用 气油)
mud pool	níjiāngchí 泥漿池(泥浆池)
mud pump	níjiāngbèng 泥漿泵(泥浆泵)
mud recirculation	níjiāng xúnhuán 泥漿循環(泥浆 循环)
naphtha oil	shínǎoyóu 石腦油(石脑油)
natural bitumen	tiānrán lìqīng 天然瀝青(天然沥 青)
natural flowing production	zìpēn cǎiyóu 自噴採油(自喷采 油)
natural gas	tiānránqì 天然氣(天然气)
new-field wild-catting	xīnqū shìtàn zuànjǐng 新區試探 鑽井(新区试探钻井)
offshore drilling	hǎishàng zuànjǐng 海上鑽井(海

上钻井）

offshore drilling unit	hǎishàng zuānjǐng zhuāngzhì 海上鑽井裝置(海上钻井装置)
offshore field	hǎishàng yóutián 海上油田
oil	yóu 油; yóumiáo 油苗
oil expelling pressure in the rock strata	yáncéngzhōng páijǐ shíyóude yālì 岩層中石油的排擠壓力(岩层中石油的排挤压力)
oil nozzle	pēn yóuzuǐ 噴油嘴(喷油咀)
oil occurrence	yóucáng 油藏
oil pipe pressure meter	yóuguǎn yālìbiǎo 油管壓力錶 (油管压力表)
oil pumping unit	chōuyóujī 抽油機(抽油机)
oil reserve under water	shuǐxià chǔyóuliàng 水下儲油量 (水下储油量)
oil sand	yóushā 油砂
oil saturation	yóubǎohélǜ 油飽和率 (油饱和率)
oil shale	yóuyèyán 油頁岩(油页岩)
oil sheet	bóyóucéng 薄油層(薄油层)
oil show	jǐngxià shǒucì xiànyóu 井下首次現油(井下首次现油)
oil zone	hányóudài 含油帶(含油带)
oscillograph	shìbōqì 示波器
oscilloscope	shìbōqì 示波器; shìbōguǎn 示波管
outdoor oil circuit breaker	lùtiānyóu duànlùqì 露天油斷路器(露天油断路器)
outdoor switchyard	lùtiān kāiguānchǎng 露天開關場 (露天开关场)
paraffin	shílà 石蠟(石蜡)
paraffin oil	shílàyóu 石蠟油(石蜡油)

percussion drill	chōngjīshìzuànjī 衝擊式鑽機(沖擊式钻机)
percussion drilling	chōngjīshìzuānjǐng 衝擊式鑽井(沖擊式钻井)
permeability	shèntòuxìng 滲透性(渗透性)
petroleum	shíyóu 石油
petroleum coke	shíyóu jiāo 石油焦
petroleum drilling	shíyóu zuànjǐng 石油鑽井(石油钻井)
petroleum exploration	shíyóu kāntàn 石油勘探
petroleum grease	shíyóu rùnhuázhī 石油潤滑脂(石油润滑脂)
petroleum secondary recovery	èrcì cǎiyóu 二次探油(二次采油)
platform	píngtái 平臺(平台)
pool of the continental shelf	dàlùjià yóuchuáng 大陸架油床(大陆架油床)
porosity	kǒngxìdù 孔隙度
power locating	dònglì dìngwèi 動力定位(动力定位)
power unit	dònglìjī 動力機(动力机)
pressure differential	yāchā 壓差(压差)
production of oil	cǎiyóu 探油(采油)
prospect drilling	zuānjǐng kāntàn 鑽井勘探(钻井勘探)
prospecting, survey	kāntàn 勘探; kāncè 勘測(勘测)
pumping well	chōuyóujǐng 抽油井
radioactivity logging	fàngshèxìng cèjǐng 放射性測井(放射性测井)
radioactivity prospecting (survey)	fàngshèxìng kāntàn 放射性勘探
rate of penetration	zuānjìn sùdù 鑽進速度(钻进速

	度)
reconnaissance survey	pǔchá 普查
reflection wave	fǎnshèbō 反射波
refraction wave	zhéshèbō 折射波
repressuring of gas	yāhuíqì 壓回氣(压回气)
reservoir behavior	yóuchǔcéng xìngnéng 油儲層性 能(油储层性能)
residual fuel	cánzhā ránliào 殘渣燃料(残渣 燃料)
rig	jǐngjià 井架
rigging up	zuānjī ānzhuāng 鑽機安裝(钻机 安装)
rocks	yánshí 岩石
rotary drill	xuánzhuǎnshì zuànjī 旋轉式鑽 機(旋转式钻机)
rotary table	xuánpán 旋盤(旋盘)
rust preventive	fángxiùjì 防銹劑(防锈剂)
seismic	dìzhènde 地震的
seismic detector	dìzhèn jiǎnbōyí 地震檢波儀(地 震检波仪)
seismic event	dìzhènbō 地震波
seismic instrument car	dìzhèn yíqìchē 地震儀器車(地 震仪器车)
seismic reflection pros- pecting (survey)	dìzhèn fǎnshèfǎ kāntàn 地震反 射法勘探
seismograph	dìzhènyí 地震儀(地震仪)
self-contained platform	zìjǐde píngtái 自給的平臺(自给 的平台); zìbèi dònglìde píng- tái 自備動力的平臺(自备动力 的平台)
self-propelling	zìdòng tuījìn 自動推進(自动推 进)

semi-submersible type platform	bànqiánshì píngtái 半潛式平臺 (半潜式平台)
sit-on-bottom type platform	zhuódǐshì píngtái 着底式平臺 (着底式平台)
solution gas drive, dissolved gas drive	róngjiě qìyālì 溶解氣壓力(溶解气压力); róngjiě qìqū 溶解氣驅(溶解气驱)
spacing of well	zuànkǒng jiānjù 鑽孔間距(钻孔间距); jǐngjù 井距(井距)
spudding in	kāizuàn 開鑽(开钻)
sputtering	jiànshè 濺射(溅射)
stacking	duīfàng 堆放
striking oil	zuànchū shíyóu 鑽出石油(钻出石油)
submersible type platform	qiánshuǐshì píngtái 潛水式平臺 (潜水式平台)
subsurface well-surveying instrument	dìxià cèjǐng yíqì 地下測井儀器 (地下测井仪器)
surface casing	dìmiàn tàoguǎn 地面套管(地面套管)
trial pit	chūtàn qiǎnjǐng 初探淺井(初探浅井)
turbo drill	wōlún zuànjī 渦輪鑽機(涡轮钻机)
valve casing	fámén tàoguǎn 閥門套管(阀门套管)
valve for well repair	xiūjǐng zhámén 修井閘門(修井闸门)
viscosity of petroleum	shíyóude niándù 石油的粘度
water drive	shuǐqū 水驅(水驱)
well deliverability of gas	qìjǐng měitiān pēnqìliàng 氣井每天噴氣量(气井每天喷气量)

well's potential	yóujǐng shēngchǎn qiánlì 油井 生產潛力(油井生产潜力)
white oil	báiyóu 白油
winch	jiǎochē 絞車(绞车)

4. Conservation

acid rain	suānyǔ 酸雨
afforestation	zàolín 造林
agroecosystem	nóngyè shēngtài xìtǒng 農業生態系統(农业生态系统)
aquatic mammal	shuǐshēng bǔrǔ dòngwù 水生哺乳動物(水生哺乳动物)
arid land	gānhàn dì 乾旱地(干旱地)
Asiatic wild ass	yělǘ 野驢(野驴)
atmospheric monitoring system	dàqì jiāncè xìtǒng 大氣監測系統(大气监测系统)
beneficial insect	yìchóng 益蟲(益虫)
binturong	shèmāo 麝貓(麝猫)
biogas	zhǎoqì 沼氣(沼气)
biome	shēngwù qúnluò 生物羣落
biosphere	shēngwùjiè 生物界; shēngwùquān 生物圈
biota	shēngwùqún 生物羣
black finless porpoise	jiāngtún 江豚
black ibis	hēihuán 黑鸛(黑鹮)
black muntjac	hēijǐ 黑麂
black-necked crane	hēijǐnghè 黑頸鶴(黑颈鹤)
black snub-nosed monkey	hēijīnsīhóu 黑金絲猴(黑金丝猴)
black stork	hēiguàn 黑鸛(黑鹳)
blood pheasant	xuèzhì 血雉
blue-eared pheasant	lánmǎjī 藍馬雞(蓝马鸡)
brown-eared pheasant	hèmǎjī 褐馬雞(褐马鸡)
camel	luòtuó 駱駝(骆驼)

195

catchment area	shòuyǔqū 受雨區(受雨区); huìshuǐqū 滙水區(汇水区)
central heating	jízhōng gōngrè 集中供熱(集中供热)
Chinese alligator	yángzǐ'è 楊子鰐(杨子鳄)
Chinese copper pheasant	tóngjī 銅雞(铜鸡)
Chinese merganser	zhōnghuá qiūshāyā 中華秋沙鴨(中华秋沙鸭)
Chinese monal	lùwěihóngzhì 綠尾虹雉(绿尾虹雉)
Chinese river dolphin	báiqítún 白鰭豚
Chinese sturgeon	zhōnghuáxún 中華鱘(中华鲟)
Chinese water deer	yázhāng 牙獐
chiru (Tibetan antelope)	zànglíng 藏羚
christmas tree	cǎiyóushù 採油樹(采油树)
clearcutting	jiéfá 皆伐
clouded leopard	yúnwèn bào 雲紋豹(云纹豹)
common seal	hǎibào 海豹
coral reef	shānhújiāo 珊瑚礁
crane	báitóuhè 白頭鶴(白头鹤)
crested ibis	zhūhuán 朱鵬(朱鹮)
crop residue	zuòwù jiégǎn 作物秸杆
data bank	shùjùkù 數據庫(数据库)
deforestation	sēnlín lànfá 森林濫伐(森林滥伐)
desertification	shāmòhuà 沙漠化
deterioration	tuìhuà 退化
discharge	páifàng 排放
dugong	rúgèn 儒艮
ecological balance	shēngtài pínghéng 生態平衡(生态平衡)

196

ecology	shēngtàixué 生態學(生态学)
ecosystem	shēngtài xìtǒng 生態系統(生态系统)
Eld's deer	hǎinánpōlù 海南坡鹿
endangered species	bīnyúmièjuéde wùzhǒng 瀕於滅絕的物種(濒于灭绝的物种)
environmental impact assessment	huánjìng yīngxiǎng gūjì 環境影響估計(环境影响估计)
environmental protection	huánjìng bǎohù 環境保護(环境保护)
eutrophication	fùyíngyǎnghuà 富營養化(富营养化)
flood plain	màntān 漫灘(漫滩)
fly ash	fēihuī 飛灰(飞灰)
food chain	shíwùliàn 食物鏈(食物链)
fossil fuel	kuàngwù ránliào 礦物燃料(矿物燃料)
Francois' leaf monkey	hēiyèhóu 黑葉猴(黑叶猴)
fuel wood	xīncái 薪材
Fukien tragopan	huángfùjiǎozhì 黃腹角雉
gene bank	jīyīnkù 基因庫(基因库)
geothermal energy	dìrènéng 地熱能(地热能)
giant panda	dàxióngmāo 大熊貓(大熊猫)
gibbon	chángbìhóu 長臂猴(长臂猴)
ginkgo	yínxìng 銀杏(银杏)
glossy ibis	cǎihuán 彩鸛(彩鹮)
golden cat	jīnmāo 金貓(金猫)
golden monkey	jīnsīhóu 金絲猴(金丝猴)
great white crane	báihè 白鶴(白鹤)
green peafowl	lǜkǒngquè 綠孔雀(绿孔雀)
grey peacock pheasant	kǒngquèzhì 孔雀雉
habitat	shēngjìng 生境

heat island	rèdǎo 熱島（热岛）
hog deer	túnlù 豚鹿
hooded crane	báitóuhè 白頭鶴（白头鹤）
hornbill	xīniǎo 犀鳥（犀鸟）
human settlement	rénlèi jūzhùqū 人類居住區（人类居住区）
Impeyan monal	zōngwěihóngzhì 棕尾虹雉
Indian elephant	yàzhōuxiàng 亞洲象（亚洲象）
Japanese white crane	báihè 白鶴（白鶴）
land fill	tiánmái 填埋
langur (entellus monkey)	chángwěiyèhóu 長尾葉猴（长尾葉猴）
leopard	bào 豹
lesser panda (red)	xiǎoxióngmāo 小熊貓
life-support system	shēngmìng zhīchí xìtǒng 生命支持系統（生命支持系统）
lizard	yáoshānèxī 瑤山鰐蜥（瑤山鳄蜥）
lynx	shēlìsūn 猞猁猻（猞猁狲）
mangrove swamp	hóngshùlín zhǎozédì 紅樹林沼澤地（红树林沼泽地）
marine life	hǎiyáng shēngwù 海洋生物
migratory species	yíqī wùzhǒng 移棲物種（移栖物种）
monitoring	jiāncè 監測（监测）
musk deer	shè 麝
national park	guójiā gōngyuán 國家公園（国家公园）
natural enemy	tiāndí 天敵（天敌）
nitrogen fixation	gùdàn 固氮
noise pollution	zàoshēng wūrǎn 噪聲污染（噪声污染）

non-pollutive technology	wúwūrǎn jìshù 無污染技術(无污染技术)
non-renewable re-sources	bùkěhuīfùde zīyuán 不可恢復的資源(不可恢复的资源)
oil spill	hǎishàng piāoyóu 海上漂油
overgrazing	guòdù fàngmù 過度放牧(过度放牧)
ozone layer	chòuyǎngcéng 臭氧層(臭氧层)
photochemical smog	guānghuàxué yānwù 光化學烟霧(光化学烟雾)
pollution control	wūrǎn kòngzhì 污染控制
primary treatment	chūjí chǔlǐ 初級處理(初级处理); yījí chǔlǐ 一級處理(一级处理)
radioactive waste	fàngshèxìng fèiwù 放射性廢物(放射性废物)
rangeland	mùdì 牧地
red crested crane (red crowned)	dāndǐnghè 丹頂鶴(丹顶鶴)
red serow	chìbānlíng 赤斑羚
red tide	hóngcháo 紅潮(红潮)
renewable energy source	kězàishēng néngyuán 可再生能源
river dolphin	hétún 河豚
run-off	jìngliú 逕流(径流)
sable	zǐdiāo 紫貂
saiga	sàijiālíngyáng 賽加羚羊(赛加羚羊)
salamander	róngyúan 蠑螈(蝾螈); dàní 大鯢(大鲵)
sand dune fixation	shāqiū gùdìng 沙丘固定
sarus crane	chìjǐnghè 赤頸鶴(赤颈鶴)

Sclater's monal	báiwěishāohóngzhì 白尾稍虹雉
secondary treatment	èrjí chǔlǐ 二級處理(二级处理)
serow	lièlíng 獵羚(猎羚)
sewage	wūshuǐ 污水
shelduck	guānyā 冠鴨(冠鸭); máyā 麻鴨(麻鸭)
shelter belt	fánghùlín 防護林(防护林)
shifting cultivation	lúnzuò 輪作(轮作)
Sika deer	Rìběnlù 日本鹿
silver pheasant	báixián 白鷴(白鹇)
silver pine	yínshān 銀杉(银杉)
slow loris	lǎnhóu 懶猴; fēnghóu 蜂猴
snow leopard	xuěbào 雪豹
solar energy	tàiyángnéng 太陽能(太阳能)
solid waste	gùtǐ fèiwù 固體廢物(固体废物)
species	wùzhǒng 物種(物种)
stork	hēiguàn 黑鸛(黑鹳)
sulfur dioxide	èryǎnghuàliú 二氧化硫
sustainable development	chíxù kāifā 持續開發(持续开发)
Taiwan blue pheasant	lánxián 藍鷴(蓝鹇)
Taiwan macaque	míhóu 獼猴(猕猴); táiwānhóu 臺灣猴(台湾猴)
tarpan	yěmǎ 野馬(野马)
tertiary treatment	sānjí chǔlǐ 三級處理(三级处理)
thermal pollution	rèwūrǎn 熱污染(热污染)
Tibetan-eared pheasant	zàngmǎjī 藏馬雞(藏马鸡)
tiger	hǔ 虎
toxic chemical	yǒudú huàxuéwù 有毒化學物(有毒化学物)
trans-boundary pollution	yuèjiè wūrǎn 越界污染
tropical forest	rèdài sēnlín 熱帶森林(热带森

林)

tufted deer	máoguānlù 毛冠鹿
urbanization	chéngshìhuà 城市化
urban sprawl	chéngshì kuòzhǎn 城市擴展(城市扩展)
vegetation	zhíbèi 植被
waste treatment	fèiwù chǔlǐ 廢物處理(废物处理)
water body	shuǐtǐ 水體(水体)
water fowl	shuǐqín 水禽
watershed forest	shuǐyuán hányǎnglín 水源涵養林(水源涵养林)
wetland	shīdì 濕地(湿地)
whale	jīng 鯨
whaling	bǔjīng 捕鯨(捕鲸)
white-backed snub-nosed monkey	qiánjīnsīhóu 黔金絲猴(黔金丝猴)
white-headed langur	báitóuyèhóu 白頭葉猴(白头叶猴)
white ibis	báihuān 白鹮(白鹮)
white-lipped deer	báichúnlù 白唇鹿
white-naped crane	báizhěnhè 白枕鶴(白枕鹤)
white stork	báiguàn 白鸛(白鹳)
white sturgeon	báixún 白鱘(白鲟)
wild camel	yěluòtuo 野駱駝(野骆驼)
wildlife	yěshēng shēngwù 野生生物
wild ox	yěniú 野牛
windbreak	fángfēnglín 防風林(防风林)
wind erosion	fēngshí 風蝕(风蚀)
wolverine	lánghuān 狼獾(狼獾)
Xiamen lancelet	Xiàmén wénchāngyú 廈門文昌魚(厦门文昌鱼)

yak	yěmáoniú 野牦牛
zone of silence	jìngqū 靜區(静区)
zooecology	dòngwù shēngtàixué 動物生態 學(动物生态学)

5. Insurance

abandonment of a ship	qìchuán 棄船(弃船)
acceptance	jiēshòu 接受; chéngbǎo 承保
accident insurance	yìwài bǎoxiǎn 意外保險(意外保险)
account	zhàng 帳務(帐务); zhànghù 帳戶(帐户)
acquisition cost	jiēbàn chéngběn 接辦成本(接办成本); zhǎnyèfèi 展業費(展业费)
actual loss	shíjì sǔnshī 實際損失(实际损失)
actuary (insurance)	(bǎoxiǎnyè)tǒngjìyuán (保險業)統計員((保险业)统计员)
actual total loss	shíjì quánsǔn 實際全損(实际全损)
addendum	fùyuē 附約(附约)
adjustment of loss	sǔnshī lǐsuàn 損失理算(损失理算)
administration cost	guǎnlǐfèi 管理費(管理费)
advance payment of premium	yùjiǎo bǎofèi 預繳保費(预缴保费)
age of vessel	chuánlíng 船齡(船龄)
agency agreement	dàilǐ hétong 代理合同
agency commission	dàilǐ shǒuxùfèi 代理手續費(代理手续费)
agent	dàilǐrén 代理人
agreed value	yuēdìng jiàzhí 約定價值(约定价值)

agricultural insurance	nóngyè bǎoxiǎn 農業保險(农业保险)
aircraft all risks	fēijī yíqièxiǎn 飛機一切險(飞机一切险)
aircraft hull insurance	fēijī jīshēnxiǎn 飛機機身險(飞机机身险)
air transport insurance	kōngyùn bǎoxiǎn 空運保險(空运保险)
all risks	zōnghéxiǎn 綜合險(综合险); yíqièxiǎn 一切險(一切险)
amicable settlement	héjiě 和解
amount ceded	fēnchū jīn'é 分出金額(分出金额)
amount insured	bǎoxiǎn jīn'é 保險金額(保险金额)
amount retroceded	zhuǎnfēnbǎo jīn'é 轉分保金額(转分保金额)
annual report	niánbào 年報(年报)
applicant	tóubǎorén 投保人
appraisal of damage	gūsǔn 估損(估损)
arbitration	zhōngcái 仲裁
arson	zònghuǒ 縱火(纵火)
assured	bèibǎoxiǎnrén 被保險人(被保险人)
assurer	bǎoxiǎnshāng 保險商(保险商)
auditor	cházhàngyuán 查帳員(查帐员)
automatic reinstatement clause	zìdòng xùbǎo tiáokuǎn 自動續保條欵(自动续保条款)
automatic sprinkler installation	zìdòng pēnsǎ zhuāngzhì 自動噴灑裝置(自动喷洒装置)
automobile insurance	qìchē bǎoxiǎn 汽車保險(汽车保险)

average	hǎisǔn 海損(海损)
average rate	píngjūn bǐlǜ 平均比率
aviation insurance	hángkōng yùnshū bǎoxiǎn 航空運輸保險(航空运输保险)
aviation liability insurance	hángkōng zérèn bǎoxiǎn 航空責任保險(航空责任保险)
basic premium	jīchǔ bǎofèi 基礎保費(基础保费)
basic rate	jīběn bǐlǜ 基本比率; jīběn yùnfèi lǜ 基本運費率(基本运费率)
belated claim	chísuǒde péikuǎn 遲索的賠款(迟索的赔款)
bid	chūjià 出價(出价); tóubiāo 投標(投标)
bill of lading	tídān 提單(提单)
binding	yuēshù 約束(约束)
blanket policy	gàibǎodān 概保單(概保单); zǒngbǎodān 總保單(总保单)
boiler insurance	guōlú bǎoxiǎn 鍋爐保險(锅炉保险)
bordereau	(fēnbāo)míngxìbiǎo (分保)明細表((分保)明细表); (bǎoxiǎn kuàiji)zhāiyàobù (保險會計)摘要薄((保险会计)摘要薄)
breakdown of machinery	jīqì gùzhàng 機器故障(机器故障)
broker	jīngjìrén 經紀人(经纪人)
brokerage	jīngjìrén shǒuxùfèi 經紀人手續費(经纪人手续费); yòngjīn 佣金
builders' risks	jiànzàoxiǎn 建造險(建造险)

205

burden of proof	jǔzhèng zérèn 舉証責任(举证责任)
business interruption insurance	qǐyè tíngdùn bǎoxiǎn 企業停頓保險(企业停顿保险)
cancel	zhùxiāo 注銷(注销)
cancellation notice	zhùxiāo tōngzhī 注銷通知(注销通知)
cargo transportation insurance	huòwù yùnshūxiǎn 貨物運輸險(货物运输险)
cash loss	xiànjīn péikuǎn 現金賠欵(现金赔款)
cause of fire	qǐhuǒ yuányīn 起火原因
certificate of insurance	bǎoxiǎn píngzhèng 保險憑証(保险凭证)
civil commotion	mínbiàn 民變(民变)
class of risk	wēixiǎn lèibié 危險類別(危险类别)
co-insurance	gòngbǎo 共保
collapse	dǎotā 倒塌
collision	pèngzhuàng 碰撞
commission	yòngjīn 佣金; shǒuxùfèi 手續費(手续费)
compensation	bǔcháng 補償(补偿)
comprehensive insurance	zōnghé bǎoxiǎn 綜合保險(综合保险)
compulsory third party insurance	dìsānzhě zérèn qiángzhì bǎoxiǎn 第三者責任強制保險(第三者责任强制保险)
consequential loss insurance	zāihòu sǔnshī bǎoxiǎn 災後損失保險(灾后损失保险); cóngshǔ sǔnshī bǎoxiǎn 從屬損失保險(从属损失保险)

206

consignment	jìshòu 寄售; jiāoyùn huòwù 交運貨物(交运货物)
contractor's all risks insurance	chéngjiànzhě yíqièxiǎn 承建者一切險(承建者一切险)
cover note	chéngbǎodān 承保單(承保单)
depreciation	zhéjiù 折舊(折旧); biǎnzhí 貶值(贬值)
depreciation of value	biǎnzhí 貶值(贬值)
earthquake	dìzhèn 地震
employer's liability insurance	gùzhǔ zérèn bǎoxiǎn 雇主責任保險(雇主责任保险)
excess of loss	chāo'é péikuǎn 超額賠欵(超额赔款)
excess of loss cover	chāo'é péikuǎn bǎozhàng 超額賠欵保障(超额赔款保障)
excess of loss reinsurance treaty	chāo'é péikuǎn fēnbǎo hétóng 超額賠款分保合同(超额赔款分保合同)
ex gratia payment	tōngróng fùkuǎn 通融付欵; yōuhuì fùgěi 優惠付給(优惠付给)
expiration of policy	bǎodān mǎnqī 保單滿期(保单满期)
expiry date	yǒuxiàoqī 有效期; dàoqīrì 到期日
facultative reinsurance	línshí fēnbǎo 臨時分保(临时分保)
fidelity guarantee insurance	zhígōng bǎozhèng bǎoxiǎn 職工保証保險(职工保证保险)
fire alarm	huǒjǐng 火警
fire damage	huǒsǔn 火損(火损)
fire insurance	huǒzāi bǎoxiǎn 火災保險(火灾

保險）

fire peril	huǒzāi wēixiǎn 火災危險（火灾危險）
fire resistance	nàihuǒdù 耐火度
floating policy	liúdòng bǎoxiǎndān 流動保險單（流动保险单）
flood	shuǐzāi 水災（水灾）
force majeure	bùkě kànglì 不可抗力
fortuitous event	yìwài shìgù 意外事故
franchise, deductible	juéduì miǎnpéi'é 絕對免賠額（绝对免赔额）
free alongside ship（F.A.S.）	chuánbiān jiāohuò（jià）船邊交貨（價）（船边交货（价））
free from particular average（F.P.A.）	dāndú hǎisǔn bupéicháng 單獨海損不賠償（单独海损不赔偿）
general agent	zǒngdàilǐrén 總代理人（总代理人）
gross premium	máobǎoxiǎnfèi 毛保險費（毛保险费）; bǎoxiǎnfèi zǒng'é 保險費總額（保险费总额）
gross rate	máofèilǜ 毛費率（毛费率）
group insurance	tuántǐ bǎoxiǎn 團體保險（团体保险）
group life insurance	tuántǐ rénshòuxiǎn 團體人壽險（团体人寿险）
householder's comprehensive policy	zhùhù zōnghé bǎoxiǎndān 住戶綜合保險單（住户综合保险单）
houseowner's comprehensive policy	yèzhǔ zōnghé bǎoxiǎndān 業主綜合保險單（业主综合保险单）
inland marine insurance	nèilù shuǐshàngyùnshū bǎoxiǎn 內陸水上運輸保險（内陆水上运输保险）

208

inland transportation	nèilù yùnshū 內陸運輸(内陆运输)
insurable interest	kěbǎo quányì 可保權益(可保权益)
insurable value	kěbǎo jiàzhí 可保價值(可保价值)
insurance	bǎoxiǎn 保險(保险)
insurance against all risks	yíqièxiǎn 一切險(一切险)
insurance agent	bǎoxiǎn dàilǐrén 保險代理人(保险代理人)
insurance certificate	bǎoxiǎn zhèngmíngshū 保險證明書(保险证明书); bǎoxiǎn dān 保險單(保险单)
insurance claim	bǎoxiǎn suǒpéi 保險索賠(保险索赔)
insurance cover	bǎoxiǎn fànwéi 保險範圍(保险范围)
insurance coverage	bǎoxiǎn fànwéi 保險範圍(保险范围)
insurance on goods	duì huòwù de bǎoxiǎn 對貨物的保險(对货物的保险)
insurance policy	bǎoxiǎndān 保險單(保险单)
insurance risk of shortage in weight and quantity	duǎnliàngxiǎn 短量險(短量险)
insured	bèibǎoxiǎnrén 被保險人(被保险人)
insurer	bǎoxiǎnshāng; chéngbǎorén 保險商(保险商); 承保人(承保人)
jettison of cargo	pāoqì huòwù 拋棄貨物(抛弃货

209

物）

kinds of insurance	bǎoxiǎn zhǒnglèi 保險種類（保險种类）
legal expenses	fǎlǜ fèiyòng 法律費用（法律費用）; sùsòngfèi 訴訟費（诉讼費）
legal liability	fǎlǜ zérèn 法律責任（法律责任）
letter of cancellation	jiěyuēshū 解約書（解约书）
liability	zérèn 責任（责任）
liability insurance	zérèn bǎoxiǎn 責任保險（责任保險）
limitation of liability	zérèn xiàn'é 責任限額（责任限額）
livestock insurance	shēngchù bǎoxiǎn 牲畜保險（牲畜保險）
livestock transit insurance	shēngchù yùnshū bǎoxiǎn 牲畜運輸保險（牲畜运输保险）
long-term insurance	chángqī bǎoxiǎn 長期保險（长期保險）
loss prevention	fángsǔn 防損（防损）
loss report	sǔnshī bàogàoshū 損失報告書（损失报告书）
machinery breakdown insurance	jīqì sǔnhuài bǎoxiǎn 機器損壞保險（机器损坏保險）
malicious act	èyì xíngwéi 惡意行爲（恶意行为）
marine cargo insurance	hǎiyùn huòwù bǎoxiǎn 海運貨物保險（海运货物保險）
marine hull insurance	chuánshēn bǎoxiǎn 船身保險（船身保險）
marine insurance	hǎiyùn bǎoxiǎn 海運保險（海运保險）; shuǐxiǎn 水險（水险）

maximum amount	zuìgāo'é 最高額(最高额)
maximum liability	zuìgāo zérèn 最高責任(最高责任); zuìdàde fùzhài 最大的負債(最大的负债)
maximum limit	zuìgāo xiàn'é 最高限額(最高限額)
misrepresentation	wù bào 誤報 (误报); bùshí-shēnbào 不實申報 (不实申报)
monthly report	yuèbào 月報(月报)
motorcar insurance	qìchē bǎoxiǎn 汽車保險(汽车保险)
motorcar liability insurance	qìchē zérèn bǎoxiǎn 汽車責任保險(汽车责任保险)
motorcycle insurance	mótuōchē bǎoxiǎn 摩托車保險(摩托车保险)
negligence	shūhu 疏忽
net premium	jìngtiēshuǐ 淨貼水(净贴水); jìngbǎoxiǎnfèi 淨保險費(净保险费)
net premium rate	jìngfèilù 淨費率(净费率)
non-reciprocal reinsurance	fēi hùhuì fēnbǎo 非互惠分保
notice of loss	sǔnshī tōngzhī (shū) 損失通知(書)(损失通知(书))
open cover	yùyuē chengbǎotiáo 預約承保條(预约承保条); yùyuēbǎoxiǎndān 預約保險單(预约保险单)
open policy	kāikǒu bǎoxiǎndān 開口保險單(开口保险单); yùyuē bǎoxiǎndān 預約保險單(预约保险

211

over insurance	chāo'é bǎoxiǎn 超額保險（超額保险）
parcel post insurance	yóubāo bǎoxiǎn 郵包保險（邮包保险）
passenger liability insur-	lǚkè zérèn bǎoxiǎn 旅客責任保險（旅客责任保险）
performance bond	lǚyuē bǎozhèngshū 履約保證書（履约保证书）
perils insured against	suǒ chēngbǎode fēngxiǎn 所承保的風險（所承保的风险）
perils of the seas	hǎishàng fēngxiǎn 海難（海难）
personal accident insur-ance	gèrén rénshēn yìwài shānghài bǎoxiǎn 個人人身意外傷害保險（个人人身意外伤害保险）
personal effects	sīrén wùpǐn 私人物品
pilferage	tōudào 偷盗
plate glass insurance	bōlí bǎoxiǎn 玻璃保險（玻璃保险）
power interruption insur-ance	diànliú zhōngduàn bǎoxiǎn 電流中斷保險（电流中断保险）
power of attorney, proxy	shòuquánshū 授權書（授权书）; dàilǐ zhèngshū 代理證書（代理证书）
premium	bǎoxiǎnfèi 保險費（保险费）
premium, annual	niánbǎoxiǎnfèi 年保險費（年保险费）
premium, deposit	yùfù bǎoxiǎnfèi 預付保險費（预付保险费）
premium earned	shíshōu bǎoxiǎnfèi 實收保險費（实收保险费）
premium, pro rata	ànrìjìsuànde bǎoxiǎnfèi 按日計

	算的保險費(按日计算的保险費)
premium, provisional	línshí bǎoxiǎnfèi 臨時保險費(临时保险费)
products liability	chǎnpǐn zérèn 產品責任(产品责任)
property insurance	cáichǎn bǎoxiǎn 財產保險(财产保险)
pro rata	ànrì jìsuàn 按日計算(按日计算)
reinsurance	zàibǎoxiǎn 再保險(再保险); fēnbǎo 分保
reinstatement value	chóngjiàn jiàzhí 重建價值(重建价值)
reinsurance commission	fēnbǎo shǒuxùfèi 分保手續費(分保手续费)
retention	zìliú'é 自留額(自留额); bǎoyǒu'é 保有額(保有额)
retroactive effect	yǒuzhuīsù xiàolì 有追溯效力
retrocede	zhuǎnfēnbǎo 轉分保(转分保)
right of cancellation	zhùxiāoquán 注銷權(注销权)
robbery insurance	dàojié bǎoxiǎn 盜劫保險(盗劫保险)
salvage	jiùzhù 救助; jiùzhùfèi 救助費(救助费)
self-insurance	zìbǎo 自保
smoke damage	yānxūn sǔnshī 烟燻損失(烟熏损失)
subrogate	dài wèi qiú cháng 代位求償(代位求偿); quánlì zhuǎnràng 權利轉讓(权利转让)
subrogation form	dài wèi qiú chang shū 代位求償書(代位求偿书); quányì

213

	zhuǎnràngshū 權益轉讓書(权益转让书)
theft (burglary) insurance	tōuqiè (shíqiè) bǎoxiǎn 偷竊(失竊)保險(偷窃(失窃)保险)
third party liability	dìsānzhě zérèn 第三者責任(第三者责任)
transportation insurance	yùnshū bǎoxiǎn 運輸保險(运输保险)
underwriter	chéngbǎorén 承保人
water damage insurance policy	shuǐzì bǎoxiǎndān 水漬保險單(水渍保险单)
worker's compensation	láogōng péicháng 勞工賠償(劳工赔偿)
workmen's compensation insurance	láogōngxiǎn 勞工險(劳工险)

6. Commerce

act of God	tiānzāi 天災(天灾)
actual budget	juésuàn 決算(决算)
affiliated company	fùshǔ gōngsī 附屬公司(附属公司); zǐgōngsī 子公司
analysis certificate, laboratory report	huàyàn zhèngmíngshū 化驗證明書(化验证明书); huàyàn bàogào 化驗報告(化验报告)
arbitration	zhōngcái 仲裁
attachment	fùjiàn 附件; cháfēng 查封
authority to pay	shòuquán fùkuǎn 受權付款(受权付款)
authority to purchase	wěituō gòumǎizhèng 委托購買證(委托购买证)
barter	wùwùjiāohuàn 物物交換(物物交換); yǐhuòyìhuò 以貨易貨(以货易货)
bill of lading (B/L)	tíhuòdān 提貨單(提货单)
binding contract	yǒuxiào hétong 有效合同
brand, trademark	shāngbiāo 商標(商标); páizi 牌子
business law	shāngyèfǎ 商業法(商业法)
buy back	fǎnxiāo 返銷(返销)
capital financing	tígōng zīběn 提供資本(提供资本)
capital gain	zīběn déyì 資本得益(资本得益)
capital influx	zījīn liúrù 資金流入(资金流入)
capital loss	zīběn sǔnshī 資本損失(资本损失)

catalogue	shāngpǐn mùlù 商品目錄(商品目录)
certificate	zhèngmíng 證明(证明); zhèngshū 證書(证书)
China Council for the Promotion of International Trade	Zhōngguó Guójì Màoyì Cùjìnhuì 中國國際貿易促進會(中国国际贸易促进会)
commerce	shāngyè 商業(商业)
commercial law	shāngyèfǎ 商業法(商业法)
commercial treaty	màoyì tiáoyue 貿易條約(貿易条约)
commission rate	yòngjīnlǜ 佣金率
commodity	shāngpǐn 商品
company	gōngsī 公司
compensation	péicháng 賠償(赔偿)
compensation trade policy	bǔcháng màoyì zhèngcè 補償貿易政策(补偿贸易政策)
contract	hétong 合同
cost price	chéngběn jiàgé 成本價格(成本价格)
date of shipment	zhuāngyùn rìqī 裝運日期(裝运日期)
deficit in revenue	shōurù bùzú 收入不足
delivery	jiāohuò 交貨(交货)
delivery date	jiāohuò rìqī 交貨日期(交货日期)
direct investment	zhíjiē tóuzī 直接投資(直接投资)
distribution	fēnpèi 分配; jīngxiāo 經銷(经销)
dividend, yield	gǔxī 股息; hónglì 紅利(红利)
document	wén jiàn 文件; zhèngquàn 證券

（证券）

economic aid	jīngjì yuánzhù 經濟援助(经济援助)
enquiry, enquiring	xúnjià 詢價(询价)
establishment of L/C	kāi xìnyòng zhèng 開信用證(开信用证)
expenses	fèiyong 費用(费用)
expiry date of L/C	xìnyòngzhèng yǒuxiàoqī 信用证有效期(信用证有效期)
export of services	láowù shūchū 勞務輸出(劳务输出)
export of technology	jìshù shūchū 技術輸出(技术输出)
finance and trade (commerce)	cáizhèng yǔ màoyì 財政與貿易(财政与贸易)
financial capital	jīnróng zīběn 金融資本(金融资本)
financial year	cáizhèng niándù 財政年度(财政年度); kuàijì niándù 會計年度(会计年度)
fiscal year	cáizhèng niándù 財政年度(财政年度); kuàijì niándù 會計年度(会计年度)
fixed capital	gùdìng zīběn 固定資本(固定资本)
force majeure	bùkěkànglì 不可抗力
free trade policy	zìyóu màoyì zhèngcè 自由貿易政策(自由贸易政策)
free trade zone	zìyóu màoyìqū 自由貿易區(自由贸易区)
import and export business	jìnchūkǒu jiāoyì 進出口交易(进出口交易)

217

import and export figures (total)	jìnchūkǒu zǒngé 進出口總額（进出口总额）
import of services	láowù shūchū 勞務輸入（劳务输入）
inland revenue	guónèi shuìshōu 國內稅收（国内税收）
inspection certificate, testing certificate	jiǎnyàn zhèngmíngshū 檢驗證明書（检验证明书）
investment	tóuzī 投資（投资）
investment in capital goods	jīběn shèbèi tóuzī 基本設備投資（基本设备投资）
inward (documentary bill)	jìnkǒu yāhuìpiào 進口押滙票（进口押汇票）
joint enterprise	liánhé qǐyè 聯合企業（联合企业）
joint venture	héyíng qǐyè 合營企業（合营企业）
law	fǎlǜ 法律
letter of credit, L/C	xìnyòngzhèng 信用證（信用证）
liquid assets	liúdòng zīchǎn 流動資產（流动资产）
liquid capital	liúdòng zīběn 流動資本（流动资本）
loan capital	jièdài zīběn 借貸資本（借贷资本）
long-term investment	chángqī tóuzī 長期投資（长期投资）
making a budget	biānzhì yùsuàn 編製預算（编制预算）
management	guǎnlǐ 管理
memorandum	bèiwànglù 備忘錄（备忘录）
merchandise	shāngpǐn 商品

monetary policy	Huòbì zhèngcè 貨幣政策
multi-national (trans-national) company	kuàguó gōngsī 跨國公司(跨国公司)
negotiable L/C	yìfù xìnyòngzhèng 議付信用證 (议付信用证); rànggòu xìnyòngzhèng 讓購信用證(让購信用證)
negotiation	tánpàn 談判(谈判); rànggòu 讓購(让购); yìfù 議付(议付)
opening of L/C	kāizhèng 開證(开证)
operating cost	jīngyíngfei 經營費(经营费)
order	dìngdān 訂單(订单)
outward (documentary bill)	chūkǒu yāhuìpiào 出口押滙票 (出口押滙票)
parent company	mǔ gōngsī 母公司; fù gōngsī 父公司
patent	zhuānlìquán 專利權(专利权)
point in question	zhēngzhídiǎn 爭執點(争执点)
power of attorney, proxy	shòuquán shū 授權書(授权书); dàilǐ zhèngshū 代理證書(代理证书)
price	jiàgé 價格(价格)
private investment	sīrén tóuzī 私人投資(私人投资)
profit	lìrùn 利潤(利润)
protective trade policy	bǎohùzhǔyì màoyì zhèngcè 保護主義貿易政策(保护主义贸易政策)
protocol	yìdìngshū 議定書(议定书)
proxy	shòuquánshū 授權書(授权书); wěituōshū 委託書(委托书)
purchase, buy	gòumǎi 購買(购买)
receipt	shōujù 收據(收据)

reciprocal trade policy	hùhuì màoyì zhèngcè 互惠貿易政策(互惠贸易政策)
representative sample	yǒu dàibiǎoxìng de huòyàng 有代表性的貨樣(有代表性的货样)
revenue	shōuyì 收益
revised budget	dìng zhèngde yùsuàn 訂正的預算(订正的预算)
sales	xiāoshòu 銷售(销售)
sample	yàngpǐn 樣品(样品)
services	láowù 勞務(劳务)
shipment	zhuāngyùn 裝運(装运)
source of revenue	shōuyì láiyuán 收益來源(收益来源)
specification	guīgé 規格(规格)
standard	biāozhǔn 標準(标准); biāozhǔnwù 標準物(标准物)
standard contract	biāozhǔn hétong 標準合同(标准合同)
subsidiary company	fùshǔ gōngsī 附屬公司(附属公司); zǐgōngsī 子公司
supply and demand	gōngqiú (qíngkuàng) 供求(情况)
syndicate	xīndíjiā 辛迪加; cáituán 財團(财团)
tangible trade	yǒuxíng màoyì 有形貿易(有形贸易)
taxation	zhēngshuì 徵稅(征税)
terms of payment	fùkuǎn tiáojiàn 付款條件(付款条件)
total dividend	zǒnghónglì 總紅利(总红利)
total revenue	zǒngshōurù 總收入(总收入)

trade	màoyì 貿易(贸易)
trade agreement	màoyì xiédìng 貿易協定(贸易协定)
trade fair	shāngpǐn jiāoyìhuì 商品交易會(商品交易会)
trade policy	màoyì zhèngcè 貿易政策(贸易政策)
transferring funds by drafts and bills of exchange	lìyòng qīpiào huò huìpiào huàhuì 利用期票或滙票劃滙(利用期票或汇票划汇)
valid contract	yǒuxiào hétong 有效合同
validity of L/C	xìnyòngzhèng yǒuxiàoqī 信用證有效期(信用证有效期)
visible trade	yǒuxíng màoyì 有形貿易(有形贸易)
waiver	qì quán 棄權(弃权)
working budget	shíxíngde yùsuàn 實行的預算(实行的预算)
working capital	zhōuzhuǎn zījīn 週轉資金(周转资金); yíngyùn zījīn 營運資金(营运资金)
working cost	jīngyíngfei 經營費(经营费)
world standard	shìjiè biāozhǔn 世界標準(世界标准)

7. Finance

administer, manage   guǎnlǐ 管理

agreement   xiédìng 協定(协定)

allocation of funds   bōkuǎn 撥款(拨款)

amortization (depre-   tānxiāofèi 攤銷費(摊销费); zhé-
ciation)charge   jiù kāizhi 折舊開支 (折旧开
                                        支)

appendix   fùlù 附錄(附录)

appropriation for buying   shèbèi tiānzhì hé gēngxīn bōku
new equipment and re-   ǎn 設備添置和更新撥款(设备
novating existing ones   添置和更新拨款)

appropriation of funds   bōkuǎn 撥款(拨款)

arbitrage   tàohuì 套滙(套汇)

bank   yínháng 銀行(银行)

banking   yínháng yè 銀行業(银行业)

blocked currency   bùnéngduìhuàn de huòbì 不能
                                        兌換的貨幣 (不能兑换的货
                                        币)

budget   yùsuàn 預算(预算)

budget deficit   yùsuàn chìzì 預算赤字(预算赤
                                        字)

budget estimate   gàisuàn 概算

budgeting for the coming   wèi xiàyìniándù biānzhì yù-
year   suàn 爲下一年度編製預算
                                        (为下一年度编制预算)

budget proposal   yùsuàn tí'àn 預算提案(预算提
                                        案)

budget surplus   yùsuàn yíngyú 預算盈餘(预算
                                        盈余)

buying price	mǎijià 買價（买价）
buying rate	yínháng mǎijià 銀行買價（银行买价）; mǎirù huìlǜ 買入滙率（买入汇率）
capital	zīběn 資本（资本）
capital expenditure	jīběn jiànshè fèiyong 基本建設費用（基本建设费用）; gùdìng zīchǎn zhīchū 固定資產支出（固定资产支出）
cash control	xiànjīn guǎnlǐ 現金管理（现金管理）
cash on delivery, C.O.D.	huò dào fù kuǎn 貨到付款（货到付款）
cashier's check	yínháng běnpiào 銀行本票（银行本票）
check, cheque	zhīpiào 支票
commercial bank	shāngyè yínháng 商業銀行（商业银行）
commission	yòngjīn 佣金
consortium	guójì cáituán 國際財團（国际财团）
conversion table	huànsuànbiǎo 換算表（换算表）
convertible currency	kěduìhuàn huòbì 可兌換貨幣（可兑换货币）
credit	xìnyòng 信用; dàifāng 貸方（贷方）
credit card	xìnyòngkǎ 信用卡
cross exchange	tàohuì 套滙（套汇）
currency	huòbì 貨幣（货币）
currency devaluation, currency depreciation	huòbì biǎnzhí 貨幣貶值（货币贬值）
current exchange rate	xiànxíng huìlǜ 現行滙率（现行

汇率)

deficit	kuīsǔn 虧損(亏损); chìzì 赤字
deficit spending	chìzì kāizhī 赤字開支(赤字开支)
deflation	tōnghuò jǐn suō 通貨緊縮(通货紧缩)
depreciation	biǎnzhí 貶值(贬值)
depreciation provision, depreciation fund	zhéjiù chǔbèijīn 折舊儲備金(折旧储备金)
devaluation	biǎnzhí 貶值(贬值)
document	wénjiàn 文件; zhèngquàn 證券(证券)
documentary bill	gēndān huìpiào 跟單匯票(跟单汇票)
earnings from foreign exchange	wàihuì shōurù 外滙收入(外汇收入)
estimate	gūjì 估計(估计); gūjiàdān 估價單(估价单)
estimation	gūjì 估計(估计); yùsuàn 預算(预算)
exchange quotation	wàihuì hángqíng 外滙行情(外汇行情)
exchange rate	duìhuànlǜ 兌換率
exchange table	huìduì huànsuànbiǎo 滙兌換算表(汇兑换算表)
expenditure	zhīchū 支出; suìchū 歲出(岁出)
extending credit	yáncháng xìndài 延長信貸(延长信贷)
financial system	cáizhèng tǐzhì 財政體制(财政体制)
floating rate	fúdòng huìlǜ 浮動滙率(浮动汇率)

224

foreign currency	wàiguó huòbì 外國貨幣（外国货币）
foreign exchange	wàihuì 外匯（外汇）
foreign trade	duìwài màoyì 對外貿易（对外贸易）
franchise	miǎnpéilǜ (é) 免賠率（額）（免赔率（额））
fund	zījīn 資金（资金）; jījīn 基金
gross profit	máolì 毛利
Import and Export Bank	jìnchūkǒu yínháng 進出口銀行（进出口银行）
inflation	tōnghuò péngzhàng 通貨膨脹（通货膨胀）
in pounds sterling	yǐ yīnbàng kāijià 以英鎊開價（以英镑开价）
in Renminbi	yǐ rénmínbì kāijià 以人民幣開價（以人民币开价）
interest rate	lìlǜ 利率
in US dollars	yǐ měiyuán kāijià 以美圓開價（以美圆开价）
legal tender, lawful money	fǎdìng huòbì 法定貨幣（法定货币）
liabilities	fùzhài 負債（负债）
making up the deficit	míbǔ chìzì 彌補赤字（弥补赤字）
maximum profit	zuìgāo lìrùn 最高利潤（最高利润）
minimum profit	zuìdī lìrùn 最低利潤（最低利润）
money changing	duìhuàn huòbì 兌換貨幣（兑换货币）
money, finances	huòbì 貨幣（货币）; jīnróng 金融
net profit	chúnlì 純利（纯利）; jìnglì 淨利
normal profit	zhèngcháng lìrùn 正常利潤（正

225

常利潤)

offer, offering	bàojià 報價、(报价); fāpán 發盤(发盘)
official exchange rate	fǎdìng huìlǜ 法定匯率(法定汇率)
People's Bank of China	Zhōngguó Rénmín Yínháng 中國人民銀行(中国人民银行)
profit	lìrùn 利潤(利润)
profit margin	lìrùnlǜ 利潤率(利润率)
profit sharing system	lìrùn fēnchéng zhìdù 利潤分成制度(利润分成制度)
quality	pǐnzhì 品質(品质)
quota system	pèiézhì 配額制(配额制)
quotation	bàojià 報價(报价); hángqíng 行情
rate of exchange	huìjià 匯價(汇价); huìlǜ 匯率(汇率)
remittance	huìkuǎn 匯款(汇款)
selling price	màijià 賣價(卖价)
selling rate	màichū huìlǜ 賣出滙率(卖出汇率); yínháng màijià 銀行賣價(银行卖价)
total value of foreign trade	duìwài màoyì zǒngé 對外貿易總額(对外贸易总额)
traveller's check	lǚxíng zhīpiào 旅行支票
written agreement	shūmiàn xiédìng 書面協定(书面协定)

8. Customs and Tax

application for customs clearance	chūkǒu jiéguān shēnbàoshū 出口結關申報書(出口结关申报书)
bonded factory	bǎoshuì jiāgōngchǎng 保稅加工廠(保税加工厂)
bonded warehouse	bǎoshuì cāngkù 保稅倉庫(保税仓库)
category of taxes	shuìzhǒng 稅種(税种)
classification of imports and exports under customs tariff	jìnchūkǒu huòwùde shuìzé guīlèi 進出口貨物的稅則歸類(进出口货物的税则归类)
corporation income tax	gōngsī suǒdéshuì 公司所得稅
customs	hǎiguān 海關(海关)
customs bureau	hǎiguān zǒngshǔ 海關總署(海关总署)
customs duty	guānshuì 關稅(关税)
customs formality	hǎiguān shǒuxù 海關手續(海关手续)
(The) Customs Import and Export Tariff Regulations of the People's Republic of China	Zhōnghuá Rénmín Gònghéguó Hǎiguān Jìnchūkǒu Shuìzé 中華人民共和國海關進出口稅則(中华人民共和国海关进出口税则)
customs law	hǎiguānfǎ 海關法(海关法)
customs rules and regulations	hǎiguān guīzhāng zhìdù jí fǎlìng 海關規章制度及法令(海关规章制度及法令)
customs tariff	guānshuì shuìzé 關稅稅則(关税

税則）

declaration	shēnbào 申報（申报）; shēnbào-dān 申報單（申报单）
departure permit	chūjìng xǔkězhèng 出境許可證（出境许可证）
direct tax	zhíjiēshuì 直接稅
duty receipt	wánshuì shōujù 完稅收據（完稅收据）
duty to be paid at port of import	kǒuàn nàshuì 口岸納稅
entry permit	rùjìng xǔkězhèng 入境許可證（入境许可证）
excise tax	xiāofèishuì 消費稅（消费稅）
exemption and rebatement of duty	guānshuìde jiǎnmiǎn 關稅的減免（关稅的减免）
exit permit	chū kǒu xǔkězhèng 出口許可證（出口许可证）
export declaration	chūkǒu shēnbào 出口申報（出口申报）
export duty	chūkǒushuì 出口稅
import declaration	jìnkǒu shēnbào 進口申報（进口申报）
import duty	jìnkǒushuì 進口稅（进口稅）
indirect tax	jiànjiēshuì 間接稅（间接稅）
individual income tax	gèrén suǒdéshuì 個人所得稅（个人所得稅）
normal rate, normal tariff	pǔtōng shuìlǜ 普通稅率
permit	xǔkězhèng 許可證（许可证）
port of entry	tōngguāngǎng 通關港（通关港）; jìnkǒugǎng 進口港（进口港）
preferential tariff	tèhuì guānshuì 特惠關稅（特惠关稅）

(The) Provisional Customs Law of the People's Republic of China	Zhōnghuá Rénmín Gònghéguó Zànxíng Hǎiguānfǎ 中華人民共和國暫行海關法(中华人民共和国暂行海关法)
release	fàngxíng 放行
tariff	shuìlǜ 税率; guānshuì biǎo 關税表(关税表)
tax	shuì 税
tax exemption	miǎnshuì 免税
tax law	shuìwù fǎlìng 税務法令(税务法令)
tax policy	shuìshōu zhèngcè 税收政策
tax reduction	jiǎnshuì 減税
transit duty	tōngxíngshuì 通行税
verification	jiǎnyàn 檢驗(检验); jiàndìng 鑒定(鉴定)

9. Mail, Telephone and Telex

airmail	hángkōng yóujiàn 航空郵件(航空邮件)
airmail stamp	hángkōng yóupiào 航空郵票(航空邮票)
booking form for telex service	diànchuán guàhàodān 電傳掛號單(电传挂号单)
cablegram, telegram	hǎidǐ diànbào (海底)電報((海底)电报)
collect call, reverse charge call	shòuhuàrén fùfèi diànhuà 受話人付費電話(受话人付费电话)
express mail	kuàidì yóujiàn 快遞郵件(快递邮件)
facsimile room, xerox room	chuánzhēnjīshì 傳眞機室(传真机室)
insured mail	bǎojià yóujiàn 保價郵件(保价邮件)
letters, mail	xìnjiàn 信件
letter in reply, to answer a letter, to reply by letter	huíxìn 回信
long distance call	chángtú diànhuà 長途電話(长途电话)
mail, post(v.)	jì 寄
person-to-person call	jiàorén diànhuà 叫人電話(叫人电话)
postcard	míngxìnpiàn 明信片
post office	yóujú 郵局(邮局)
post and telegraph office	yóudiànjú 郵電局(邮电局)

registered mail	guàhào yóujiàn 掛號郵件(挂号邮件)
stamp	yóupiào 郵票(邮票)
station-to-station call	jiàohào diànhuà 叫號電話(叫号电话); júijiàn diànhuà 局間電話(局间电话)
surface mail	pǔtōng yóujiàn 普通郵件(普通邮件); píng yóu 平郵(平邮)
telegram	diànbào 電報(电报)
telegraph	diànbào 電報(电报)
telegraph form	diànbàozhǐ 電報紙(电报纸)
telegraph office	diànbàojú 電報局(电报局)
telephone	diànhuà 電話(电话)
telephone number	diànhuà hàomǎ 電話號碼(电话号码)
telex	diànchuán 電傳(电传)
telex switchboard	diànchuán zǒngjī 電傳總機(电传总机)
trunk call	chángtú diànhuà 長途電話(长途电话)
urgent telegram	jiājí diànbào 加急電報(加急电报)
xerox room, facsimile room	chuánzhēnjīshì 傳真機室(传真机室)

10. Sports

archery	shèjiàn 射箭
badminton	yǔmáoqiú 羽毛球
ball games	qiúlèi yùndòng 球類運動 (球类运动); qiúlèi bǐsài 球類比賽 (球类比赛)
baseball	bàngqiú 棒球
basketball	lánqiú 籃球 (篮球)
billiards	táiqiú 檯球 (台球); dànzǐqiú 彈子球 (弹子球)
bowling	bǎolíngqiú 保齡球 (保龄球)
boxing	quánjī 拳擊 (拳击)
canoeing	dúmùzhōu yùndòng 獨木舟運動 (独木舟运动)
chess	guójì xiàngqí 國際象棋 (国际象棋)
Chinese chess	zhōngguó xiàngqí 中國象棋 (中国象棋)
cricket	bǎnqiú 板球
croquet	chuíqiú 槌球
cycling	zìxíngchē yùndòng 自行車運動 (自行车运动)
diving	tiàoshuǐ 跳水
dragon boat race	lóngzhōu bǐsài 龍舟比賽 (龙舟比赛)
fencing	jījiàn 擊劍 (击剑)
football, association football, soccer	zúqiú 足球
go	wéiqí 圍棋 (围棋)

golf	gāoěrfūqiú 高爾夫球(高尔夫球)
handball	shǒuqiú 手球
high jump	tiàogāo 跳高
high swing	gāoqiūqiān 高鞦韆(高秋千)
hockey	qūgùnqiú 曲棍球
horse race	sàimǎ 賽馬(赛马)
ice hockey	bīngqiú 冰球
judo	róu dào 柔道; róu shù 柔術(柔術)
karate	kōngshǒudào 空手道
long-distance running	chángpǎo 長跑(长跑)
long jump, broad jump	tiàoyuǎn 跳遠(跳远)
modern pentathlon	xiàndài wǔxiàng yùndòng 現代五項運動(现代五项运动)
mountaineering	dēngshān yùndòng 登山運動(登山运动)
mountain climbing	páshān 爬山
motor-boating	mótuōtǐng yùndòng 摩托艇運動(摩托艇运动)
motor-cycling	mótuōchē yùndòng 摩托車運動(摩托车运动)
pelota, jai alai	huílìqiú 回力球
playing on the swing	dàngqiūqiān 蕩鞦韆(荡秋千)
pole climbing	págān 爬桿(爬杆)
polo	mǎqiú 馬球(马球)
physical exercises, gymnastics	tǐcāo 體操(体操)
rope climbing	páshéng 爬繩(爬绳)
rope skipping	tiàoshéng 跳繩(跳绳)
rowing	huáchuán yùndòng 划船運動(划船运动)
rubber-band skipping	tiàoxiàngpíjin 跳橡皮筋

Rugby (football), rugger	gǎnlǎnqiú 橄欖球(橄榄球)
running	pǎobù 跑步
sailing	hánghǎi yùndòng 航海運動(航海运动)
see-saw jumping	tiào qiāoqiāobǎn 跳蹺蹺板(跳跷跷板)
shooting	shèjī 射擊(射击)
skating	huábīng 滑冰
skating (wheels)	lúnshì liūbīng 輪式溜冰(轮式溜冰)
skiing	huáxuě 滑雪
skittles, ninepins	gǔnqiúxì 滾球戲(滚球戏); jiǔzhùxì 九柱戲(九柱戏)
softball	lěiqiú 壘球(垒球)
springboard	tiàobǎn 跳板
sumo	xiàngpū 相撲(相扑)
swimming	yóuyǒng 游泳
table tennis	pīngbāngqiú 乒乓球
tennis	wǎngqiú 網球(网球)
track and field	tiánjìng yùndòng 田徑運動(田径运动)
tug-of-war	báhé 拔河
volleyball	páiqiú 排球
water polo	shuǐqiú 水球
water skiing	huáshuǐ 滑水
wrestling	shuāijiāo 摔跤(摔跤)
yak race	sàimáoniú 賽氂牛(赛牦牛)
yachting	kuàitǐng yùndòng 快艇運動(快艇运动); qīng fānchuán yùndòng 輕帆船運動(轻帆船运动)

11. Room

ball room	wǔtīng 舞廳(舞厅)
banquet room	yànhuìtīng 宴會廳(宴会厅)
bar	jiǔbājiān 酒吧間(酒吧间)
barber's	lǐfàshì 理髮室(理发室)
bathroom	yùshì 浴室
bedroom	wòshì 臥室
billiard room	tái qiúshì 檯球室(台球室); dàn-zǐfáng 彈子房(弹子房)
cashier's office	cáiwùshì 財務室(财务室); chū-nàshì 出納室(出纳室)
cloak room	cúnyīchù 存衣處(存衣处)
conference room	huìyìshì 會議室(会议室)
dining hall	fàntīng 飯廳(饭厅)
dining room	cānshì 餐室
double room	shuāngrénfáng 雙人房(双人房)
guest room	kèfáng 客房
kitchen	chúfáng 廚房
living room	kètīng 客廳(客厅)
reading room	yuèlǎnshì 閱覽室(阅览室)
reception room	huìkèshì 會客室(会客室)
recreation room	yóuyìshì 游藝室(游艺室)
room	fángjiān 房間(房间)
single room	dānrénfáng 單人房(单人房)
study room	shūfáng 書房(书房)
suite	tàofáng 套房
toilet	cèsuǒ 廁所(厕所)
vacant room	kōngfáng 空房
washroom	guànxǐshì 盥洗室; cèsuǒ 廁所(厕所)

235

12. Family

aunt

gūmā (father's sister) 姑媽;
yímā (mother's sister) 姨媽;
jiùmā (wife of mother's
brother) 舅媽

aunty

āyi 阿姨; bómǔ 伯母

boy

nánhái 男孩

brother

xiōngdì 兄弟

brother-in-law

jiěfú (husband of one's elder
sister) 姐夫; mèifù (husband
of one's younger sister)妹夫;
nèixiōng(elder brother of one's
wife) 內兄; nèidì(younger
brother of one's wife)內弟;
dàbō (elder brother of one's
husband) 大伯; xiǎoshū
(younger brother of one's
husband) 小叔

children

háizi (mén) 孩子(們)(孩子
(们))

cousin

tángjiě (elder female on
father's side) 堂姐; tángmèi
(younger female on father's
side) 堂妹; tángxiōng (elder
male on father's side) 堂兄;
tángdì (youngermale on
father's side) 堂弟; biǎojiě
(elder female on mother's
side) 表姐; biǎomèi (youn-

ger female on mother's side)
表妹; biǎoxiōng (elder male
on mother's side) 表兄
biǎodì (younger male on
mother's side) 表弟

daughter	nǚér 女兒(女儿)
daughter-in-law	ér xífù 兒媳婦(儿媳妇)
elder brother	gēge 哥哥
elder sister	jiějie 姐姐
father	fùqīn 父親; bàba 爸爸
father-in-law	yuèfù (father of one's wife) 岳父; zhàngrén 丈人; gōnggong (father of one's husband) 公公
girl	nǚhái 女孩
grand-daughter	sūnnǚ (daughter of one's son) 孫女(孙女); wàisūnnǚ (daughter of one's daughter) 外孫女(外孙女)
grand father	yéye (on father's side) 爺爺(爷爷); wàigōng (on mother's side) 外公
grand mother	zǔmǔ (on father's side) 祖母; nǎinai 奶奶; wàipó (on mother's side) 外婆; pópo 婆婆; lǎolao 姥姥
grand son	sūnzi (son of one's son) 孫子(孙子); wàisūn (son of one's daughter) 外孫(外孙)
husband	zhàngfu 丈夫
mother	mǔqīn 母親(母亲); māma 媽媽(妈妈)

mother-in-law	pópo (mother of one's husband) 婆婆; yuèmǔ (mother of one's wife) 岳母; zhàngmǔniáng 丈母娘
nephew	zhízi (son of one's brother) 侄子; wàisheng (son of one's sister) 外甥
niece	zhínǚ (daughter of one's brother) 侄女; wàishengnǚ (daughter of one's sister) 外甥女
sister-in-law	sǎozi 嫂子
sisters, elder and younger	jiěmèi 姐妹
son	érzi 兒子 (儿子)
son-in-law	nǚxu 女婿
uncle	bófù (elder brother of one's father) 伯父; shūshu (younger brother of one's father) 叔叔; gūfù (husband of a brother of one's mother) 姑父; yífù (husband of a sister of one's mother) 姨父; jiùfù (brother of one's mother) 舅父
wife	qīzi 妻子; lǎopo 老婆
younger brother	dìdi 弟弟
younger sister	mèimei 妹妹

13. Clothes

apron	wéiqún 圍裙(围裙)
belt	yāodài 腰带(腰带)
blouse	nǔ chènyī 女襯衣(女衬衣)
bodice, corset	jǐnshēnxiōngyī 緊身胸衣(紧身胸衣)
bonnet	nǔmào 女帽
boots	xuēzi 靴子
braces, suspenders	bēidài 背带(背带)
brassiere, breastform	rǔzhào 乳罩
buckle	yāodàikòu 腰带扣(腰带扣)
cap	biànmào 便帽
cape	duǎndǒupeng 短斗篷
clothes; dress; garment	yīfu 衣服
coat	shàngyī 上衣
collar	lǐngzi 領子(领子)
combination	liánshānkù 連衫褲(连衫裤)
cotton shoes	bùxié 布鞋
cuff	xiùkǒu 袖口
dinner jacket, tuxedo	xiǎo yèlǐfú 小夜禮服(小夜礼服)
divided skirt	qúnkù 裙褲(裙裤)
double-breasted suit	shuāngpáiniǔ shàngyī 雙排鈕上衣(双排钮上衣)
dressing gown; bathrobe	yùyī 浴衣
evening dress	wǎnlǐfú 晚禮服(晚礼服)
felt hat	nímào 呢帽
flared skirt	lǎbāqún 喇叭裙
fur coat	pídàyī 皮大衣

239

galoshes, overshoes	yǔxié 雨鞋; tàoxié 套鞋
gloves	shǒutào 手套
handkerchief	shǒupà 手帕
hat	màozi 帽子
top hat	dàlǐmào 大禮帽(大礼帽)
high-heel shoes	gāogēnxié 高跟鞋
jacket	duǎnshàngyī 短上衣; jiákè 夾克(夾克)
kimono (Japanese)	héfú 和服
leather shoes	píxié 皮鞋
military uniform	jūnfú 軍服(军服)
mini skirt	chāoduǎnqún 超短裙
night gown, night dress	nǚshuìyī 女睡衣
overcoat	dàyī 大衣
overcoat with fur collar	pílǐng dàyī 皮領大衣(皮领大衣)
overalls	gōngzuòfú 工作服
panties	sānjiǎokù 三角褲(三角裤)
pantihose	liánkùwà 連褲襪(连裤袜)
pants, slacks	kù 褲(裤)
parka	fēngxuě dàyī 風雪大衣(风雪大衣)
pleated skirt	bǎizhéqún 百摺裙(百折裙)
pyjamas	shuìyī 睡衣
raincoat, mackintosh	yǔyī 雨衣
robe, dress	liányīqún 連衣裙(连衣裙)
sandal	liángxié 涼鞋
scarf; muffler	wéijīn 圍巾(围巾)
shawl	pījiān 披肩; tóujīn 頭巾(头巾)
shirt	chènyī 襯衣(衬衣)
shoe brush	xiéshuā 鞋刷
shoe laces (or strings)	xiédài 鞋帶(鞋带)
shoe polish	xiéyóu 鞋油

shorts	duǎnkù 短褲(短裤)
single-breasted suit	dānpáiniǔ shàngyī 單排鈕上衣 (单排钮上衣)
skirt	qúnzi 裙子
skirt pants	qúnkù 裙褲(裙裤)
sleeve	xiùzi 袖子
slippers	tuōxié 拖鞋
socks	duǎnwà 短襪(短袜)
sportswear	yùndòngfú 運動服(运动服)
stocking suspenders	diàowàdài 吊襪帶(吊袜带)
stockings	chángtǒngwà 長筒襪(长筒袜)
straw hat	cǎomào 草帽
suspenders; garters	diàowàdài 吊襪帶(吊袜带)
sweater	máoyī 毛衣
swimming suit, bathing suit	yóuyǒngyī 游泳衣
swimming trunks	yóuyǒngkù 游泳褲(游泳裤)
T-shirt	(duǎnxiù)yùndòngshān (短袖) 運動衫((短袖)运动衫)
tie, necktie	lǐngdài 領帶(领带)
bow tie	lǐngjié 領結(领结)
tie clip, tie pin	lǐngdàijiā 領帶夾(领带夹)
tights	jǐshēn yīkù 緊身衣褲(紧身衣 裤)
trousers; slacks	chángkù 長褲(长裤)
underpants	nèikù 內褲(内裤); kùchǎ 褲衩 (裤衩)
undershirt	hànshān 汗衫; hànbèixīn 汗背 心
underwear	nèiyī 內衣
uniform	zhìfú 制服
veil	miànshā 面紗(面纱)

vest waist-coat	xīfú bèixīn 西服背心
walking shoes	píngdǐxié 平底鞋
wedding gown	hūnlǐfú 婚禮服（婚礼服）
windbreaker	fēngyī 風衣（风衣）

14. Color

beige	mǐsè 米色
black	hēisè 黑色
blue	lánsè 藍色 (蓝色)
brown	zōngsè 棕色; hèsè 褐色
color	yánsè 顏色 (颜色)
dark	shēnsè 深色
golden	jīnsè 金色
gray	huīsè 灰色
green	lùsè 綠色 (绿色)
light	qiǎnsè 淺色 (浅色); dànsè 淡色
orange	júhuángsè 橘黃色
pink	fěnhóngsè 粉紅色 (粉红色)
purple	zǐsè 紫色
red	hóngsè 紅色 (红色)
silvery	yínsè 銀色 (银色)
white	báisè 白色
yellow	huángsè 黃色

15. Food

breakfast	zǎocān 早餐
dinner	wǎnfàn 晚飯 (晚饭)
dish (a kind of)	yídào cài 一道菜
food	shípǐn 食品
food (chinese)	zhōngcān 中餐
food (western)	xīcān 西餐
hors d'oeuvre	xiǎochī 小吃
lunch	wǔfàn 午飯 (午饭)
meal, (have a)	chīfàn 吃飯 (吃饭)
menu	càidān 菜單 (菜单); càipǔ 菜譜 (菜谱)
restaurant	fàngguǎn 飯館 (饭馆)
soup (thick)	gēng 羹
soup (thin)	tāng 湯 (汤)
boiled	zhǔ(de) 煮(的)
fried	jiān(de) (in shallow oil) 煎 (的)
fried	zhá(de) (in deep fat) 炸(的)
steamed	zhēng(de) 蒸(的)
stir-fried	chǎo(de) 炒(的)
roast	kǎo(de) 烤(的)
acid	suān 酸
bitter	kǔ 苦
hot, peppery	là 辣
salty	xián 鹹 (咸)
sour taste	suān 酸

244

sweet taste	tián 甜
bowl	wǎn 碗
chopsticks	kuàizi 筷子
fork	chāzi 叉子
glass	bōlibēi 玻璃杯; bēizí 杯子
knife	dāozi 刀子
napkin	cānjīn 餐巾
pepper shaker	hújiāopíng 胡椒瓶
plate	pánzi 盤子(盘子)
salt cellar	yánpíng 鹽瓶(盐瓶)
spoon	chí匙; sháozi 勺子
table cloth	zhuōbù 桌布
teapot	cháhú 茶壺(茶壶)
tooth picks	yáqiān 牙籤(牙签)
utensil	yòngjù 用具
bacon	yānròu 醃肉(腌肉)
beef	niúròu 牛肉
beef（curry）	gālí niúròu 咖喱牛肉
beef steak	niúpái 牛排
bird（swallow）nest soup	yànwōtāng 燕窩湯(燕窝汤)
chicken	jī 鷄(鸡)
coldmeat platter	pīnpán 拼盤(拼盘)
duck	yāzi 鴨子(鸭子)
duck（roast）	kǎoyā 烤鴨(烤鸭)
egg	jīdàn 鷄蛋(鸡蛋)
egg（preserved）	sōnghuādàn 松花蛋; pídàn 皮蛋
egg white	dànbái 蛋白
goat（meat）	shānyángròu 山羊肉
goose	é 鵝(鹅)
ham	huǒtuǐ 火腿

lamb	yángròu 羊肉
lamb chop	yángpái 羊排
Mongolian hot pot	huǒguō 火鍋(火锅); shuànyáng-ròu 涮羊肉
pork	zhūròu 猪肉
pork chop	zhūpái 猪排
rice-flour meat	mǐfěnròu 米粉肉
soup (sour-pepper)	suānlàtāng 酸辣湯(酸辣汤)
sausage	xiāngcháng 香腸(香肠)
veal cutlet	xiǎoniúpái 小牛排
abalone	bàoyú 鮑魚(鲍鱼)
carp	lǐyú 鯉魚(鲤鱼)
carp (silver)	báilián yú 白鰱魚(白鲢鱼)
clam	géli 蛤蜊
crab	pángxiè 螃蟹
crabmeat	xièròu 蟹肉
cuttle fish	mòyú 墨魚(墨鱼)
eel	shànyú 鱔魚(鳝鱼)
fish	yú 魚(鱼)
fish in sweet and sour sauce	tángcùyú 糖醋魚(糖醋鱼)
jelly fish	hǎizhé 海蜇
lobster	lóngxiā 龍蝦(龙虾)
mandarin fish	guìyú 鱖魚(鳜鱼)
oyster	háo 蠔(蚝); mǔlì 牡蠣(牡蛎)
prawn	dàxiā 大蝦(大虾)
scallop	gānbèi 乾貝(干贝)
seafoods	hǎixiān 海鮮(海鲜)
sea slug, sed cucumber	hǎishēn 海參(海参)
shark's fin	yúchì 魚翅(鱼翅)
shark's fin soup	yúchìtāng 魚翅湯(鱼翅汤)

shrimp	xiǎoxiā 小蝦(小虾)
squid	yóuyú 魷魚(魷鱼)
tuna fish	jīnqiāngyú 金槍魚(金枪鱼)
turtle	jiǎyú 甲魚(甲鱼)
white bait	yínyú 銀魚(银鱼)
bamboo shoots	sǔn 筍(笋)
bean	dòu 豆
bean curd	dòufu 豆腐
bean sprouts	dòuyá 豆芽
broad beans	cándòu 蠶豆(蚕豆)
cabbage	juǎnxīncài 捲心菜(卷心菜)
cabbage	dàbáicài 大白菜
carrots	húluóbo 胡蘿蔔(胡萝卜)
cauliflower	càihuā 菜花
celery	qíncài 芹菜
chilli	làjiāo 辣椒
cucumber	huángguā 黃瓜
eggplant	qiézi 茄子
fungus	mùěr 木耳
garlic	dàsuàn 大蒜
ginger	jiāng 薑(姜)
kelp	hǎidài 海帶(海带)
lettuce	wōjù 萵苣(莴苣)
lotus root	ǒu 藕
mushroom	mógu 磨菇
onion	yángcōng 洋葱
peanuts	huāshēng 花生
peas	wāndòu 豌豆
potato	tǔdòu 土豆
radish	xiǎohóngluóbo 小紅蘿蔔(小红萝卜)

spinach	bōcài 菠菜
string beans	càidòu 菜豆
tomato	xīhóngshì 西紅柿(西红柿)
turnip	luóbo 蘿蔔(萝卜)
vegetables	shūcài 蔬菜; qīngcài 青菜
chilli oil	làjiāoyóu 辣椒油
mustard	jièmo 芥末
pepper	hújiāo 胡椒
pickles	pàocài 泡菜
salad dressing	shālàyóu 沙拉油
salt	yán 鹽(盐)
soy sauce	jiàngyóu 醬油(酱油)
sugar	táng 糖
tomato sauce	fānqiéjiàng 蕃茄醬(蕃茄酱)
vinegar	cù 醋
bread	miànbāo 麵包(面包)
bun, steamed	bāozi 包子; mántóu 饅頭(馒头)
butter	huángyóu 黃油(黄油)
cake	bǐng 餅(饼); dàngāo 蛋糕
chocolate	qiǎokèlì 巧克力
cookies	xiǎotiánbǐng 小甜餅(小甜饼); bǐnggān 餅乾(饼干)
corn	yùmǐ 玉米
dessert	tiánshí 甜食
dimsum	diǎnxin 點心(点心)
dumpling (boiled)	shuǐjiǎo 水餃(水饺); jiǎozi 餃子(饺子)
dumpling (fried)	guōtiē 鍋貼(锅贴)
dumpling (steamed)	zhēngjiǎo 蒸餃(蒸饺)
macaroni	tōngxīnfěn 通心粉

noodles	miàntiáo 麵條(面条)
pancake	làobǐng 烙餅(烙饼)
pastry	gāodiǎn 糕點(糕点)
pastry roll	dànjuǎn 蛋卷
pie	tiánxiànbǐng 甜餡餅(甜馅饼)
pudding	bùdīng 布丁
rice	mǐ 米
rice gruel	xīfàn 稀飯(稀饭); zhōu 粥
rice (steamed)	mǐfàn 米飯(米饭)
roll (steamed)	mántóu 饅頭(馒头); huājuǎn 花捲(花卷)
roll (twisted)	huājuǎn 花捲(花卷)
salad	shālā 沙拉
toast	kǎomiànbāo 烤麵包(烤面包)
wonton	húntún 餛飩(馄饨)
apple	píngguǒ 蘋果(苹果)
apricot	xìng 杏
banana	xiāngjiāo 香蕉
cherry	yīngtáo 櫻桃(樱桃)
date	zǎo 棗(枣)
fruits	shuǐguǒ 水果
grape	pútáo 葡萄
grape fruit	pútáoyòu 葡萄柚
jam	guǒjiàng 果醬(果酱)
lemon	níngméng 檸檬(柠檬)
lichee	lìzhī 荔枝
melon	guā 瓜; sīguā 西瓜
orange	júzi 橘子(橘子); chénzi 橙子
peach	táozi 桃子
pear	lí 梨
persimmon	shìzi 柿子

249

pineapple	bōluó 菠蘿(菠萝)
strawberry	cǎoméi 草莓
water melon	xīguā 西瓜
beer	píjiǔ 啤酒
brandy	báilándì 白蘭地(白兰地)
coffee	kāfēi 咖啡
drinks	yǐnliào 飲料(饮料); jiǔ 酒
fruit juice	guǒzhī 果汁
ice cream	bīngqílín 冰淇淋
ice cube	bīngkuàir 冰塊兒(冰块儿)
liquor	lùjiǔ 露酒
lemonade	níngméngshuǐ 檸檬水(柠檬水)
maotai	máotái 茅台
milk	niúnǎi 牛奶
mineral water	kuàngquánshuǐ 礦泉水(矿泉水)
orange juice	júzhī 橘汁
orange soda	júzi qìshuǐ 橘子汽水
soda water	qìshuǐr 汽水兒(汽水儿)
spirits	lièjiǔ 烈酒
tea (black)	hóngchá 紅茶(红茶)
tea (green)	lǜchá 綠茶(绿茶)
tea (jasmine)	huāchá 花茶; xiāngpiàn 香片
vodka	fútèjiā 伏特加
water (boiled)	kāishuǐ 開水(开水)
water (cold drinking)	liángkāishuǐ 涼開水(凉开水)
whisky	wēishìjì 威士忌
wine	pútáojiǔ 葡萄酒
yellow wine	huángjiǔ 黄酒
yogurt	suānniúnǎi 酸牛奶

| I want to make a reservation. | wǒ xiǎng yùdìng zuòwèi 我想预定座位。(我想预定座位。) |
| I want to order··· | wǒ xiǎngdiǎn 我想點···(我想点···) |

16. Weights and Measures

Weight	**Zhòngliàng 重量(重量)**
Avoirdupois	chánghéng 常衡
1 long ton=2,240 pounds = 1.016 metric tons	1 chángdūn = 2,240 bàng= 1.016 gōngdūn 1長噸=2,240 磅=1.016公噸
1 short ton= 2,000 pounds=0.907 metric tons	1 duǎndūn=2,000 bàng= 0.907 gōngdūn 1短噸 = 2,000磅=0.907公噸
1 hundredweight=(U.K.) 112 lb.= 50.802 kg.	1 yīngdàn=(Yīng)112 bàng= 50.802 gōngjīn 1英担= (英)112磅= 50.802公斤
1 hundredweight=(U.S.) 100 lb.= 45.359 kg.	1 Yīngdàn= (Měi) 100 bàng = 45.359 gōngjīn 1英担= (美) 100磅=45.359公斤
1 pound=16 oz.=0.454 kg.	1 bàng =16 àngsī =0.454 gōngjīn 1磅=16盎司=0.454 公斤
1 ounce= 16 dr. = 28.35g.	1 àngsī =16 Yīng qián =28.35 kè 1盎司 =16英錢 =28.35 克
1 dram =1.771 g.	1 Yīngqián =1.771 kè 1英錢 =1.771克
Troy	jīnhéng 金衡
1 pound =12 oz.t. = 0.373 kg.	1 bàng =12 àngsì =0.373 gōngjīn 1磅 =12盎司 = 0.373公斤
1 ounce =20 dwt. 31.103 g.	1 àngsī =20 Yīngqián =31.103 kè 1盎司 =20英錢 =

1 pennyweight =24 gr. =1.555 g.	1 Yīngqián =24 lí =1.555 kè 1英錢 =24喱 =1.555克
1 grain =64.8 mg.	1 lí =64.8 háokè 1喱 =64.8 毫克

Apothecaries' Yàohéng 藥衡(药衡)

1 pound =12 oz. ap. = 0.373 kg.	1 bàng =12 àngsī =0.373 gōngjīn 1磅 =12盎司 = 0.373公斤
1 ounce =8 dr. ap. = 31.103 g.	1 àngsì =8 Yīngqián =31.103 kè 1盎司 =8英錢 =31.103 克
1 dram =3 scr. ap. = 3.887 g.	1 Yīngqián =3 fēn =3.887 kè 1英錢 =3吩 =3.887克
1 scruple =20 gr. =1.295 g.	1 fēn =20 lí =1.295 kè 1吩 =20喱 =1.295克
1 grain =64.8 mg.	1 lí =64.8 háokè 1喱 =64.8 毫克

Capacity Róngliàng 容量

Dry Measure gānliàng 乾量(干量)

1 bushel =4 pks. (U.K.) =36.368 litres	1 pushìer =4 pèikè (Yīng) = 36.368 shēng 1蒲式耳 =4 配克 (英)=36.368升
1 bushel =4 pks. (U.S.) =35.238 litres	1 pǔshìer =4 pèikè (Měi) = 35.238 shēng 1蒲式耳 =4 配克 (美)=35.238升
1 peck =8 qts. (U.K.) = 9.092 litres	1 pèikè =8 kuàtuò (Yīng) = 9.092 shēng 1配克 =8夸 脱 (英)=9.092升
1 peck =8 qts. (U.S.) = 8.809 litres	1 pèikè =8 kuàtuò(Měi) = 8.809 shēng 1配克 =8夸 脱 (美)=8.809升

1 gallon ＝4 qts. ＝4.546
   litres

1 jiālún ＝4 kuàtuò ＝4.546shēng
1加侖 ＝4夸脱 ＝4.546升

1 quart ＝2 pts. (U.K.) ＝
   1.136 litres

1 kuàtuò ＝2 pīntuò (Yīng) ＝
1.236 shēng 1夸脱 ＝2品
脱 (英) ＝1.136升

1 quart ＝2 pts. (U.S.)
   1.101 litres

1 kuàtuò ＝2 pīntuò (Měi) ＝
1.101 shēng 1夸脱 ＝2品
脱 (美) ＝1.101升

1 pint (U.K.) ＝0.568
   litres

1 pīntuò (Yīng) ＝0.568 shēng
1品脱 (英) ＝0.568升

1 pint (U.S) ＝0.55 litres

1 pīntuò (Měi) ＝0.55 shēng
1品脱 (美) ＝0.55升

Liquid Measure

yèliàng 液量

1 gallon ＝4 qts. (U.K.)
   ＝4.546 litres

1 jiālún ＝4 kuàtuò (Yīng) ＝
4.546 shēng 1加侖 ＝4夸脱
(英) ＝4.546升

1 gallon ＝4 qts. (U.S.)
   ＝3.785 litres

1 jiālún ＝4 kuàtuò (Měi) ＝
3.785 shēng 1加侖 ＝4夸脱
(美) ＝3.785升

1 quart ＝2 pts. (U.K.) ＝
   1.136 litres

1 kuàtuò ＝2 pīntuò (Yīng) ＝
1.136 shēng 1夸脱 ＝2品脱
(英) ＝1.136升

1 quart ＝2 pts. (U.S.) ＝
   0.946 litres

1 kuàtuò ＝2 pīntuò (Měi) ＝
0.946 shēng 1夸脱 ＝2品脱
(美) ＝0.946升

1 pint ＝4 gi. (U.K.) ＝
   0.568 litres

1 pīntuò ＝4jiěr (Yīng) ＝0.568
shēng 1品脱 ＝4及耳 (英)
＝0.568升

1 pint ＝4 gi. (U.S.) ＝
   0.473 litres

1 pīntuò ＝4 jiěr (Měi) ＝0.473
shēng 1品脱 ＝4及耳 (美) ＝
0.473升

1 gill (U.K.) ＝0.142 litres

1 jiěr (Yīng) ＝0.142 shēng 1

	及耳（英）＝0.142升
1 gill (U.S.)＝0.118 litres	1 jiěr（Měi）＝0.118 shēng　1 及耳（美）＝0.118升

Length

1 mile＝880 fm.＝1.609 km.

chángdù 長度（长度）

1 Yīng lǐ＝880 xún＝1.609 gōnglǐ　1英里＝880噚＝1.609公里

1 fathom＝2 yd.＝1.829 m.

1 xún＝2 mǎ＝1.829 mǐ　1噚＝2碼＝1.829米

1 yard＝3 ft.＝0.914 m.

1 mǎ＝3 Yīngchǐ＝0.914 mǐ 1碼＝3英尺＝0.914米

1 foot＝12 in.＝30.48 cm.

1 Yīngchǐ＝12 Yīngcùn＝30.48 límǐ　1英尺＝12英寸＝30.48厘米

1 inch＝2.54 cm.

1 Yīngcùn＝2.54 límǐ　1英寸＝2.54厘米

Area

1 square mile＝640 a.＝2.59 sq.km.

miànjī 面積（面积）

1 píngfāng yīnglǐ＝640 Yīngmǔ＝2.59 pingfāng gōnglǐ　1平方英里＝640英畝＝2.59平方公里

1 acre＝4,840 sq. yd.＝4,047 sq.m.

1 Yīngmǔ＝4,840 píngfāngmǎ＝4,047 píngfāngmǐ　1英畝＝4,840平方碼＝4,047平方米

1 square yard＝9 sq.ft.＝0.836 sq.m.

1 píngfānmǎ＝9 píngfāng Yīngchǐ＝0.836 píngfāngmǐ　1平方碼＝9平方英尺＝0.836平方米

1 square foot＝144 sq.in.＝929 sq.cm.

1 píngfāng Yīngchǐ＝144píngfāng Yīngcùn＝929 píngfāng límǐ　1平方英尺＝144平方英

寸 ＝929平方厘米

1 square inch ＝6.451 sq.cm.

1 píngfāng yīngcùn ＝6.451 píngfānglímǐ 1平方英寸 ＝ 6.451平方厘米

Comparison

bǐjiào 比較（比较）

1 Chinese foot ＝ .333meters ＝1.094 feet

1 shìchǐ ＝.333 mǐ ＝1.094 Yīngchǐ 1市尺 ＝.333米 ＝ 1.094英尺

1 li ＝.5 kilometers ＝ .311 miles

1 shìlǐ ＝.5 gōnglǐ ＝.311 Yīnglǐ 1市里 ＝.5公里 ＝ .311英里

1 mu ＝.066 hectares ＝ .164 acres

1 shìmǔ ＝.066 gōngqīng ＝ .164 Yīngmǔ 1市畝 ＝.066 公頃 ＝.164 英畝

1 foot ＝.305 meters ＝ .914 Chinese feet

1 Yīngchǐ ＝.305 mǐ ＝.914 shìchǐ 1英尺 ＝.305米 ＝ .914市尺

1 mile ＝1.609 kilometers ＝3.219 li

1 Yīnglǐ ＝1.609 gōnglǐ ＝ 3.219 shìlǐ 1英里 ＝1.609公 里 ＝3.219市里

1 acre ＝6.072 mu

1 Yīngmǔ ＝6.072 shìmǔ 1英 畝 ＝6.072市畝

1 meter ＝3 Chinese feet ＝＝3.281 feet

1 mǐ ＝3 shìchǐ ＝3.281 Yīng- chǐ 1米 ＝3市尺 ＝3.281英尺

1 kilometer ＝2li ＝.621 miles

1 gōnglǐ ＝2 shìlǐ ＝.621 Yīng- lǐ 1公里 ＝2市里 ＝.621英里

1 square metre ＝9 Chinese sq. feet

1 píngfāngmǐ ＝9 píngfāngshì- chǐ 1平方米 ＝9平方市尺

1 square kilometre＝4 sq.li

1 píngfāng gōnglǐ ＝4 píngfāng shìlǐ 1平方公里 ＝4平方市里

1 hectare ＝15 mu ＝2.47 acres

1 gōngqīng ＝15 shìmǔ ＝2.47 Yīngmǔ 1公頃 ＝15市畝 ＝

2.47英畝

1 catty =.5 kilograms
1.102 pounds

1 shìjīn =.5 gōngjīn =1.102 bàng　1市斤 =.5公斤 = 1.102磅

1 pound =.454 kilograms = .907 catties

1 bàng =.454 gōngjīn =.907 shìjīn　1磅 =.454公斤 = .907市斤

1 kilogram =2 catties = 2.205 pounds

1 gōngjīn =2 shìjin =2.205 bàng　1公斤 =2市斤 =2.205 磅

APPENDICES

1. 漢語拼音和威妥瑪式拼法音節對照表
Chinese Phonetic Alphabet and Wade System

漢語拼音	威妥瑪拼法	漢語拼音	威妥瑪拼法
a	a	chi	ch'ih
ai	ai	chong	ch'ung
an	an	chou	ch'ou
ang	ang	chu	ch'u
ao	ao	chua	ch'ua
ba	pa	chuai	ch'uai
bai	pai	chuan	ch'uan
ban	pan	chuang	ch'uang
bang	pang	chui	ch'ui
bao	pao	chun	ch'un
bei	pei	chuo	ch'o
ben	pên	ci	tz'ŭ (ts'ŭ)
beng	pêng	cong	ts'ung
bi	pi	cou	ts'ou
bian	pien	cu	ts'u
biao	piao	cuan	ts'uan
bie	pieh	cui	ts'ui
bin	pin	cun	ts'un
bing	ping	cuo	ts'o
bo	po	da	ta
bu	pu	dai	tai
ca	ts'a	dan	tan
cai	ts'ai	dang	tang
can	ts'an	dao	tao
cang	ts'ang	de	tê
cao	ts'ao	deng	têng
ce	ts'ê	di	ti
cen	ts'ên	dian	tien
ceng	ts'êng	diao	tiao
cha	ch'a	die	tieh
chai	ch'ai	ding	ting
chan	ch'an	diu	tiu
chang	ch'ang	dong	tung
chao	ch'ao	dou	tou
che	ch'ê	du	tu
chen	ch'ên	duan	tuan
cheng	ch'êng	dui	tui

258

漢語拼音	威妥瑪拼法	漢語拼音	威妥瑪拼法
dun	tun	hou	hou
duo	to	hu	hu
e	ê	hua	hua
ê	eh	huai	huai
ei	ei	huan	huan
en	ên	huang	huang
eng	êng	hui	hui
er	êrh	hun	hun
fa	fa	huo	huo
fan	fan	ji	chi
fang	fang	jia	chia
fei	fei	jian	chien
fen	fên	jiang	chiang
feng	fêng	jiao	chiao
fo	fo	jie	chieh
fou	fou	jin	chin
fu	fu	jing	ching
ga	ka	jiong	chiung
gai	kai	jiu	chiu
gan	kan	ju	chü
gang	kang	juan	chüan
gao	kao	jue	chüeh, chüo
ge	kê, ko	jun	chün
gei	kei	ka	k'a
gen	kên	kai	k'ai
geng	kêng	kan	k'an
gong	kung	kang	k'ang
gou	kou	kao	k'ao
gu	ku	ke	k'ê, k'o
gua	kua	ken	k'ên
guai	kuai	keng	k'êng
guan	kuan	kong	k'ung
guang	kuang	kou	k'ou
gui	kui	ku	k'u
gun	kun	kua	k'ua
guo	kuo	kuai	k'uai
ha	ha	kuan	k'uan
hai	hai	kuang	k'uang
han	han	kui	k'ui
hang	hang	kun	k'un
hao	hao	kuo	k'uo
he	hê, ho	la	la
hei	hei	lai	lai
hen	hên	lan	lan
heng	hêng	lang	lang
hong	hung	lao	lao

漢語拼音	威妥瑪拼法	漢語拼音	威妥瑪拼法
le	lê, lo	ne	nê
lei	lei	nei	nei
leng	lêng	nen	nên
li	li	neng	nêng
lia	lia	ni	ni
lian	lien	nian	nien
liang	liang	niang	niang
liao	liao	niao	niao
lie	lieh	nie	nieh
lin	lin	nin	nin
ling	ling	ning	ning
liu	liu	niu	niu
long	lung	nong	nung
lou	lou	nou	nou
lu	lu	nu	nu
lü	lü	nü	nü
luan	luan	nuan	nuan
lüe	lüeh	nüe	nüeh
	lüo		nüo
	lio		nio
lun	lun		no
luo	luo	nuo	no
ma	ma	o	o
mai	mai	ou	ou
man	man	pa	p'a
mang	mang	pai	p'ai
mao	mao	pan	p'an
me	me	pang	p'ang
mei	mei	pao	p'ao
men	mên	pei	p'ei
meng	mêng	pen	p'ên
mi	mi	peng	p'êng
mian	mien	pi	p'i
miao	miao	pian	p'ien
mie	mieh	piao	p'iao
min	min	pie	p'ieh
ming	ming	pin	p'in
miu	miu	ping	p'ing
mo	mo	po	p'o
mou	mou	pou	p'ou
mu	mu	pu	p'u
na	na	qi	ch'i
nai	nai	qia	ch'ia
nan	nan	qian	ch'ien
nang	nang	qiang	ch'iang
nao	nao	qiao	ch'iao

260

漢語拼音	威妥瑪拼法	漢語拼音	威妥瑪拼法
qie	ch'ieh	shuan	shuan
qin	ch'in	shuang	shuang
qing	ch'ing	shui	shui
qiong	ch'iung	shun	shun
qiu	ch'iu	shuo	sho
qu	ch'ü	si	sǔ, szǔ, ssǔ
quan	ch'üan	song	sung
	ch'üeh	sou	sou
	ch'üo	su	su
qun	ch'ün	suan	suan
ran	jan	sui	sui
rang	jang	sun	sun
rao	jao	suo	so
re	jê	ta	t'a
ren	jên	tai	t'ai
reng	jêng	tan	t'an
ri	jih	tang	t'ang
rong	jung	tao	t'ao
rou	jou	te	t'ê
ru	ju	teng	t'êng
ruan	juan	ti	t'i
rui	jui	tian	t'ien
run	jun	tiao	t'iao
ruo	jo	tie	t'ieh
sa	sa	ting	t'ing
sai	sai	tong	t'ung
san	san	tou	t'ou
sang	sang	tu	t'u
sao	sao	tuan	t'uan
se	sê	tui	t'ui
sen	sên	tun	t'un
seng	sêng	tuo	t'o
sha	sha	wa	wa
shai	shai	wai	wai
shan	shan	wan	wan
shang	shang	wang	wang
shao	shao	wei	wei
she	shê	wen	wên
shei	shei	weng	wêng
shen	shên	wo	wo
sheng	shêng	wu	wu
shi	shih	xi	hsi
shou	shou	xia	hsia
shu	shu	xian	hsien
shua	shua	xiang	hsiang
shuai	shuai	xiao	hsiao

漢語拼音	威妥瑪拼法	漢語拼音	威妥瑪拼法
xie	hsieh	zen	tsên
xin	hsin	zeng	tsêng
xing	hsing	zha	cha
xiong	hsiung	zhai	chai
xiu	hsiu	zhan	chan
xu	hsü	zhang	chang
xuan	hsüan	zhao	chao
xue	hsüeh, hsüo	zhe	chê
xun	hsün	zhei	chei
ya	ya	zhen	chên
yan	yen	zheng	chêng
yang	yang	zhi	chih
yao	yao	zhong	chung
ye	yeh	zhou	chou
yi	yi	zhu	chu
yin	yin	zhua	chua
ying	ying	zhuai	chuai
yo	yo	zhuan	chuan
yong	yung	zhuang	chuang
you	yu	zhui	chui
yu	yü	zhun	chun
yuan	yüen	zhuo	cho
yue	yüeh	zi	tzǔ (tsǔ)
yun	yün	zong	tsung
za	tsa	zou	tsou
zai	tsai	zu	tsu
zan	tsan	zuan	tsuan
zang	tsang	zui	tsui
zao	tsao	zun	tsun
ze	tsê	zuo	tso
zei	tsei		

2. 漢語拼音聲母韻母和國際音標對照表

Consonants and Vowels of the Chinese Phonetic Alphabet and their Corresponding International Phonetic Symbols

漢語拼音	國際音標	漢語拼音	國際音標
b	[p]	ê	[ɛ]
p	[pʻ]	er	[ər]
m	[m]		
f	[f]	ai	[ai]
d	[t]	ei	[ei]
t	[tʻ]	ao	[au]
n	[n]	ou	[əu]
l	[l]	an	[ʌn]
g	[k]	en	[ən]
k	[kʻ]	ang	[aŋ]
h	[x]	eng	[əŋ]
j	[tɕ]	ong	[uŋ]
q	[tɕʻ]	ia	[ia]
x	[ɕ]	ie	[iɛ]
z	[ts]	iao	[iau]
c	[tsʻ]	iu, iou	[iəu]
s	[s]	ian	[ian]
zh	[tʂ]	in	[in]
ch	[tʂʻ]	iang	[iaŋ]
sh	[ʂ]	ing	[iŋ]
r	[ʐ]	iong	[yŋ]
		ua	[ua]
y	[j]	uo	[uə]
w	[w]	uai	[uai]
		ui, uei	[uei]
a	[a]	uan	[uan]
o	[o]	un, uen	[uən]
e	[ə]	uang	[uaŋ]
i	[i]	üe	[yɛ]
u	[u]	üan	[yan]
ü	[y]	ün	[yn]
-i	[ɿ] [ʅ]ʻ		

ʻ〔ɿ〕用於 z c s 後，〔ʅ〕用於 zh ch sh r 後。

263

3. 聲調示意圖
Figure Showing the Four Tones

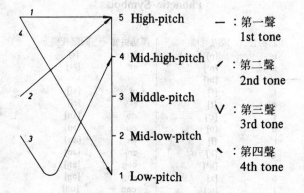

— :	第一聲 1st tone
╱ :	第二聲 2nd tone
∨ :	第三聲 3rd tone
╲ :	第四聲 4th tone